PRINCETON UNIVERSITY'S
INDUSTRIAL RELATIONS SECTION
IN HISTORICAL PERSPECTIVE:
1922–2015

LAWRENCE DAMIAN ROBINSON

Copyright © 2016 by the Industrial Relations Section

ISBN 0-9773544-9-0

Designed by Laurel Masten Cantor, University creative director, Office of Communications, Princeton University
Edited by Beth Chute

Contents

FOREWORD — FROM HENRY S. FARBER

We began work on this history of the Industrial Relations Section early in 2012 in order for its publication to be part of the celebration of our 90th anniversary during academic year 2012-2013. That we are now only publishing this work in the second half of 2015 is the result of a combination of factors. First, writing the history of the section proved to be a much more involved process than we had anticipated. Second, two important changes to our faculty contributed to the delay: Cecilia Rouse was selected to serve as Dean of the Woodrow Wilson School beginning September 1, 2012 and David S. Lee, the Director of the section through the 2012-2013 academic year, was named Provost of Princeton University, July 1, 2013. These appointments continue a long tradition, described in this history, of members of the Industrial Relations Section serving in leadership positions within the University.

We have endeavored to revise our original text to reflect the changes that have occurred during the past two years. In addition to the faculty changes above, we have welcomed Will Dobbie as an Assistant Professor of Economics and Public Affairs. Will holds a joint appointment in the Department of Economics and the Woodrow Wilson School. We were also pleased to welcome Alan Krueger back from Washington, where he served as Chairman of President Barack Obama's Council of Economic Advisers and was a Member of the Cabinet from November 2011 to August 2013. As well as these changes to our faculty, we reactivated the Clarence J. Hicks Memorial Fellowship in Industrial Relations and added the William G. Bowen Award for the Outstanding Book on Labor and Public Policy.

— HENRY S. FARBER, DIRECTOR
AUGUST 2015

The 2012-2013 academic year coincides with the 90th anniversary of the Princeton Industrial Relations Section's founding. This is both a significant milestone and an opportunity to reflect on the section's evolution as a unique center for research, teaching, and public policy engagement on labor issues as it enters its 10th decade. It is also an opportunity to honor the many talented, dedicated scholars and professionals who have served in the section over the years and advanced the field of labor economics in such meaningful ways.

The Industrial Relations Section was founded in 1922 as an unbiased clearinghouse for information on employment policies and practices among U.S. corporations. It quickly became known for its intellectual rigor, doctrinal neutrality, and clear analysis of issues from the management, labor, and government perspectives. This reputation—which endures today—allowed it to play an influential part in many of the most important labor developments of the twentieth century. The section's role in public policymaking stretches from Doug Brown's work for Presidents Hoover and Roosevelt and Orley Ashenfelter's groundbreaking tenure as Director of Evaluation at the Department of Labor, to the presence of several section faculty—Alan Krueger, Alexandre Mas, and Cecilia Rouse—in various senior policy roles in both the Clinton and Obama Administrations.

Over time, both technological and methodological advancements have changed the daily activities of the Industrial Relations Section. Nevertheless, certain themes run throughout its history to the present day and are characteristic of its values. These include the application of its appreciation and knowledge of various institutions and their perspectives, to a detailed understanding of how the world of economics and labor markets works, as well as the positive influence of the section's physical environment. Its lab-like setting fosters the development of highly effective, enduring academic interactions and an exchange of ideas and perspectives like those the section was founded to promote.

Drawing on historical and contemporary sources and the firsthand insights of many individuals who have helped to shape Princeton University's Industrial Relations Section in recent decades, author Damian Robinson puts the section and its academic significance into a historical perspective that is engaging and informative. It is thus with the present volume that the section marks its 90th anniversary, and looks forward to its approaching centennial with deep gratitude to all those who have contributed to its rich, fruitful, and storied past.

— DAVID S. LEE, DIRECTOR
DECEMBER 2012

When I was first asked to consider writing a history of Princeton University's Industrial Relations Section, my immediate reaction was to be daunted by the task. As I saw it, there were three principal challenges I would have to overcome. First, while my background encompassed more than a passing understanding of finance and economics, I knew relatively little about labor economics per se, and even less about the field of industrial relations. I would therefore need to do a significant amount of research in a relatively short space of time in order to familiarize myself enough with the subject just to begin an earnest inquiry into the section's history.

Second, I already had some competition, so to speak. A history of the Industrial Relations Section had previously been produced (principally by one of its faculty associates, the late Richard Lester) in the mid-1980s. That brochure, which had rendered a summary account of many of the section's activities from 1922 to 1985, was written in what can perhaps best be described as a taxonomic fashion; and while it contained a wealth of information that turned out to be enormously helpful—and which I have certainly incorporated into my own version of the section's history—my goal was to produce a very different kind of document. I wanted, in fact, to write something that would be of interest to both labor economists and to a more general readership of Princeton faculty, staff, students, and alumni with a wide range of interests—in effect, something that would put the section's history in the context of the larger University, and of the national community in which it exists.

And, third, I had a not-so-small prejudice to overcome. In the absence of any real familiarity with the subject, I initially imagined the 90-year-old Industrial Relations Section to be something of a musty, ivory-tower relic of a bygone era, with little relevance to modern-day life. As I soon learned, however, nothing could be further from the truth. In fact, after researching the subject in a fair amount of depth, I became convinced that, in the history of American education, there are relatively few fields of study—and even fewer distinct academic units—that can trace their very origins to questions of immediate and practical existential significance to some of the major structural elements of our society. The field of industrial relations, along with its successor discipline of labor economics, and Princeton University's Industrial Relations Section are among them.

Born of the deeply divisive labor strife of the late 19th and early 20th centuries, the field of industrial relations has had an enormous and fundamental impact—on areas from the organized labor movement, to contemporary management and human resources practices, to the legislation behind some of our most basic social protections like Social Security—which reverberates throughout our society and our economy today. And, as one of the firstborn academic institutions of that discipline, Princeton's Industrial Relations Section has long stood at the forefront of its development and its evolution.

The section's significance, however, is far from a simple matter of having a historical connection to esoteric questions about how, when, and where Americans work. Rather, Princeton's Industrial Relations Section and the many fascinating personalities associated with it over the course of its 90-year history have consistently made—through a combination of high-caliber empirical research, teaching, and public policy work—real and lasting contributions to both the fields of industrial relations and labor economics, and to society as a whole. From questions as fundamental to our nation as how governments, unions, corporations, and other institutions relate to one another, to the connection between quality of education and future success in work and life, Princeton's Industrial Relations Section has influenced not only the terms of reference, but also the quality of the public policy debate.

In my estimation, in an era in which history often seems to be repeating itself with a vengeance, an examination of the history of Princeton University's Industrial Relations Section can provide some surprising insights into questions of major socioeconomic significance today. Thus it has been my extraordinary privilege to attempt to provide a small glimpse into a little known but important chapter in the history of Princeton University and its venerable Industrial Relations Section—and, indeed, of our country as a whole.

I would like to express my deep appreciation to the many faculty and staff members—both present and former—of Princeton's Industrial Relations Section, economics department, and Firestone Library, who have been of enormous assistance to me during the writing of this history. In particular, I would also like to thank the section's longtime director and "godfather," Orley Ashenfelter; its current director, David Lee; its other faculty associates, Henry Farber, Alan Krueger, David Lee, Alex Mas, and Cecilia Rouse; and former faculty associate David Card, for being as generous with their insights as they were with their time. It is my fervent hope that the present history does adequate justice to the Industrial Relations Section's fascinating story.

— LAWRENCE DAMIAN ROBINSON
DECEMBER 2012

About the author: Lawrence Damian Robinson holds a bachelor's degree in chemistry from Harvard University and a master's degree from the School of Advanced International Studies of the Johns Hopkins University. He has worked in fields as diverse as government, biomedical research, and financial services, and is currently an independent consultant and freelance writer.

Introduction

In a 1968 study of contemporary research for a regional meeting of the International Industrial Relations Association, University of Minnesota economist and director of the school's Industrial Relations Center, Herbert G. Heneman, Jr., made what would today seem to be a rather remarkable declaration:

> The two most important disciplines of the first half of this century were mathematics and physics; beyond reasonable doubt industrial relations is the most important discipline of the second half.[1]

While the contours of the study of industrial relations have changed considerably since then, one thing is certain: for the better part of the last 150 years, the often tumultuous relationship between labor and capital has been one of the overriding themes in American society with enormous political and economic ramifications for our way of life. Furthermore, one need only look as far as the issues that preoccupy American society today—from unemployment to the legislative debate over the collective bargaining rights of public sector unions, to healthcare reform and the future of Social Security and Medicare—to conclude that the study of the labor market in all its facets has remained as important in our own times as it was when Heneman made his bold pronouncement more than 40 years ago.

It is therefore through this lens, multifocal and variegated as it may be, that one must view the history and the significance of Princeton University's

---

[1] Herbert G. Heneman, Jr., "Contributions of Current Research" in The Role of Industrial Relations Centers: *Proceedings of a Regional Meeting of the International Industrial Relations Association in Chicago, Illinois, May 17-18, 1968* (Madison, WI: International Industrial Relations Association, 1968), 49 [as cited in Bruce E. Kaufman, *The Origins and Evolution of the Field of Industrial Relations in the United States* (Ithaca, NY: ILR Press, 1993), 103-104].

Industrial Relations Section in the aftermath of its 90th anniversary in the 2012-2013 academic year. And in so doing, one may arrive at a better understanding of, and appreciation for, the many and often surprising contributions made by the section and the people associated with it since its inception in 1922—contributions that still have a major influence on the lives of millions of Americans and on the vigorous political and economic debate taking place in our society today.

Foundations

With the trauma of World War I still fresh in memory

and in a time of violent clashes between workers and their employers, the "labor problem" loomed large in the United States in 1922. Laborers and their capitalist bosses of the mines and factories across the land were still arming themselves, and strikes were still being settled in bloodshed. From this chaotic environment emerged a new approach to industrial relations, espoused by reform-minded men like John D. Rockefeller, Jr., and Clarence J. Hicks. Their vision of a mutually beneficial employer-employee partnership led to the founding of the Industrial Relations Section at Princeton University.

Library of Congress, Prints and Photographs Division, NYWT&S Collection, LC-USZ62-132521.

Aftermath of the Wall Street bombing, September 16, 1920, New York City. Library of Congress, Prints and Photographs Division, NYWT&S Collection, LC-DIG-ggbain-31205. http://www.loc.gov/pictures/item/ggb2006006717/

Nineteen twenty-two, the year in which Princeton University founded its Industrial Relations Section, was a time of great change in America, both socially and economically.

Only a few years after the "war to end all wars," it was, on the one hand, the beginning of a time of optimism buoyed by progressive social innovations and major technological changes, and fueled by rapid economic growth and a surge of rampant consumerism. On the other hand, it was also a time in which the memory of persistent and often violent labor disputes, as well as fears of potential socialist revolution, underlined by the establishment of the Soviet Union and punctuated by a recent, deadly anarchist bombing on Wall Street, were still fresh in the national consciousness.

In the aftermath of the First World War, many countries, including the United States, experienced a prolonged and severe deflationary period known as the Depression of 1920-21. Wages in many industries fell by as much as one-half during an 18-month period, while U.S. unemployment skyrocketed from a national average of 5.2 percent to 8.7 percent.[2] For many workers, it seemed that the hard-won wage and benefit gains that had been accumulated as the result of decades of collective bargaining action had been erased in just a few short years.

In fact, the plight of the working class, and the conditions of labor and the relations between employer and the employed in general, were topics of such serious concern on the national and international stages that an entire section of the 1919 Treaty of Versailles, which had officially ended World War I just three years before, was devoted to the establishment of an International Labour Office of the League of Nations—the predecessor organization to what would later become the International Labour Organization, or ILO. In the preamble to the organization's constitution,

---

[2] Christina Romer, "Spurious Volatility in Historical Unemployment Data," *The Journal of Political Economy* 91: 1-37.

the signatories to the treaty, including the United States government, stated their intention clearly: that the great social issue of the late 19th and early 20th centuries—the so-called Labor Problem—must be addressed in order to preserve the hard-won peace. In their words:

> WHEREAS conditions of labour exist involving such injustice, hardship, and privation to large numbers of people as to produce unrest so great that the peace and harmony of the world are imperilled; and an improvement of those conditions is urgently required: as, for example, by the regulation of the hours of work, including the establishment of a maximum working day and week, the regulation of the labour supply, the prevention of unemployment, the provision of an adequate living wage, the protection of the worker against sickness, disease and injury arising out of his employment, the protection of children, young persons and women, provision for old age and injury, protection of the interests of workers when employed in countries other than their own recognition of the principle of freedom of association, the organisation of vocational and technical education and other measures.[3]

Furthermore, in Article 427 of the treaty, they enumerated a list of general principles intended to guide the policymaking of the members of the League of Nations with respect to industrial relations, which began with the following:

> The High Contracting Parties, recognising that the well-being, physical, moral and intellectual, of industrial wage-earners is of supreme international importance, have framed, in order to further this great end, the permanent machinery provided for in Section I and associated with that of the League of Nations. They recognise that differences of climate, habits, and customs, of economic opportunity and industrial tradition, make strict uniformity in the conditions of labour difficult of immediate attainment. But, holding as they do, that labour should not be regarded merely as an article of commerce, they think that there are methods and principles for regulating labour conditions which all industrial communities should endeavour to apply, so far as their special circumstances will permit.[4]

---

[3] Preamble, *Constitution and standing orders of the International Labour Organisation* (Geneva: International Labor Office, 1936), http://www.ilo.org/dyn/normlex/en/f?p=1000:62:0::NO:62:P62_LIST_ENTRIE_ID:2453907:NO.

[4] Article 427, *Constitution and standing orders of the International Labour Organisation* (Geneva: International Labor Office, 1936), http://www.ilo.org/dyn/normlex/en/f?p=1000:62:0::NO:62:P62_LIST_ENTRIE_ID:2453907:NO.

Industrial relations and the "labor problem" were thus topics of major import in the first decades of the 20th century, not only at the international level, but also on the American national scene. Working conditions in the recently industrialized regions of the United States were such that a new working-class consciousness, having emerged over the course of more than a generation, had become more self-aware, increasingly militant, and well organized. In the words of Yale University labor historian David Montgomery:

Armored "Death Car" used against striking mine workers at Trinidad, Colorado, c. 1913.

> To understand the scope and nature of that development, however, it is necessary to look beyond the iron and steel craftsmen and their amalgamation struggle. They have served to bring to our attention the interlocking character of the skilled workers' "managerial" role, the social structure of the mill, the craft basis of nineteenth-century trade unionism, the mutualistic culture and ideology of the epoch's labor movement, and the workers' increasingly aggressive drive for collective control in the face of the increasingly awesome ability of the firms' owners to impose their will in the workplace. Moreover, their workplace conflicts spilled over into community and political life, raising fundamental questions about the nature of the American republic itself....[5]

In the years leading up to the First World War, numerous large-scale strikes had swept through one industry after another across the country, often ending in bloodshed and the tragic loss of life. Incidents such as the Pennsylvania Homestead Strike of 1892 and the Colorado Ludlow Massacre of 1914 had created an increasing sense of urgency among industrialists, company managers, and civil authorities that methods must be found to reduce the commercial and social disruption caused by these labor wars.

For some, the solution to the labor problem took the form of increasingly harsh, and in many cases repressive tactics. For example, according to an official publication of the state of West Virginia:

> Unionization had always met fierce resistance from coal operators, who used eviction, termination, blacklisting, yellow dog contracts, court injunctions, coercion, and intimidation to prevent workers from joining unions and to stifle union organizers. By the early twentieth century, especially in the eastern United

---

[5] David Montgomery, *The Fall of the House of Labor* (Cambridge: Cambridge University Press, 1987), 46.

In his "And in the Meantime the Lady Drowns," which first appeared in *Life* on May 8, 1919, cartoonist Harry Grant Dart lampoons the state of contemporary labor relations.

States, coal operators held and exercised exclusive political control and strongly influenced local and state governments, literally dictating state policies that would insure coal profits, prevent labor organization, and guarantee a passive work force. Such tight control was necessary, coal operators maintained, because of the "boom and bust" nature of the coal mining industry, the instability of consumer demand, competition at home and abroad, and constantly fluctuating coal prices. Except for a brief period during the Anthracite Strike of 1902, when the federal government openly sided with labor organizations against recalcitrant mine owners, the companies had successfully resisted attempts by miners to unionize.[6]

When, in the summer of 1921, the coal operators' coercive anti-union tactics failed to prevent labor leaders from organizing mine workers in Mingo County, West Virginia, one of the largest and most violent labor disputes in American history—the so-called Battle for Blair Mountain—erupted with deadly consequences.

On August 20, 1921, nearly five thousand miners, armed with rifles and an old machine gun with three thousand rounds of ammunition, assembled at Marmet. Their commander, "General" Bill Blizzard, a twenty-eight year old man of proven leadership in District 17, formed the men into a column and began the march toward Logan. Along the way new recruits swelled the column until it reached fifteen to twenty thousand men. Informed of "Blizzard's Army," Secretary of War Weeks directed General Read, on August 23, to place the Nineteenth Infantry in readiness, and sent Major Thompson to Charleston to investigate. Realizing that two years of cumulative "insurrectionary fury" were

---

[6] Clayton D. Laurie, "The United States Army and the Return to Normalcy in Labor Dispute Interventions: The Case of the West Virginia Coal Mine Wars, 1920-1921," *West Virginia History,* vol. 50 (1991): 1-24.

about to explode in the coalfields, Governor Morgan, on August 25, asked President Warren Harding for one thousand troops and military aircraft.[7]

After several days of skirmishes between the armed miners and local authorities aligned with the coal operators, the U.S. Army was finally forced to intervene in order to end the violence that claimed as many as a score of lives.

For others, however, a different approach—one that sought to promote the unity of interests between employer and employed—held infinitely greater promise for lasting industrial peace. Driven by motives such as the larger questions of social justice, economic reform, and the desire to preserve the capitalist system by improving it, and influenced by the principles of scientific management—or what came to be known as Taylorism[8]—proponents of a more collaborative view of the labor-capital relationship were convinced that the careful application of scientific methods of personnel management and the prudent integration of workplace reforms could result in a sustainable balance between operational efficiency and worker well-being.

Among the proponents of this "personnel management" brand of industrial relations were two men who would play a critical role in the establishment and the initial financial sponsorship of Princeton's Industrial Relations Section: Clarence J. Hicks and John D. Rockefeller, Jr. Because of their importance to the Industrial Relations Section's early history, it is fitting to offer a few words about them here.

John D. Rockefeller, Jr.

On the morning of April 20, 1914, after seven months of strikes by coal miners organized by the United Mine Workers of America and a number of violent confrontations between the miners and militia units comprised of company-employed guards and Colorado National Guardsmen, a major gun battle broke out at the site of a massive tent colony near Ludlow, Colorado. By the end of the day, dozens of people, including eleven children, were dead, and the tent colony—home to as many as 1,200 striking workers and their families—had been burned to the ground. A newspaper account at the time described the events:

John D. Rockefeller, Jr. Detail from a photo of Calvin Coolidge with Judge Elbert Henry Gary and John D. Rockefeller, Jr., January 8, 1925. Library of Congress, Prints and Photographs Division, LC-USZ62-106305.

---

[7] Ibid.

[8] Originally introduced and advocated by American engineer Frederick W. Taylor in the late 1800s, "Taylorism" was a theory of management that emphasized the use of engineering methods (including the analysis of workflows and time utilization) to improve labor efficiency, particularly in the manufacturing industries.

IT'S ALWAYS AFTER THE FAKE MEDICINES
FAIL THAT THE DOCTOR IS CALLED IN.

This illustration by cartoonist Edwin Marcus, first published in the July 16, 1922 edition of the *The New York Times,* is reproduced by permission of the Marcus Family.

Forty-five dead, more than two-thirds of them women and children, a score missing, and more than a score wounded, is the result known to-night [sic] of the fourteen-hour battle which raged with uninterrupted fury yesterday between State troops and striking coal miners in the Ludlow district, on the property of the Colorado Fuel and Iron Company, the Rockefeller holdings. The Ludlow camp is a mass of charred débris, and buried beneath it is a story of horror unparalleled in the history of industrial warfare. In the holes which had been dug for their protection against the rifles' fire the women and children died like trapped rats when the flames swept over them. One pit, uncovered this afternoon disclosed the bodies of ten children and two women. Further exploration was forbidden by the position of the camp, which lies directly between the militia and the strikers' positions.[9]

Not only was this incident, known as the Ludlow Massacre, the spark that touched off 10 days of deadly pitched battles between striking miners and company and state militiamen (prompting President Woodrow Wilson to order the intervention of federal troops in order to quell the violence of what became known as the Colorado Coalfield War), but it was also a public relations disaster for the big coal operators and their investors. Among these, none were more affected than the state's largest coal mining operation, the Colorado Fuel and Iron Company, and its majority shareholder, John D. Rockefeller, Jr., upon whom the events at Ludlow and their aftermath left an indelible mark. According to one biographical sketch of the wealthy industrialist:

It wasn't long before [Rockefeller's] determination to change the family's image suffered its most serious setback. In September 1913 nine thousand workers at the Rockefeller-owned Colorado Fuel and Iron Company went out on strike for union recognition, better hours, wages, and housing. The coal miners and their families, evicted from their company homes, spent the winter in tent colonies in the town of Ludlow. In March 1914, with the strike still unresolved, John D. Rockefeller Jr.,

---

[9] "45 Dead, 20 Hurt, Score Missing, in Strike War," *The New York Times,* April 22, 1914. http://query.nytimes.com/mem/archive-free/pdf?res=FA0C1EF93D5E13738DDDAB0A94DC405B848DF1D3.

a board member of the company, testified before the House Subcommittee on Mines and Mining. He upheld the "open shop" as a sacred ideal. When the strike was violently suppressed in April 1914, public opinion turned against Junior, blaming him for the deaths of two women and eleven children.[10]

In recapitulating the history of Ludlow for a mock trial competition held in 2003, the Colorado Bar Association was even more explicit with regard to the public relations consequences for Rockefeller and his corporation:

> The legal court proceedings might have gone nowhere, but it was a different story in the court of public opinion. The Ludlow Massacre had electrified the nation. Demonstrations and rallies protesting the killing of women and children erupted in cities across the country. In Denver, 5,000 people demonstrated at the state capitol, calling for Guard officers to be tried for murder and the Governor to be tried as an accessory. Nearly every newspaper and magazine in the country covered the story, with pro- and anti-company editorials run side-by-side. The New York Times carried so much news that the index of articles for three months amounted to six pages in small print. Rockefeller was scathingly censured in the press and demonized in the eyes of the American public by such prominent progressives as Upton Sinclair and John Reed. Even The Wall Street Journal, after a wait of several days following the massacre, observed that a "reign of terror" existed in southern Colorado. Grim cartoons ran in both the mainstream press and socialist publications. John Sloan's cover drawing for The Masses showed a miner, a dead baby in his arms and dead wife at his feet, returning gunfire at Ludlow. In Harper's Weekly Rockefeller was portrayed as a vulture-like creature hovering over the shambles of Ludlow with a caption that read "Success." A national speaking tour made by several women survivors of Ludlow, including Mary Petrucci—still barely coherent from the loss of her children in the "Death Pit"—brought the tragedy even closer to home for many Americans. Visits included the White House and Rockefeller's offices at 26 Broadway in New York City.[11]

As the only male child and heir to the industrial fortune of his father, by the time John D. Rockefeller, Jr. (or Junior, as he was often called) was in his early twenties, he had

---

[10] Public Broadcasting System, "People & Events, John D. Rockefeller Junior, 1874-1960," "American Experience: The Rockefellers." http://www.pbs.org/wgbh/amex/rockefellers/peopleevents/p_rock_jjr.html.

[11] "Historical Background for the 2003 Colorado Mock Trial Competition," Colorado Bar Association. http://www.cobar.org/index.cfm/ID/581/dpwfp/Historical-Foreward-and-Bibliography/.

Ruins of the Ludlow miners' camp, Trinidad, Colorado, after the massacre. April 29, 1914. Library of Congress, Prints and Photographs Division, LC-DIG-ggbain-15859.

already been groomed to become one of the wealthiest men in the world and the chief executive of a vast business empire. After graduating from Brown University in 1897, Rockefeller joined his father's Standard Oil Company, and soon became a director of that enterprise during one of the most turbulent times in its history. Throughout the 1880s and 1890s, Standard Oil was the target of numerous state and federal lawsuits accusing it (and John D. Rockefeller, Sr. in particular) of unfair business practices, which ultimately led to the company's forced breakup on anti-trust grounds in 1911.

Although the Rockefellers largely maintained control of and ultimately profited enormously from their holdings in the 34 companies that resulted from the dissolution of the Standard Oil trust, the experience left Rockefeller Jr. in many ways disillusioned and determined to improve the public perception of his family, while pursuing his philanthropic inclinations full-time. However, his personal involvement in and responsibility for the corporate empire created by his father complicated his journey from his role as one of the world's wealthiest young business moguls to that of a devoted philanthropist and industrial relations advocate. His handling of the circumstances surrounding the Ludlow Massacre and its aftermath demonstrate this complexity perhaps better than any other event in his public life, and are indicative of the transformation that ultimately led him to sponsor a number of activities devoted to his vision of industrial relations, including the Industrial Relations Section of Princeton University.

For example, three months into the strike at the Colorado Fuel and Iron Company, in December 1913, Rockefeller wrote to the company's vice president, expressing his full support for the tactics being used to break the strike. As the dispute wore on, and a mere two weeks before the massacre at Ludlow took place, he testified before a congressional committee, espousing the principle of the "open shop." Answering a question as to whether or not the killing of miners and their children was not enough to prompt him to communicate with the company's other directors and attempt to find an end to the dispute, he replied:

> We believe that the issue is not a local one in Colorado; it is a national issue, whether workers shall be allowed to work under such conditions as they may choose. And as part owners of the property, our interest in the laboring men

in this country is so immense, so deep, so profound that we stand ready to lose every cent we put in that company rather than see the men we have employed thrown out of work and have imposed upon them conditions which are not of their seeking and which neither they nor we can see are in our interest.... There is just one thing that can be done to settle this strike, and that is to unionize the camps, and our interest in labor is so profound and we believe so sincerely that that interest demands that the camps shall be open camps, that we expect to stand by the officers at any cost.[12]

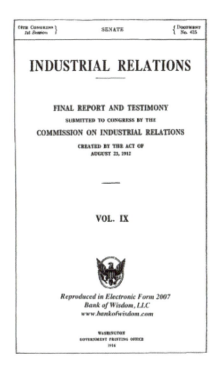

Cover of the 1,046-page final report and testimony submitted to Congress by the Commission on Industrial Relations, detailing its investigation into the 1914 Ludlow Massacre.

In other words, rather than accept unionization at the hands of what the company's management considered to be outside forces, Rockefeller believed that the mining camps should be "open," allowing workers to decide whether to align themselves with organized labor or with company-sponsored employee representation mechanisms. When asked by a member of the committee whether he would uphold this principle even at the cost of all the company's property and the lives of its employees, Rockefeller's chilling reply was: "It is a great principle."

As described above, however, in the wake of the Ludlow Massacre the situation changed dramatically. Initially, Rockefeller attempted to deny the massacre and the company's role in it. However the public reaction to the tragedy was so forceful that the congressional Commission on Industrial Relations, which had been created nearly two years earlier to investigate the conditions of labor in the principal industries in the U.S., turned its attention to the matter. The commission's chairman, labor lawyer Frank Walsh, used the congressional hearings as a platform to publicly excoriate Rockefeller for three days, and exposed the industrialist's role as a

---

[12] "Conditions in the Coal Mines of Colorado," hearings before a subcommittee of the Committee on Mines and Mining, U.S. House of Representatives, Washington: United States Government Printing Office, April 6, 1914. http://congressional.proquest.com.ezproxy.princeton.edu/congressional/result/congressional/pqpdocumentview?accountid=13314&pgId=5c84683d-2cb5-4da5-91ff-bc0751cd32c7&rsId=1398788135F.

John D. Rockefeller, Jr. testifying to the 1915 Industrial Relations Commission about labor strife at the Rockefeller-owned Colorado Fuel and Iron Company. The Ludlow Massacre of the previous year resulted in the death of three women and 11 children at a mining encampment in Trinidad, Colorado, and the resultant public humiliation was cause for a turning-point in Rockefeller's views on industrial relations. Library of Congress, Prints and Photographs Division, LC-DIG-gg-bain-18228.

leading strategist in the company's handling of the strike.

In response to this public humiliation, Rockefeller took decisive action to address the blemish to the family's image. He made a well-publicized and well-received visit to Ludlow to pay his respects to the families of the victims and to have an open dialogue with the miners. At the same time, he engaged several experts in labor relations, including future Canadian prime minister W.L. Mackenzie King, and Clarence J. Hicks, to help him devise a plan for establishing industrial peace at the corporation. This plan—known alternately as the Colorado Industrial Plan, the Colorado Plan, or the Industrial Representation Plan—included a series of physical and policy improvements at the company, and envisioned elected representation of employees in what amounted to a company union. Although several outspoken labor leaders such as Mother Jones, the United Mine Workers of America's Frank Hayes, and John Lawson decried it as little more than corporate welfare, Rockefeller's plan ultimately proved successful. It was accepted by the employees of the Colorado Fuel and Iron Company, and became a model for a number of company unions in various industries throughout the country. By 1928, these employee representation plans covered more than 1.5 million workers,[13] or about 5 percent of the total non-agricultural workforce.

Over the course of the decade following the Ludlow Massacre, Rockefeller's views on industrial relations evolved significantly. For example, in a 1918 speech before the U.S. Chamber of Commerce, Rockefeller emphasized the role of the four stakeholders in business, which he named as: capital, management, labor, and the community. "Labor," he said, "like capital, is an investor in industry"; and he credited the community with providing industry with numerous infrastructural, legal, and financial benefits, as well as the consumer who "reimburses capital for its advances and ultimately provides the wages, salaries and profits that are distributed among the other parties." He then went on to elucidate the principles he believed should govern industrial relations:

---

[13] Richard A. Lester, *The Industrial Relations Section of Princeton University, 1922 to 1985* (Princeton: Industrial Relations Section, 1986), 3.

It is frequently maintained that the parties to industry must necessarily be hostile and antagonistic. I am convinced that the opposite is true; that they are not enemies but partners; and that they have a common interest. Moreover, success cannot be brought about through the assumption by any one party of a position of dominance and arbitrary control. Rather it is dependent upon the cooperation of all four. Partnership, not enmity, is the watchword. If cooperation between the parties to industry is sound business and good social economics, why, then, is antagonism so often found in its stead?[14]

In the conclusion of his speech, Rockefeller offered up, in effect, a 10-point plan for industrial harmony—what he called his Industrial Creed.[15]

If the points which I have endeavored to make are sound, might not the four parties to industry subscribe to an industrial creed somewhat as follows?

1. I believe that labor and capital are partners, not enemies; that their interests are common, not opposed; and that neither can attain the fullest measure of prosperity at the expense of the other, but only in association with the other.

The seemingly ubiquitous power of John D. Rockefeller's Standard Oil Company is satirized in *Puck* magazine's cartoon 'Next!' by Udo J. Keppler, September 7, 1904. Library of Congress, Prints and Photographs Division, LC-DIG-ppmsca-25884.

[14] John D. Rockefeller, Jr., "Representation in Industry," from an address before the Chamber of Commerce of the United States, Atlantic City, New Jersey, December 5, 1918 [as reproduced in Daniel Bloomfield, *Problems in Personnel Management* (New York: H.W. Wilson, 1923), 518].

[15] Ibid., 526-528.

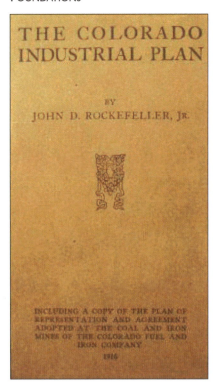

THE COLORADO INDUSTRIAL PLAN

BY
JOHN D. ROCKEFELLER, Jr.

INCLUDING A COPY OF THE PLAN OF
REPRESENTATION AND AGREEMENT
ADOPTED AT THE COAL AND IRON
MINES OF THE COLORADO FUEL AND
IRON COMPANY
1916

Inside cover of John D. Rockefeller, Jr.'s Colorado Industrial Plan, aimed at creating "open," or company, unions.

2. I believe that the community is an essential party to industry and that it should have adequate representation with the other parties.

3. I believe that the purpose of industry is quite as much to advance social well-being as material prosperity; that, in the pursuit of that purpose, the interests of the community should be carefully considered, the well-being of employees fully guarded, management adequately recognized and capital justly compensated, and that failure in any of these particulars means loss to all four parties.

4. I believe that every man is entitled to an opportunity to earn a living, to fair wages, to reasonable hours of work and proper working conditions, to a decent home, to the opportunity to play, to learn, to worship and to love, as well as to toil, and that the responsibility rests as heavily upon industry as upon government or society, to see that these conditions and opportunities prevail.

5. I believe that diligence, initiative and efficiency, wherever found, should be encouraged and adequately rewarded, and that indolence, indifference and restriction of production should be discountenanced.

6. I believe that the provision of adequate means of uncovering grievances and promptly adjusting them, is of fundamental importance to the successful conduct of industry.

7. I believe that the most potent measure in bringing about industrial harmony and prosperity is adequate representation of the parties in interest; that existing forms of representation should be carefully studied and availed of insofar as they may be found to have merit and are adaptable to conditions peculiar to the various industries.

8. I believe that the most effective structure of representation is that which is built from the bottom up; which includes all employees, which starts with

the election of representatives and the formation of joint committees in each industrial plant, proceeds to the formation of joint district councils and annual joint conferences in a single industrial corporation, and admits of extension to all corporations in the same industry, as well as to all industries in a community, in a nation, and in the various nations.

"Why Can't People Think of That Before Breaking Up All the Furniture," by Jay N. "Ding" Darling, June 7, 1919. Reproduced courtesy of the "Ding" Darling Wildlife Society.

9. I believe that the application of right principles never fails to effect right relations; that "the letter killeth but the spirit giveth life"; that forms are wholly secondary, while attitude and spirit are all important; and that only as the parties in industry are animated by the spirit of fair play, justice to all and brotherhood, will any plan which they may mutually work out succeed.

10. I believe that that man renders the greatest social service who so cooperates in the organization of industry as to afford to the largest number of men the greatest opportunity for self development [sic] and the enjoyment of those benefits which their united efforts add to the wealth of civilization.

From this brief review, it is thus possible to understand more fully the spirit behind Rockefeller's involvement in the field of industrial relations, and his support of numerous programs aimed at promoting the causes of industrial peace—support that included the initial funding of Princeton University's Industrial Relations Section in 1922.

Clarence J. Hicks, c. 1883 (detail from University of Wisconsin photo album, 1883). Reproduced by permission of the University of Wisconsin Library.

Clarence J. Hicks

Although virtually unknown by today's generation of labor economists and labor and employment relations professionals, Clarence John Hicks was no less influential in the early history of the industrial relations field than was his contemporary and patron, John D. Rockefeller, Jr. Moreover, he was undoubtedly the single most influential person associated with the founding of Princeton's Industrial Relations Section outside of those within the University itself.

A self-described "industrial relations man," Hicks was first introduced to the nascent field that was to become industrial relations as a young man in the late 1800s. Working for the YMCA (his job was to obtain permission and sponsorships from the owners and management of the numerous railroad lines crisscrossing the country, allowing the organization to establish hostels for railroad workers and day laborers on railroad property), he gradually succeeded in developing close relationships with railroad management, union leaders, and government officials in the United States and abroad. It was these relationships, and his reputation as an able and trustworthy negotiator between management and labor, which eventually brought him to the attention of the Rockefellers.[16]

When John D. Rockefeller, Jr. needed respected labor relations specialists to help devise and implement a plan for industrial peace at the Colorado Fuel & Iron Company (CF&I) after the Ludlow Massacre, Hicks, along with future Canadian prime minister, W.L. Mackenzie King, was one of those to whom he turned in 1915. Hicks, at that time a member of the executive staff dealing with industrial relations and personnel matters for the International Harvester Company, was hired as a special assistant to the president of CF&I and was put in charge of administering the employee representation plan at the company. After two years, he became the director of industrial relations at Rockefeller's Standard Oil Company of New Jersey, in the aftermath of the bitter 1915 strike in the company's Bayonne refinery. After retiring from that company in 1933, he became a member of the board of trustees—and later chairman—of the highly respected nonprofit consulting firm, Industrial Relations Counselors, Inc. (which had been founded by John D.

---

[16] In building his Standard Oil empire, John D. Rockefeller, Sr. had employed the strategy of negotiating special tariff agreements with a number of railroads, allowing him to ship petroleum and other commodities at much lower rates than his competitors—a practice that opened him up to charges of unfair business practices and contributed to the eventual forced breakup of Standard Oil on antitrust grounds. According to Hicks's memoir: "These practices, such as sourcing rebates from railroads, were very common and not illegal at that time. But Mr. Rockefeller's outstanding success in developing a large company made him a target for much unfair abuse." Clarence J. Hicks, *My Life in Industrial Relations: Fifty Years in the Growth of a Profession* (New York and London: Harper & Brothers, 1941), 45.

This is how we celebrate Nov. 13/06 on Thanksgiving : See if you find Mr. Ahens & myself.

KAUKAUNA

THANKSGIVING DINNER

RAIL ROAD Y.M.C.A.

Home to the homeless railroad man — *R.W. Gibson*

Postcard featuring the Kaukauna Railroad YMCA, 1906. Clarence Hicks began his career in industrial relations by establishing YMCA hostels for railroad laborers across North America. Image courtesy of the Kaukauna Postcard Collection, Kaukauna Public Library, Kaukauna, WI.

Rockefeller, Jr. in 1926). He also accepted a temporary appointment as a member of the staff of the National Labor Board, which was established in 1933 under the National Recovery Administration for the purpose of handling industrial disputes.

Like his longtime benefactor, Rockefeller, Hicks believed in the effectiveness of a collaborative relationship between labor and capital.

> The third basis of labor relationships is that which lays emphasis on the unity of interest of all employees, including management, in industry as organized today. In this country it is no longer a question of capital dealing with labor but of management and labor dealing with stockholders and consumers. But employees are numerous among the stockholders and consumers of our national corporations in this country. As employee, owner, and consumer, as well as voter at the polls, the American wage earner has too large a stake in his employing corporation to treat it as something to fight. Management, on its part, is no longer the unquestioned dictator, but can be increasingly regarded as the agent that brings employee, owner, and consumer together in a mutually beneficial relationship. Such a relationship requires co-operation [sic] on all sides to be successful, but most of all it requires the co-operation [sic] of the two active partners, management and men, and in promoting this co-operation [sic] management has the obligation of initiative.[17]

---

[17] Hicks, *My Life* (see note 16), 77.

During the course of his career, Hicks was influential in the establishment of several of the earliest academic industrial relations programs throughout the United States, including those at MIT, Stanford, Caltech, and the University of Michigan. However, it is the one at Princeton University of which he seems to have been particularly proud. In his 1941 memoir, *My Life in Industrial Relations,* he holds up Princeton's Industrial Relations Section as a model to be emulated by others, and describes in detail the following events surrounding its creation.

About twenty years ago [circa 1921], I accepted a Princeton invitation similar to the one received from Yale, and on a number of occasions addressed the labor-problems class which at that time was devoting itself almost exclusively to labor-union developments. Professor D.A. McCabe, who had charge of the class, had asked me to speak of the labor-relations policy of the Standard Oil Company (New Jersey). At the close of one session Professor E.W. Kemmerer and Professor F.A. Fetter, well-known experts in the Economics Department, asked me to visit with them at the Pliny Fisk Library. This library, which was devoted entirely to the financial history of American corporations, had been gathered as a private collection by Pliny Fisk of New York, and later turned over to Princeton. I found here a large number of students in economics who were studying the past and current corporation reports to stockholders of various companies over a period of years. One condition of the gift had been that Princeton should keep the library up to date from year to year. I said to these professors: "Practically every one of the corporations represented in this library has a mass of similar material concerning labor relations, most of which has been published and distributed to its employees. There is no place in America where this current material has been gathered and kept on file. If Princeton would initiate such a library, the employers would gladly furnish the material, and such up-to-date information would be far more helpful to students than any lectures that might be made by representatives of these companies." The next day I received a letter from President John G. Hibben: "What is this you have said to our Economics men? They are all stirred up about it. Will you come over to Princeton, and I will get the Economics faculty together for a dinner at my home, and we will ask you to explain what you think Princeton might well do in this direction?" I, of course, accepted the invitation and in preparation for the gathering outlined what I chose to call an Industrial Relations Section to be organized as a subdivision of the Department of Economics.

Clarence John Hicks
by Robert Brackman,
American, 1898–1980
(1863-1944) 1940.
Oil on canvas. Princeton
University, gift of John D.
Rockefeller III, Class of
1929, in 1941. PP214

Hicks goes on to outline the program he suggested to President Hibben and his "Economics men," which included:

1. Gathering of current information concerning every type of labor relationship in the United States and Canada and also current information concerning legislation on this subject throughout the world.

2. Giving unbiased instruction based on facts thus gathered rather than on theories.

3. Offering opportunities for research as to every type of labor relationship.

4. Making this current information available not only to the faculty and the students but to business men and labor-union leaders, and any others interested in this subject.

5. A budget of not less than $12,000 a year for a period of five years to cover the additional expense of this specialization; this budget to include the services of a full-time professor with the title "Director of Industrial Relations Section," an assistant, a librarian and an assistant librarian, a private secretary and a traveling-expense budget that would enable members of the staff to visit any part of the country where interesting labor developments are taking place.

This program was unanimously approved, and John D. Rockefeller, Jr., was easily persuaded to provide, as his first gift to Princeton, the budget for a five-year program, starting in 1922. President Harold W. Dodds has taken an unfailing interest in carrying out and developing the plans for this Section as originally approved by his predecessor, the late President Hibben. After the Section had been in operation for a few years, a sixth point was added to the program. It provided for an annual

STANDARD OIL MANAGER TO LECTURE HERE TODAY

Clarence J. Hicks, Industrial Relations Expert, Will Outline Modern Labor Policies.

Following its practice of bringing to Princeton leading representatives of the various fields of economic endeavor and of the groups participating in finance and industry, the Economics Department has asked Clarence John Hicks, of the Standard Oil Company of New Jersey, to lecture on the labor policies of that company in McCosh 28, at 4:30.

As Executive Assistant to the President of the Company in charge of its industrial sections program, Mr. Hicks has had many years of experience in dealing with thousands of employees. The extensive development by the Standard Oil Company of employee representation, employee stock ownership, group insurance, pensions, education and practically every other program directed toward the improvement of relations between employee and employer allows Mr. Hicks to speak with authority on these newer phases of management which have become so important since the war. Over a billion dollars of stock in employing

(Continued on Page Six)

Article announcing a lecture by Clarence Hicks at Princeton on February 20, 1929. Courtesy of *The Daily Princetonian*.

conference of executives responsible for or engaged in industrial relations work, and assured free discussion of various points of view, with the co-operative [sic] leadership of industrial executives, outstanding economists, union leaders, and government representatives.[18]

Thus were the auspicious beginnings of Princeton University's Industrial Relations Section in 1922. In a testament to the wisdom of Hicks's original proposal, the Industrial Relations Section closely followed the program he suggested for several decades following its inception, developing along the way a sterling reputation for providing independent and unbiased empirical research into matters considered highly relevant by leaders in industry, organized labor, government, and the academic community.

[18] Hicks, *My Life,* 145-148.

From the Roaring '20s to the New Deal Economy

Workers assemble auto bodies at a Ford Motor Company factory in 1920.

From the unbridled growth and optimism of the "Roaring '20s" through the depths and deprivation of the Great Depression in the 1930s, American industry and American workers endured wide swings of the economic pendulum. Against that backdrop, the Industrial Relations Section at Princeton was established and developed as a clearinghouse of unbiased information and experience for scholars, business leaders, and public policymakers.

Newspaper advertisement touting the increasing affordability of cars during the 1920s.

The Post-War Environment

The increasing power of organized labor, and the stresses of the industrial disputes of the first decades of the 20th century, had gradually led a small but influential cadre of reform-minded labor economists, industrialists, and public policymakers to pioneer new approaches to labor relations, which evolved into the field of industrial relations. But if the years immediately surrounding World War I—with their dramatic growth in both union membership and the number of strikes—were something of a heyday for the early American labor movement, the years between 1922 and 1929 were their complete antithesis.

Following the post-war Depression of 1920-21, the U.S. experienced a period of rapid domestic economic growth. Improvements in industrial efficiency over the course of the decade, due in part to technological advancements, but also to the increasingly widespread application of personnel management techniques, helped keep production costs low and spurred an unprecedented boom in manufacturing.

For the first time, various forms of consumer credit became available, and Americans in large numbers could afford many new types of household appliances and items previously thought of as luxury goods. There was a sudden explosion in the number of cars in circulation, and this in turn prompted major programs of road and highway building and other forms of construction. The expansion of the nation's electric grid, which had slowed during the war years, once again accelerated, and the enormous popularity of recent inventions, such as the radio, commercial phonographs, and, later in the decade, movies with color and sound, caused a huge surge in the entertainment and related industries. Indeed, the decade that had begun in the throes of a post-war depression soon transformed itself into what became known as the Roaring Twenties.

The Industrial Relations Field in the 1920s

For the industrial relations field itself, the 1920s was also a period of firsts. While various aspects of the employment relationship had been studied by economists and academicians from numerous other fields for decades (under names as diverse as labor relations, industrial relations, human relations, and industrial psychology), industrial relations finally began to be recognized as a distinct profession in 1920. One of the hallmark events of that year was the passage of the Kansas Industrial Court Act of 1920, which established the Kansas Court of Industrial Relations—empowered to settle labor disputes statewide through binding arbitration[19]—as the first such court of its kind in the nation.

In that same year, the Employment Managers' Association, a professional organization focused on personnel work, recreated itself as the Industrial Relations Association of America, and the country's first academic course concentration in industrial relations was established in the economics department of the University of Wisconsin, under the direction of John R. Commons.[20] Over the course of the decade, a number of other professional organizations and academic programs focused on the burgeoning field of industrial relations were likewise established. Among these were the nonprofit Industrial Relations Counselors, Inc., an early private sector think tank devoted to research and consulting on industrial relations and personnel management topics, established by John D. Rockefeller, Jr., Clarence J. Hicks, and their associates; a graduate fellowship in industrial relations at Harvard; an industrial research unit at the University of Pennsylvania's Wharton School of

[19] Kaufman, *Origins & Evolution* (see note 1), 11.

[20] Ibid., 10.

Commerce and Finance; an informal Department of Industrial Relations at Columbia University; and the nation's first autonomous academic unit dedicated specifically to Industrial Relations, the Industrial Relations Section of Princeton University.

Princeton University in the 1920s

As with the nation as a whole, Princeton University also experienced a period of rapid growth and expansion in the wake of World War I. The number of applicants for admission increased so rapidly in the years immediately following the war that, by 1922, the trustees were concerned about the University's ability to handle the size of the growing student body and instituted the principle of selective admission for the first time. Despite limiting the size of the incoming freshman class to 600 students and attempting to maintain the total pool of undergraduates at no more than 2,000, 10 years later, the overall population of the school (including undergraduate and graduate students, and full-time faculty and staff) surpassed 3,000 persons.

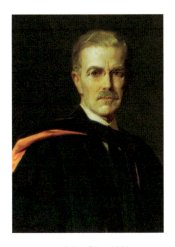

John Grier Hibben (1861–1933), Class of 1882, Ph.D. 1893. John Lamar, American, 1893-1967. Oil on canvas, 1925, 150.5 x 100 cm. (59 1/4 x 39 3/8 in.). Princeton University, commissioned by the Trustees. Photo: Bruce M. White.

In order to accommodate this growth, the University, under President John Grier Hibben, implemented an aggressive building program to expand the size and quality of the campus facilities. This so-called Campaign for the Endowment Fund, the first of Princeton's capital campaigns, was aimed at constructing new dormitories, a building for the School of Architecture, a chemistry laboratory, an extension to McCosh Hall, and a new engineering building. In addition to this program, over the course of a decade a large number of University halls, dormitories, and other facilities were built on and around a campus that nearly doubled in size to 120 acres by 1932.

More than simply expanding its student body, its physical facilities, and its capital endowment, Princeton University in the 1920s also began to experiment with new forms of organizing its academic and administrative structures. In 1923, the University adopted its New Plan of Study, which increased the flexibility of students' education and allowed them to concentrate on a specific field of study in their junior and senior years. Within a few years, this Four-Course Plan, as it was popularly known, led to the requirement of a senior thesis in almost every academic department, and "became a distinctive centerpiece of a Princeton education."[21]

---

[21] Don Oberdorfer, *Princeton University: The First 250 Years* (Princeton: Princeton University Press, 1995), 123

A page from *The Daily Princetonian*, Volume 43, Number 132, 16 November 1922.
Courtesy of *The Daily Princetonian*.

ROCKEFELLER ENDOWS INDUSTRIAL LIBRARY

Financier Pledges His Support for Five Years of Collection at Princeton.

NEW SECTION IS CREATED IN ECONOMICS DEPARTMENT

Library Material Will Include All Printed Matter Dealing with Labor Questions.

(In the following article the Director of the newly created Industrial Relations Section of the Department of Economics and Social Institutions explains 'the facts surrounding the formation and the purpose of the Industrial Relations Library.) By Professor Robert F. Foerster The suggestion for a Library of Industrial Relations at Princeton first came from a visitor to the University who, on being shown the Pliny Fisk collection of financial documents was moved to say: "This is excellent, but it is all cash. You ought to have a collection on the relations of employers to labor." Not long thereafter members of the Faculty seriously proposed that an effort be made to establish the new Library. Gift of $12,000 Yearly. This would require money. While the new collection "would consist largely of materials that would be acquired free of charge, the task of collecting and installing so many items, of classifying them and rendering them available, could not but cost a large sum. The need for additional funds was presently made known to John D. Rockefeller Jr. who on condition that the University should provide space for the Library and ordinary running expenses, generously agreed to meet its other needs by a pledge of $12,000 a year for five years. The nucleus of the Library will consist of literature describing, illustrating, or otherwise growing out of, the relations of employers and employees. It will aim to include books, pamphlets, periodicals, and documents (including unpublished documents). Its main stress will be on arrangements that are actually in operation, and on the aims and recommendations of those who are themselves 'parties to industry. More specifically, it will include the publications of industrial and railroad corporations, and of organizations representing one or another of these interests or the public interest. Interest to Outsiders. Literature of this sort is often of a fugitive character; matters of the greatest significance may be presented in leaflets or booklets whose appearances belie their importance. For this reason, and also because the literature is not usually issued by the standard publishers, but is available only in small editions and can be procured only from the issuing authorities, few libraries have gone far toward including it. To Princeton has come an opportunity that may fairly be called unique. The Library should prove of great value in connection with the efforts of Princeton students to understand labor problems, for here they can gain access to whatever is said by the participants in the work of production. Service to Labor Policy. And yet this collection would fall short of one of its greatest opportunities if it were not consulted by employers and by representatives of labor, since they are better situated than all others to plan the changes in industry which will continue to come rapidly. Such persons, it is hoped, will avail themselves of its resources both by correspondence and by personal visits. At many points the Library may be found to render a substantial service in the encouragement of better standards of labor policy. An Industrial Relations Section of the Department of Economics and Social Institutions has been created to develop the new Library. The Director of the Section will ultimately give some instruction in subjects connected with his task. During the current year especially, he will devote considerable time to contacts in the field calculated to enlarge his own understanding of significant labor relationships and developments and to supplement by personal investigation the published materials in the Library.

Undoubtedly, it was this attitude of innovation and receptivity to new ideas that in 1921 prompted President Hibben to pen his letter to Clarence Hicks, in an invitation that would eventually lead in the autumn of 1922 to the inauguration of the University's new Industrial Relations Section.

The Industrial Relations Section in the 1920s

Princeton's Industrial Relations Section was originally conceived and designed to be a clearinghouse of information and experience for scholars, business leaders, and public policymakers, on questions and practices related to employment, employment relationships and practices, and industrial labor relations. The three main pillars on which the section was built were its library, research program, and program of student instruction. Later, a series of annual conferences and seminars for business and labor leaders and government officials concerned with industrial relations issues was added to supplement its activities. Thus, according to a monograph published by the section (authored principally by one of its noted faculty affiliates, Richard A. Lester), documenting its history from 1922 to 1985:

> A primary objective of the Section was to develop a library specializing in labor subjects, designed for the use of students, faculty, and practitioners and researchers in this country and abroad. Cooperating companies and unions were solicited to supply a continuous flow of published and unpublished material so that the Section's library could serve as a comprehensive, well-catalogued storehouse of information and experience and could, thereby, provide a first-class reference service in response to requests. To facilitate functioning of the library as well as research and student instruction, provision was made that the Section's collection and operations should always be located within the main library of Princeton University.[22]

Staffed with a cohort of labor economists and research associates of diverse backgrounds (for example, Helen Baker, one of the section's earliest research librarians, had been the head of personnel at a retail department store), in its first years the

---

[22] Lester, *Industrial Relations Section*, 2.

Industrial Relations Section operated with a fairly pronounced personnel management orientation. Not only is this trend apparent from the close ties that the section
faculty and staff cultivated and maintained with the executives of many of the leading corporations of the time, but it is also reflected in the focus of its early research.
For example, the first book published under the section's aegis and co-authored
by its inaugural director, Robert F. Foerster, was *Employee Stock Ownership in the
United States,* on a topic of current interest to many corporate personnel managers. Its second publication, a book co-authored by the section's second director, J.
Douglas Brown and its first full-time librarian, Helen Baker, likewise addressed a
topical personnel management–oriented subject, the labor banking movement in the
United States.

In the section's 1986 historical monograph, Richard Lester notes:

> In the late 1920s, many large firms instituted and pursued new programs
> of personnel management. Among the items in many programs were: an
> employee representation plan, employee stock ownership, and various em-
> ployee benefit plans such as group life insurance and company pensions. In
> 1928, the coverage of employee representation plans (later dubbed "company
> unions") exceeded one and a half million workers.[23]

This early influence of a personnel-management style of industrial relations on
the section's figurative DNA is, of course, not at all surprising, considering the
pedigree of the Industrial Relations Section's original sponsors, Hicks and
Rockefeller—both of whom were greatly concerned with the human relations
aspects of the employer-employee relationship. Fortunately, however, in the expan-
sive realm that was the early field of industrial relations, it would seem that neither
of those men suffered from the malady of a rigid ideological stance. For example, in
a 1918 speech in which he advocated for multi-partite representation and collaborative relationships in industry, far from condemning the role of organized labor and
collective bargaining, Rockefeller instead had these rather pragmatic words to say
on its behalf:

> As regards the organization of labor, it is just as proper and advantageous
> for labor to associate itself into organized groups for the advancement of its

---

[23] Lester, *Industrial Relations Section,* 3.

legitimate interests as for capital to combine for the same objects. Such associations of labor manifest themselves in collective bargaining, in an effort to secure better working and living conditions, in providing machinery whereby grievances may easily and without prejudice to the individual be taken up with the management. Sometimes they provide benefit features, sometimes they seek to increase wages, but whatever their specific purpose, so long as it is to promote the well-being of the employees, having always due regard for the just interests of the employer and the public, leaving every worker free to associate himself with such groups or to work independently, as he may choose, they are to be encouraged.[24]

Citizens lining up for auditions as part of the WPA's Federal Theater Project. Courtesy of the American Studies Programs @ The University of Virginia: http://xroads.virginia.edu/~ma04/mccain/play/intro.htm

Thus, unfettered by the pressures of a particular ideological bias on the part of its financial sponsors, and steeped as it was in the objectively rigorous academic environment of Princeton's Department of Economics, the Industrial Relations Section, as it developed and grew, maintained a broad and balanced perspective on all modes of the labor-capital relationship. Whether taking into account the latter's institutional nature, encompassing the effect of the actions and policies of labor unions and governmental bodies, as well as those of corporations, on the well-being of the wage earner; or its personnel nature, such as the impact of corporate management policies and practices on employees, this perspective characterized its research program and other activities over the years. In the words of Richard Lester:

> Members of the Section's professional staff—mostly Princeton faculty—have been free to pursue research projects of their choice in the industrial relations field. That helps to explain the varied character of the Section's research as indicated in the lists of publications following the text.[25]

As will soon become clear, the section's focus on producing objective, careful research, and the respect it earned among all parties to the industrial relations debate for being a neutral and trustworthy broker of relevant information, experience, and best practices, became increasingly important in the 1930s and later into the World War II years. In fact, these were among some of the major factors that enabled it to make significant and lasting contributions during those critical years, both within its academic

---

[24] Rockefeller, "Representation in Industry," 521.

[25] Lester, *Industrial Relations Section,* 1.

A Tennessee Valley Authority public works project. Courtesy of the Industrial Relations Section.

discipline as well as in service to the nation as a whole. Another of these key factors was its particularly strong emphasis on the firsthand collection and analysis of empirical data.

Throughout the remainder of the 1920s, Princeton's Industrial Relations Section strengthened its academic program and expanded its library resources. In 1927, although the initial experimental funding period of five years had not yet expired, John D. Rockefeller, Jr. extended his support of the section for three years, thus demonstrating his confidence in its success. By the end of the 1929-1930 academic year, no fewer than 11 Ph.D. economists had graduated from Princeton, having completed their program of graduate studies under the aegis of the Industrial Relations Section. Among these was James Douglas Brown GS'27, who was to exert a major influence on the section during his nearly 30-year tenure as its director, from 1926 through 1955. Thus the nation's first independent academic unit devoted to the study of industrial relations was off to an auspicious start.

The Great Depression and the New Deal

So much has already been written about the Great Depression of the 1930s, and so much of that has generated so much controversy, that to attempt to analyze its causes here in detail would be superfluous. Instead, it is enough to refer to the words of the economist John Maynard Keynes, who described the nature of the economic system in which we live as "capable of remaining in a chronic condition of subnormal activity for a considerable period without any marked tendency either towards recovery or towards complete collapse."[26] What can be summarized relatively succinctly, however, are the dramatic effects the economic conditions of the 1930s had on the U.S. labor markets, as well as on the labor movement and the social legislation that eventually emerged under the Roosevelt Administration as the New Deal.

From 1929 to the trough of the Depression in 1933, U.S. nominal gross domestic product fell nearly in half from $103.6 billion to $56.4 billion. At the same time, total personal consumption fell by over 40 percent, from $77.4 billion to $45.9 billion, and gross private investment dropped a staggering 90 percent, from $16.5 billion to a mere $1.7 billion.[27] Meanwhile, on the labor front, the total number of private sector employees (full- and part-time) fell from 34.1 million in 1929 to about 25 million in 1933, and aggregate private sector wages declined by nearly half from about $45.5 billion to $23.9 billion over the same time period.[28]

According to the same economic indicators, by the end of the 1930s the U.S. economy had regained some of the ground it had lost, but was still well below the levels of a decade earlier. Nominal GDP in 1939 was $92.2 billion, or 11 percent below the level of 1929; total personal consumption was 13 percent below its 1929 level, at $67.2 billion; and gross private investment was still nearly 44 percent below its 1929 level, at only $9.3 billion. Likewise, on the supply side of the labor market, while the total number of full- and part-time private sector workers had recovered to 31.6 million by 1939—in other words, to almost 93 percent of the 1929 total—that year's private sector wage bill of $37.7 billion was only 83 percent of the level of a decade earlier.

The economic conditions created by the Great Depression had a profound effect on organized labor. While union membership had fallen dramatically during the boom years of the previous decade, declining from a peak of about 4.9 million members in 1920 to a low of about 2.8 million in 1933, by 1939 the number of union members in the U.S. had grown to over 6.3 million; and they more than doubled again by the end of the 1940s.[29] The galvanizing effect of the wage erosion that took place over the course of the Depression years was certainly a factor in this rapid increase in union membership, but it was by no means the only one. In fact, perhaps even more significant was the raft of new social legislation enacted under President Franklin Delano Roosevelt's New Deal promise.

[26] John Maynard Keynes, *The General Theory of Employment, Interest, and Money* (New York: Harcourt, Brace, 1936), 249

[27] U.S. Bureau of Economic Analysis, Table 1.1.5 Gross Domestic Product, as revised on May 31, 2012.

[28] U.S. Bureau of Economic Analysis, Table 6.4A Full-Time and Part-Time Employees by Industry, as revised on August 20, 2009, and Table 2.2A Wage and Salary Disbursements by Industry, as revised on August 17, 2009.

[29] Leo Troy, *Trade Union Membership,* 1897-1962, (Washington: National Bureau of Economic Research, UMI, 1965), 1.

A Depression-era scene from the Franklin D. Roosevelt Presidential Library. Photograph by John E. Allen, Inc.

From 1933 until 1938, hundreds of pieces of federal legislation and presidential executive orders were passed under the New Deal programs of the Roosevelt Administration, creating scores of new federal agencies and accompanying regulations focused on the so-called three Rs of relief, recovery, and reform. Among the better-known programs and agencies established during the New Deal period were those intended to create public works-based employment, such as the Tennessee Valley Authority and the Works Progress Administration, as well as those intended to reform and regulate the financial sector and to protect consumers, such as the Federal Deposit Insurance Corporation, the Securities and Exchange Commission, and the Federal Housing Authority.

A number of New Deal programs were highly contentious in their time, and some—such as the original Agricultural Adjustment Act in 1933—were even overturned by Supreme Court rulings soon after their enactment, only to be reconstituted and reenacted in different forms at a later time. Among the most controversial of these were programs that were to have far-reaching and long-term implications for all of American society: the 1935 National Labor Relations Act, or Wagner Act, which guaranteed a wide range of protections to labor unions and was largely responsible for a resurgence in the organized labor movement; the Fair Labor Standards Act of 1938, which enshrined into federal law the principles of a maximum work week, a minimum wage, and the prohibition of child labor; and the Social Security Act of 1935, which established the basis for today's Social Security system, unemployment insurance, and a host of other social welfare programs.

The Industrial Relations Field in the 1930s

The 1930s saw the establishment of a handful of industrial relations units at universities in the United States and Canada, several of which—as in the earlier case of the Princeton University Industrial Relations Section in 1922—were initiated through the agency of Clarence J. Hicks. Among these were the units at the University of Michigan in 1935, Stanford University in 1936, MIT in 1937, Queens University in Canada in 1937, and

Caltech in 1939. Additionally, the economics departments of many state and private universities taught courses in "labor problems," which, despite their case-study methodological orientation and their emphasis on institutional solutions, have been called the "intellectual forerunner of what is today called labor economics."[30]

As in the 1920s, much of the research that was done in the industrial relations field during this decade remained multidisciplinary, and even interdisciplinary, in nature. Moreover, some of the most important research in industrial relations was not even done in an academic setting, but was conducted by managers of commercial enterprises. For example, a series of groundbreaking experiments known as the Hawthorne experiments was conducted from 1924 to 1932 at the Hawthorne, Illinois plant of the Western Electric Company. The surprising results of these experiments—which showed that, irrespective of work conditions and operational processes, group dynamics had a significant impact on worker productivity—touched off an avalanche of interpretive and theoretical work by industrial sociologists and psychologists, and are widely considered to have been a catalyst for the so-called human relations movement and for the later development of the field of organizational behavior.

Portion of Page 81, Membership Ledger for 1934-1936, Painters Local 12 (Records of International Brotherhood of Painters and Allied Trades of the United States and Canada Local 201). Image courtesy of the University Libraries, State University of New York at Albany. From <http://library.albany.edu/speccoll/documentinglabor/unionmembers.htm>

Thus, in the 1930s, industrial relations was comprised of an assortment of industrial practitioners and scholars from a wide range of academic disciplines—from economics to history, law, sociology, and even psychology—who brought a diversity of methodological, philosophical, and ideological approaches to the field. Some focused their efforts on the more practical, experiential, or institutional aspects of the employment relationship and worker productivity, while others attempted to develop a comprehensive theoretical framework with which to describe them.

To a certain extent, it was the conditions of the Depression era, as well as the effects of the New Deal social agenda that was the Roosevelt Administration's response to them, that helped bring questions of economic theory into sharper focus among a later generation of labor economists. Nevertheless, in the 1930s, the more

---

[30] Kaufman, *Origins & Evolution,* 48.

Women in the Relay Assembly Test Room, ca. 1930. Western Electric Company Hawthorne Studies Collection, Baker Library, Harvard Business School.

applied institutional labor economics and personnel management approaches to industrial relations still dominated the field, to the point that the dean of Princeton University's graduate school and chairman of the renowned mathematics department, Luther P. Eisenhart, could say to a group of visiting industrial relations executives: "You represent one of the most important professions in the world today, because this is an industrial age, and right relations in industry are of first importance."[31]

Princeton University in the 1930s

Despite a variety of difficulties—including a suspension of some of the major building plans initiated in the previous decade, a steadily shrinking number of student applicants, a reduction in the student body's geographic and socioeconomic diversity, and a greatly increased rate of student defaults on tuition and fees that eventually required the implementation of a policy of prepayment[32]—Princeton University managed not only to weather the lean years of the 1930s soundly, but to strengthen its academic resources and its intellectual stature in a number of areas.

Harold Willis Dodds (1889–1980). Paul Trebilcock, American, 1902-1981. Oil on canvas, 1953, 178 x 103.8 cm. (70 1/16 x 40 7/8 in.). Princeton University, anonymous gift. Photo: Bruce M. White.

Under the presidency of Harold W. Dodds, which began in 1933 in the depths of the Great Depression, the University built up world-class mathematics and physics departments, augmented or added a variety of other academic departments (such as the music department, Office of Population Studies and the Creative Arts Program), nearly doubled the number of endowed professorships, and adopted a special plan of examination-free admission for high-potential students from underrepresented parts of the country. With the help of a special grant from the Rockefeller Foundation, Princeton was also able to recruit and provide safe haven for a large number of scientists fleeing the rise of fascism and national socialism in Europe. It is also worth noting that, as part of the University's ethos of service to the nation, a score of Princeton faculty members (including Dodds, who was then chairman of the newly established School of Public and International Affairs) participated in 1932 in a comprehensive examination of the government administration of the state of New Jersey, whose purpose was to recommend areas in which costs could be reduced without disrupting essential public services.

---

[31] Hicks, *My Life,* 127.

[32] Oberdorfer, *Princeton University,* 124.

A very telling description of Princeton University's intellectual environment during this period can be found in the hopeful words of President Dodds to the students and faculty in 1933. During the University's opening exercises of that year, he said:

> We are in the midst of a revolution which does not appear to be of our own seeking; our objectives are confused, our attack uncertain… [Nevertheless] the prospects of high adventure in living are more alluring today than ever. We are in a mood to experiment. In this lies the strength and hope of the present generation.[33]

Women in the Relay Assembly Test Room, ca. 1930. Western Electric Company Hawthorne Studies Collection, Baker Library, Harvard Business School.

And perhaps no other unit of the University in the 1930s embodied this "mood to experiment" of which Dodds spoke than did the Industrial Relations Section.

The Industrial Relations Section in the 1930s

From its inception in 1922 to the end of the 1929-1930 academic year, the Industrial Relations Section of Princeton University published approximately a dozen staff reports and two book-length research reports, and produced 11 Ph.D. graduates. By the end of the 1939-1940 academic year, those numbers had increased to a total of 49 reports and 34 Ph.D. graduates, among which were included two alumni—Richard A. Lester GS'36 and Frederick Harbison GS'40—who were to play important roles in the section's later development. In addition, in 1931, the section's director, J. Douglas Brown, established an annual Conference Course in Industrial Relations, which became, in the words of Richard Lester, "the principal meeting ground for industrial relations executives in this country" for at least two decades.

The importance of this annual conference series to the Industrial Relations Section, and to the industrial relations field in the United States in general cannot be underestimated. In describing it in his historical monograph on the section, Lester recounts the following:

---

[33] Oberdorfer, *Princeton University,* 127.

Each session usually was led by (a) an academic specialist like Sumner H. Slichter of Harvard, Edwin E. Witte of Wisconsin, or Leo Wolman of Columbia; (b) a company executive like Cyrus Ching of U.S. Rubber, John A. Stephens of U.S. Steel, or Chester I. Barnard of New Jersey Bell Telephone; (c) a labor union leader like Clinton S. Golden of the Steelworkers, George M. Harrison of the Railway Clerks, or Joseph A. Beirne of the Communications Workers; or (d) a government specialist like Isador Lubin, Commissioner of Labor Statistics, Harry A. Millis, when he was a member of the National Labor Relations Board, or Murray Latimer, chairman of the Railway Retirement Board....Many top industrial relations executives attended the conference year after year. To encourage free and frank exchange of views and experience, all remarks were off the record. The conference enabled Director Brown and Associate Director Baker to develop close professional relationships with many company industrial relations executives and several union officials. The research program served the same purpose.[34]

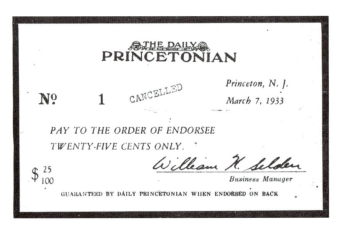

Front side of the scrip currency issued by *The Daily Princetonian,* following President Franklin Delano Roosevelt's declaration of a four-day nationwide bank holiday during the Great Depression. Courtesy of *The Daily Princetonian.*

Some of these close relationships between section faculty and staff, and key figures in industry, were to become immensely important in the nation's preparation for the Second World War, which will be discussed in more detail in the next section.

Following the success of the annual conference for senior executives, the section supplemented it, beginning in 1938, with an annual four-day seminar for junior industrial relations personnel, which was held in the week prior to the main conference. Its teaching faculty was drawn from section staff, as well as scholars from Princeton and other universities, industrial relations practitioners, and union representatives, and its program included a review of the main areas of industrial relations, labor economics, labor relations and labor legislation, and personnel management. Furthermore, the section arranged various informal on-campus meetings each year, through which interested students and staff had the opportunity to interact with labor leaders, business executives, government industrial relations experts, or university professors specializing in the labor and industrial relations fields.

As in previous years, developments in the Industrial Relations Section's program of research during the 1930s continued to reflect industrial relations trends in industry

---

[34] Lester, *Industrial Relations Section,* 5.

and the labor markets. For example, in addition to a number of studies on such familiar subjects as employee savings and investment plans and personnel management issues, research staff and faculty also prepared reports and analyses on topical issues with titles including "Company Plans for the Regularization of Plant Operation and Employment" (1930), "Company Plans for Unemployment Insurance" (1930) and "Company Plans for Unemployment Benefits" (1931), "Company Loans to Unemployed Workers" (1931), "Emergency and Permanent Policies of Spreading Work in Industrial Employment" (1931), "Dismissal Compensation" (1931), and "Hours of Work and Recovery: Summary of Fact and Opinion" (1933).

As the Depression wore on, the section's research also turned to the national public policy priorities of the time. For example, with the resurgence of union activity, in part due to the Roosevelt Administration's efforts to stabilize and raise both prices and wages in the deflationary environment of the Depression, researchers increasingly focused on issues related to collective bargaining, union-management relations, and labor legislation, publishing reports such as "Minimum Wage Legislation in the United States: Summary of Fact and Opinion" (1933), "Collective Bargaining in the Steel Industry: A Factual Summary of Recent Developments" (1937), "Group Purchase of Medical Care by Industrial Employees" (1938), and "The Seniority Principle in Union-Management Relations" (1939).

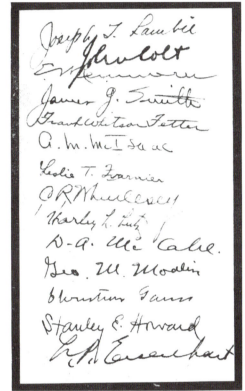

Rear side of *The Daily Princetonian's* scrip currency endorsed by faculty members from the Department of Economics and Social Institutions. Courtesy of *The Daily Princetonian.*

Finally, one of the major developments in the section's research efforts during the Depression years was its involvement in the study of employment security and social insurance—or what was to become known as Social Security. Richard Lester's historical monograph on the section describes this development in typically understated fashion:

> From 1935 on, much of the Section's staff was engaged in the study of employment security and social insurance. Director Brown had served on the old-age security part of the staff of the President's Committee on Economic Security. The Section greatly increased its library resources in social insurance, employment stabilization, and unemployment relief and issued an extensive bibliography on social security.[35]

---

[35] Lester, *Industrial Relations Section,* 3.

Princeton's J. Douglas Brown, with Gerard Swope of General Electric Co., Matthew Woll of the A.F. of L., and Philip Murray of the C.I.O., talking to Social Security Board Chairman Arthur J. Altmeyer, at the first meeting of the Social Security Advisory Council on November 5, 1937. Library of Congress, Prints and Photographs Division, photograph by Harris and Ewing, LC-DIG-hec-23544.

Given the enormous significance the 1935 Social Security Act has had for generations of Americans, and the policy debate surrounding Social Security and its related programs in the present day, it is worth noting the role that the Industrial Relations Section's director, J. Douglas Brown, played in framing the legislation that created it nearly 80 years ago.

J. Douglas Brown's long and distinguished career with Princeton University was interspersed with a number of episodes of government service, both at the federal and state levels. For example, in 1930-1931, he was appointed to President Herbert Hoover's Emergency Committee for Employment, whose purpose it was to advise and facilitate the efforts of non-federal public and private organizations in stimulating employment during the early stages of the Great Depression. As discussed in detail in the following section, he also played a significant role in advising the United States Department of War on matters of industrial efficiency and labor relations during the Second World War.

Perhaps the most impactful aspect of his national service, however, was his role as one of the original framers of the Social Security system. Serving under Secretary of Labor Frances Perkins on President Roosevelt's Committee on Economic Security from 1934 to 1935, Brown—along with others such as the committee's executive director, University of Wisconsin's Edwin E. Witte—was "one of a small number of persons who drafted the original Social Security Program enacted in 1935."[36] In addition to serving on the original drafting committee for the legislation passed in 1935, Brown was also a member of numerous federal advisory councils on Social Security (chairing the first such council from 1937 to 1938, and serving as chairman of the drafting committee for the 1957-1958 council), and was a special advisor on Social Security to the Secretary of the Treasury in 1939 and a consulting economist to the Social Security Board from 1936 until 1950.

In 1963, Brown provided some behind-the-scenes insights into the development of the original Social Security legislation in 1935. Because of its historical interest and insider perspective, his speech before a gathering of Social Security Administration executives is reproduced below in its entirety.

---

[36] Social Security Administration, Social Security Online, "History," http://www.ssa.gov/history/brown.html.

"The Birth of Old-Age Insurance, 1934-1935"

(A speech given by Princeton University's J. Douglas Brown
at a conference of Social Security District Office Managers
at Yonkers, New York on May 17, 1963)

It is not easy in 1963 to put oneself back thirty years to 1933. It is not only the time which has elapsed, but the great events which have intervened.

In 1933, the United States was flat on its back. We had the largest number of unemployed in our history. Discouragement and distress were widespread. Millions were on relief. There seemed to be little hope for getting out of a growing state of shock and paralysis.

In the fall of 1930, some of us were called to Washington to serve on President Hoover's Emergency Committee for Employment. We pushed a "Spread the Work" program with nationwide broadcasts, distributed hundreds of thousands of leaflets, prepared advertisements, and exhorted industry leaders. We proposed a $450,000,000 appropriation for highway construction, and President Hoover fired us after four months for being too radical. I came back to Princeton with a deep sense of the immensity of the problem of insecurity, and put our staff at the Industrial Relations Section to work on what could be done.

The election of Roosevelt in 1932 made the first great change in the downward drift of the country, but the bottom did not come until early 1933 with the closing of the banks. The N.R.A. and a rapid succession of programs, C.C.C., C.W.A., W.P.A., P.W.A., began to chip away at the vast glacier of despair and distress which had spread over the country.

Again some of us that had made Hoover so unhappy were called back to Washington. Several of us were assigned the job of working [o]ut a way of taking care of the vast unemployment on the railroads and, at the same time, of getting the roads into a more economical shape. We developed the basis of the Railroad Retirement Act and various other programs. With the help of the C.W.A., we employed hundreds of unemployed railway clerks to build the records for the new retirement system.

In 1933, Roosevelt was too busy putting out fires to think of more permanent solutions to insecurity. But ideas were being pushed in Wisconsin, Ohio, New York, and other states. Abe Epstein and I. M. Rubinow had written persuasive books. College professors were studying and writing articles. By the summer of 1934, Roosevelt started the push for a long-run attack by setting up a cabinet Committee on Economic Security.

Frances Perkins, then Secretary of Labor, was chairman of the cabinet committee. Professor Ed Witte of the University of Wisconsin was appointed Executive Director of its staff. On August 4, 1934, Witte tried to reach me by phone. A letter requesting me to come to Washington immediately reached me on vacation. From then on, it was a long year's battle to develop what became the Social Security Act from a "gleam in the eye" to a statute on the books.

The staff of the Committee on Economic Security was divided into the unemployment group, the old-age group, the health group, and some others. The health group immediately got into trouble with the American Medical Association and never got off the ground. The unemployment group got the major attention from everybody since millions were unemployed and Wisconsin, well represented in the staff, already had an unemployment insurance plan. Perhaps it was lucky that our little old age group was out of the spot light. It gave us a chance to work out something new.

Our group consisted of Professor Barbara Armstrong of the University of California Law School, Murray Latimer of the Industrial Relations Counselors in New York, and myself. Latimer and I had worked on the Railroad Retirement Act. Otto Richter of the American Telephone and Telegraph Company helped us as an actuary, and later Robert Myers, the present actuary of the Social Security Administration. Armstrong knew foreign social insurance and constitutional law. Latimer knew private annuity programs, and I added the economic approach.

It was obvious from the first that the old age security problem of the United States was vastly bigger than the alleviation of the distress caused by a single depression. The more we studied the shifting age balance in the country, the more we were convinced that we were dealing with a great secular trend which the current depression had, for the first time, made all too apparent.

Our conclusion was that we must build a contributory old age insurance system which, year by year, over the decades ahead would prevent distress among old people by a life-long system of contributions. We knew that old age assistance had to be widely extended and improved to meet the immediate and residual problem. But to rely on assistance alone we were convinced, was both socially bad and fiscally dangerous.

From then on, our battle was first to develop the best plan for old age insurance we could which would fit the United States; second, to design a way to make it constitutional; and third, to rise the obvious need for old age assistance to get political support for contributory old age insurance by marrying the two together by every argument we could muster. We had to be ready by the opening of Congress in January 1935.

In developing the plan for old age insurance, we had the tremendous advantage that, no matter how little we knew, nobody around Washington knew any more! To enumerate a few of our skirmishes:

1. We decided that the system must be a national one. It was the only way it could work. We scared off the "state-by-state" opposition by showing how ridiculous it would be for a man becoming 65 to get insurance checks from a dozen states; by showing how impossible 48 state reserves, 48 state actuarial controls, and 48 state benefit, structures would be to operate, and warning of the effects state plans would have on life-long mobility.

2. We decided that equal contributions by employers and employees were necessary, with the government contributing a third share as an offset to the assistance costs to be saved. I remember getting Bill Green's approval to this on the way into the White House. He was then the President of the American Federation of Labor.

3. Age 65 seemed the right age for the beginning of benefits. There was no great justification for it, but it seemed about right. Nobody ever questioned it.

4. We wanted the widest coverage we could get without stirring up opposition from farmers, housewives, police or firemen. Also, we wanted coverage of

Political collateral in support of the Townsend Plan, c. 1936. Photographs of these items courtesy of the David B. Holcomb collection of American political memorabilia.

everyone for a basic segment of protection. We strongly opposed "contracting out" of existing industrial programs.

5. We tried our best to prevent the accumulation of a gigantic reserve fund by working out a gradual rise in contributions as the benefit load rose. We were licked on this by Secretary Morgenthau, but Congress later reversed itself by delaying the rise in the rates of contribution.

In the second main battle, to assure constitutionality, we got the advice of some of the best professors of constitutional law in the country to help us design a doublebarrelled [sic] law: one barrel covering the contributions, based on the taxing power; the other barrel covering the benefit payments, based on the appropriation power. The only link was the wage records, a sort of coincidental hyphen between the two titles of the Act. Thanks to the genius of Justice Cardozo, helped by a beautiful brief by Charlie Wyzanski, the plan worked.

President Franklin Delano Roosevelt signing the Social Security Act, 1935. Social Security Administration.

The third main battle, to keep the old age insurance program in the Social Security Act, was the hardest of all. Our success was President Roosevelt's great contribution, supported by some glorious infighting.

We got tremendous unintended help from the Townsendites. That winter thirty million postcards came into Washington supporting their $200 a month scheme. It was crazy, but it scared Congress green. Their most effective propaganda was a postcard with two pictures, side by side: one, "Over the Hill to the Poor House," showing an old couple trudging up a road in the winter snow to the poor house over the hill. The other picture was "Comfort in Old Age," showing the same couple in front of a cozy fire, the man smoking his pipe and the woman knitting. Under the picture was printed "Vote Townsend Plan," signed by the sender.

Our argument was a simple one, if you don't provide adequate assistance, the Townsend Plan will win! If you do provide adequate assistance, the shifting age

ANTICIPATION

Artwork by Jerry Doyle. "Anticipation: To J. Douglas Brown, Esq., Looking forward to the realization of a great idea." Courtesy of the Industrial Relations Section.

balance will cause it to grow in cost to billions and billions! The only way to control this vastly mounting cost was to start contributory old age insurance immediately. Our plea was to prevent dependency in old age, rather than just to relieve it after it had occurred.

It is difficult now to recall how new and radical the idea of a national old age insurance scheme was to those congressmen and senators who considered social insurance first cousin to socialism. But the shadow of a great depression and the brilliant leadership of a great President swung hundreds of congressional votes. It was an example of grand opportunism, of satisfying a great unfilled want for security—the political urge—with a plan of truly constructive design which most politicians had to take on faith. Roosevelt could understand the ways of academicians and politicians—both—and was able to use the contributions of both for the benefit of the people.

I remember well the day of crisis for the old age insurance program. The Senate Finance Committee, in executive session, was coming to the moment of truth. Should the old-age insurance titles stay in the bill? Ed Witte and I were the only so-called "experts" permitted in the committee room. Pat Harrison, the Chairman, under orders from F.D.R., had been jockeying section after section through, watching which senators were present for each vote. Just before the old-age insurance titles were up for vote en bloc, Senator King, the senior minority member, read a strong statement against the plan. Senator LaFollette asked that it be answered by the staff and indicated Witte. Although I was supposed to handle old-age insurance, Witte got up, trembling like a ship in a storm, and made the best ten-minute defense of the old-age insurance plan I have ever heard. Senator Harrison immediately called for the vote and we won 9 to 4.

There were further battles, but that is enough history for now. I could tell of the two-year job of revising the program to its present basic structure in 1937-38, when I was chairman of the Advisory Council on Social Security. But people approaching 65 should know when to stop talking, even about old-age insurance.

The War Years

The Memorial Hall
in the lobby of
Nassau Hall,
Princeton University

As the horrors of World War II rocked the world,

the American economy and workforce were simultaneously transformed by unprecedented growth. Likewise, the field of industrial relations grew and matured during the war years and afterward. Director J. Douglas Brown and many staff members of Princeton's Industrial Relations Section played an active role in assisting the U.S. government during the war, keeping true to Princeton's informal motto of being "in the nation's service."

Photograph by Nick Barberio, Office of Communicatons, Princeton University

The invasion of Poland on September 1, 1939 by Germany opened one of the most epic chapters of human strife in recorded history.

Over the nearly six-year duration of the Second World War, tens of millions of people were killed, millions more were injured or displaced, and the productive capacity of entire nations was obliterated. The war was a key turning point in modern history, both for the world as a whole, and for the United States in particular. Humbled by the Great Depression just a few short years before, America emerged from the conflict as an economic powerhouse, a global military superpower, and, for at least a short time, the world's only nuclear nation.

The experience of World War II was transformational for American society on many fronts, not the least of which was the economic one. According to statistics from the Bureau of Economic Analysis, in the ten years from 1930 to 1939, nominal GDP increased from $91.2 billion to just $92.2 billion. By contrast, in the years from 1940 to 1949, GDP rose from $101.4 billion to $267.2 billion, with nearly two-thirds of that change coming from growth in personal consumption.

Women working at the Douglas Aircraft Co. plant in Long Beach, Calif., during World War II. Library of Congress, Prints and Photographs Division, FSA/OWI Collection, LC-USW33-028626-C. From <http://www.pophistorydig.com/?tag=women-aircraft-workers>

In regard to labor, the changes were equally dramatic. In 1940, the year before the United States' entry into the war, the U.S. military employed roughly 793,000 people. By war's end in 1945, that number had climbed to more than 11.3 million service men and women. Meanwhile, in the same period, full- and part-time employment in domestic private industry grew from 33.5 million to 38.2 million. A sizeable portion of this increase in employment, which included the temporary substitution of millions of workers who had entered military service, was made possible by the large-scale absorption of women into the industrial workforce for the first time ever. Moreover, as a result of the dramatic growth experienced by organized labor during the Depression era (in part due to the effects of pro-union New Deal social legislation), by the eve of World War II, union membership represented as much as 30 percent of the total non-agricultural workforce. Along with this growth in numbers there was also a concomitant increase in the number and severity of labor disputes.

The entry of the United States into World War II had a temporary restraining effect on the ability of the labor unions to leverage their growing influence. The imperative to curb inflation by keeping wage and price increases in check, and to ensure that industrial disputes did not disrupt wartime production, prompted the federal government to create the War Labor Board, with the power to set wage and price controls and to resolve labor disputes. At the close of the war, however, many of the restrictions on collective bargaining and strike action were eased, and as business and union leaders sought to make up for what they perceived as lost ground, a period of massive labor disputes ensued.

These developments, together with the economic impact of millions of returning troops and the transition from wartime industry back to a civilian economy with years of pent-up demand, were to have significant effects on economic growth, wages and price levels, and on the influence and power of organized labor over the next two decades. In the words of one historian of industrial relations:

> Once the war was over, these companies were intent on recapturing their losses. Many unions also looked forward to the end of wartime controls, for they too were intent on making up for lost bargaining opportunities, particularly with regard to wages, which had badly lagged behind both prices and corporate profits. The prospect, therefore, was for renewed labor-management conflict at the end of the war on a scale as large or larger than when the war began five years earlier. (This prospect became a reality in 1946 when the economy experienced a strike wave of unprecedented proportions.) From the perspective of 1945, then, employer-employee relations, and labor violence and unrest in particular, was suddenly the number-one domestic issue confronting the nation.[37]

In his monograph on the history of Princeton's Industrial Relations Section, Richard Lester further encapsulates the situation as follows:

> By 1946, the labor relations situation in this country had changed considerably from the prewar years, and a great deal of attention was being devoted to labor matters. Between 1941 and 1945, union membership increased from 10.5 million to almost 15 million. The return to free collective bargaining meant an upsurge in strikes, which had largely been avoided in war production by provision for National War Labor Board decisions to settle labor disputes. Strikes increased in

[37] Kaufman, *Origins & Evolution,* 62-63.

the latter part of 1945, and reached an all-time peak in 1946, with almost 5,000 strikes involving 14.5 percent of the employed industrial workers and resulting in a direct loss of 116 million "man-days" of work.[38]

Reflective of the significance of this issue in the postwar period was the passage of the Employment Act of 1946, which articulated the position that government could play a constructive role in maintaining and improving the stability of the national economy. In framing this legislation, Congress declared that:

> [I]t is the continuing policy and responsibility of the Federal Government to use all practicable means consistent with its needs and obligations and other essential considerations of national policy, with the assistance and cooperation of industry, agriculture, labor, and State and local governments, to coordinate and utilize all its plans, functions, and resources for the purpose of creating and maintaining, in a manner calculated to foster and promote free competitive enterprise and the general welfare, conditions under which there will be afforded useful employment opportunities, including self-employment, for those able, willing, and seeking to work, and to promote maximum employment, production, and purchasing power.[39]

Nevertheless, in contrast to the pro-labor policies of the Depression years, the federal government's concern for full employment in the immediate postwar years did not result in blanket support for organized labor. Significantly, in reaction to a number of wartime labor disputes and a series of massive strikes in 1946, and over the veto of President Truman, Congress passed the Taft-Hartley Act of 1947, imposing important restrictions on unions' ability to strike and prohibiting various types of organizing activities which it deemed to be unfair labor practices. Bitterly opposed by organized labor, this legislation was one of the first in a series of setbacks to union influence that would reverberate for decades.

Workers install fixtures and assemblies to a tail fuselage section of a B-17F bomber, October 1942. Library of Congress, Prints and Photographs Division, FSA/OWI Collection, LC-DIG-fsac-1a35356.

---

[38] Lester, *Industrial Relations Section,* 8.

[39] Gardner Ackley, Otto Eckstein and Arthur M. Okun, *Annual Report of the Council of Economic Advisers, January 1966* (Washington: United States Government Printing Office), 170.

The Industrial Relations Field
in the 1940s

As alluded to above, the decade of the 1940s was a pivotal time for the field of industrial relations. Prior to the Second World War it had been a young discipline that was, in many respects, still in a process of self-discovery—indeed, a field in which labor economists and sociologists could work side by side with non-academic practitioners from industry, researching new topics and developing new methodologies by which to explore the questions of interest to them. While its overall character remained multidisciplinary well into the 1950s, the 1940s saw the beginning of a rapid process of institutionalization and specialization into a number of increasingly distinct and more formalized areas of study, characterized by the creation of industrial relations units at many universities across the country, as well as by the establishment of a professional association dedicated to industrial relations research and the field's first academic journal.

Among the universities that established industrial relations programs during the course of the decade were Cornell University (in 1945), which a couple of years later also began publishing America's first peer review journal dedicated to industrial relations, the *Industrial and Labor Relations Review;* Yale University, the University of Minnesota, and the Universities of Chicago and California, Berkeley and Los Angeles, also in 1945; the University of Illinois, in 1946; Rutgers University and the University of Wisconsin, in 1947; New York University, the University of Hawaii, and Canada's McGill University, in 1948; and the University of Utah, in 1949. Each of these programs was structured differently, offering a variety of permutations of undergraduate- and graduate-level courses and degree programs, and with some even offering extension courses for business managers and labor union representatives. However, one of the common elements they shared was their multidisciplinary character.

[I]n keeping with the original conception of the field, the new units were also explicitly organized on a multidisciplinary basis. Thus, all the units brought together faculty and course subjects from the several disciplines that touched on the employment relationship and, more specifically, on the pressing labor problems of the times. The intellectual rationale…was that the study and resolution of labor problems would be materially advanced by an interdisciplinary melding and integration of ideas and research methods, an intellectual cross-fertilization that would take place only if faculty from the various disciplines were brought together in one administrative unit.... [40]

In addition to stimulating this blossoming of new industrial relations units, the experience of the developments in the labor markets of the Great Depression and World War II eras also had a galvanizing effect on the institutional labor economics branch of the field. Having observed the ineffectiveness of the purely theoretical labor supply and demand functions to explain completely the economic conditions of the 1930s, and having seen firsthand the effects of the federal government's wage and price control efforts of the 1940s, a new generation of classically trained labor economists—men such as the University of California's Clark Kerr, Harvard's John T. Dunlop, Princeton's Richard A. Lester, and Yale's Lloyd G. Reynolds, and others—advanced the effort to incorporate their understanding of institutional factors, and particularly of the impact of labor unions and collective bargaining practices on wage and price economics, into neoclassical economic theory. In Lester's words:

> Work in war agencies in Washington and in the field taught academic labor economists much about pricing, wage structures and variation, and collective bargaining, in actual practice....Many labor economists, including some associated with the Section in the past, got an education in real-world wage-setting, employee benefits, and grievance procedures from serving as neutral members of panels, boards, and commissions under the War Labor Board and its regional offices. Such wartime experience had a major influence on developments in industrial relations research in the postwar years.[41]

Concerning these developments, MIT's historian of labor economics, Paul McNulty, recounts how, in 1948, renowned labor economist Edwin E. Witte reviewed the book *Insights into Labor Issues* edited by Richard Lester and Joseph Shister. He concluded that the group of young labor economists represented in it were well-positioned to make a significant contribution to the field of industrial relations by bringing together both a strong grasp of theory and a knowledge of the practical, or institutional, aspects of the labor markets. According to McNulty:

> What Witte discovered in this book—the integration of economic analysis with labor studies to a more pronounced extent than had been the case in the preceding

---

[40] Kaufman, *Origins & Evolution,* 67.

[41] Lester, *Industrial Relations Section,* 6-7.

decades—has become the distinguishing characteristic of labor economics in more recent years. It is this, more than any other single feature, that distinguishes contemporary labor economics from the pre–World War II period.[42]

Industrial relations historian Bruce Kaufman, in his *The Origins and Evolution of the Field of Industrial Relations in the United States* (recipient of the Princeton Industrial Relation Section's Richard A. Lester Award in 1992), comments further on this development, saying:

> These economists turned labor economics away from a historical, descriptive analysis of labor problems and toward an analytical study of labor markets. They were clearly in the neoclassical tradition in that they sought to refashion labor economics so that it would more nearly resemble other areas of economic analysis. At the same time, they continued to have many links with the institutionalists, particularly in their use of the case study, inductive method of research; their focus on the pervasiveness and importance of imperfections in the labor market; their favorable view of collective bargaining and protective labor legislation…and their desire to broaden economic theory beyond the study of market forces by bringing in nonmarket considerations from other disciplines.[43]

He also identifies—as one of the leading voices within labor economics in this progression from a more qualitative study of labor problems to a more empirical, theoretical analysis of labor markets—Princeton's Richard Lester, about whom he writes the following:

> The clearest dividing line between the labor problems and labor markets approach to labor economics is provided by Richard Lester's text Economics of Labor (1941). Three features of the book distinguish it from earlier labor problems texts: its focus on labor markets rather than labor problems per se, the important role it gives to the determination of labor market outcomes by demand and supply conditions, and the use of analytical techniques such as graphical representation of demand and/or supply curves. The text also represents an interesting middle ground between the institutionalism of [John R.] Commons and the neoclassical economics of [John R.] Hicks. Lester clearly follows Hicks and the neoclassical

---

[42] Paul J. McNulty, *The Origins and Development of Labor Economics,* (Cambridge, MA: MIT Press), 177.

[43] Kaufman, *Origins & Evolution,* 85.

approach to labor economics in that he focuses attention on the operation of labor markets and demand and supply, but he clearly follows the institutional perspective in the amount of attention given to the imperfect nature of labor markets and in the relatively favorable treatment of unions and protective labor legislation.[44]

It was largely in this spirit that Lester and the University of Illinois's William McPherson used the occasion of the American Economic Association's January 1947 meeting to organize a group of like-minded labor economists and to found the Industrial Relations Research Association. According to Lester:

The aim [of the association] was to have a professional association for persons engaged in industrial relations research—economists, sociologists, political scientists, psychologists, and law professors—and those using the results of such research in teaching and in practice in industry. [J. Douglas] Brown and [Richard A.] Lester played a leading role in the creation of the IRRA. At the time of its first annual meeting in December 1948, IRRA had a membership of 1,025; the printed proceedings of that meeting ran to 233 pages.[45]

Princeton's first Army Specialized Training Program graduation, held in Richardson Auditorium, January 1, 1944. From Historical Photograph Collection, Campus Life Series. From <http://www.princeton.edu/~mudd/databases/warbook.html>

The intensified focus on industrial relations during the 1940s involved not only academicians, but industry specialists and governmental policymakers as well. For example, in 1947, the National Planning Board launched a broad-based research program under the heading "The Causes of Industrial Peace under Collective Bargaining." According to Richard Lester:

A committee of twenty-nine prominent persons, chaired by Clinton S. Golden [head of the United Steelworkers union], was appointed to oversee the project. It included J. Douglas Brown, Frederick Harbison (executive officer of the Chicago Industrial Relations Center), George W. Taylor (chairman of the War Labor Board), Clark Kerr, and John T. Dunlop. In seeking to determine the factors that contribute to constructive relations under collective bargaining, detailed case studies were made of twelve large plants, in different competitive industries, that had important industrial relations problems to solve. The individual studies and the final report received wide publicity during the years 1948 to 1953.[46]

---

[44] Ibid., 226 (Note 17).

[45] Lester, *Industrial Relations Section,* 9.

[46] Ibid.

Thus, with an outpouring of interest in industrial and labor relations in a number of influential academic centers across the country, the growing efforts by institutional labor economists to incorporate their ideas and real-world experiences into the theoretical framework of economics, and the foundation of a professional society by some of the field's leading scholars, it was during the 1940s that industrial relations became firmly established as an academic field. As Kaufman asserts:

> Just as the labor conflict engendered by World War I precipitated the birth of the field, the labor conflict of the Depression and World War II years led to the emergence of industrial relations as a widely recognized, fully institutionalized academic field of study. Industrial relations had come of age.[47]

Princeton University in the 1940s

Dating back to Woodrow Wilson's famed speech at Princeton's sesquicentennial celebrations in 1896, the unofficial motto of the university was "Princeton in the Nation's Service."[48] Perhaps at no other time in the University's living memory was this motto tested more than during the decade of the 1940s.

Under the leadership of its president, Harold W. Dodds, who had already so ably guided the University through the challenge of the Depression years, Princeton began making preparations as early as the summer of 1940 for the United States' entry into the Second World War. At that time, Dodds created a committee on national defense, which prepared a detailed study of the potential contributions that could be made to the war effort by individual faculty members and academic departments. The University's preparations and service to the nation, moreover, did not stop there.

In the wake of the First World War, Dodds' predecessor, President John G. Hibbens, had urged students to enroll in the University's fledgling ROTC program. Thus, by the time the United States entered the Second World War, more than 2,000 Princetonians had been commissioned as Army reserve officers, and many of them served in active duty during the war.[49] In addition, during the war years, Princeton's campus served as a hub for the training of hundreds of military personnel. According to one history of the University:

---

[47] Kaufman, *Origins & Evolution,* 63.

[48] This motto was later modified under Princeton University's 18th president, Harold T. Shapiro, to "Princeton in the Nation's Service, and in the Service of All Nations."

[49] Richard D. Challener, "Reserve Officers Training Corps (R.O.T.C.)" in Alexander Leitsch, ed., *A Princeton Companion* (Princeton: Princeton University Press, 1978).

The war years were especially difficult. Princeton adopted an accelerated program to give its students an opportunity to graduate before they entered the armed services. At the same time the army and navy sent hundreds of young men to the campus for general or specialized training. The number of students fluctuated widely from month to month. A faculty depleted by enlistments or calls to government service had to teach unfamiliar subjects at break-neck speed. Yet the basic ideals of a Princeton education were maintained and a remarkably high percentage of undergraduates who had left the University for military service returned after the war.[50]

The University's contributions to the war effort were a major priority throughout the first half of the 1940s, but they were of course not the only one. Despite the turbulence of the period, the University continued its expansion efforts, and a number of significant programs and projects were completed. Between 1941 and 1946, the number of faculty members grew by more than 30 percent, to more than 500, while the student body increased by nearly half, to just under 4,000 undergraduate and graduate students. Meanwhile, plans for a number of new academic departments were initiated, resulting in the creation of the departments of religion (1940), aeronautical engineering (1941), and Near Eastern studies (1947), and the University's undergraduate plan of study was revised to include for the first time a set of core distribution requirements. The resources, faculty, and student body of the newly renamed Woodrow Wilson School of Public and International Affairs were also greatly expanded in the years immediately following the war, in part through the creation of a new graduate program.[51]

The growing numbers of students, faculty, and administrative staff on the University's campus required an expansion of Princeton's physical plant as well. During the 1940s, a number of educational, research, and residential facilities were purchased, constructed, or improved, including such noted structures as Dillon Gymnasium in 1947 and Firestone Library in 1948. To help offset the costs associated with this expansion, as well as to meet its general operating expenses, the University began its first systematic annual alumni appeal efforts in 1940, raising $80,000 in that year.

Finally, while there were many other significant developments at the university in the second half of the 1940s that could be enumerated, one in particular stands out due to the notable participation of the Industrial Relations Section's own J. Douglas Brown:

---

[50] Joseph R. Strayer, "Dodds, Harold Willis," in Leitsch, *A Princeton Companion.*

[51] An initial key ingredient of the Woodrow Wilson School's new graduate program was the recruitment of high-potential former military servicemen under a combination of GI benefits and special fellowship grants. One of its first participants was Robert F. Goheen of the Class of 1940, who later became the University's 16th president.

Princeton University's bicentennial, celebrated during the 1946-1947 academic year with a year-long series of events. These are described in Alexander Leitsch's *A Princeton Companion:*

> The bicentennial of Princeton's founding on October 22, 1746, was celebrated in a year-long series of events in 1946-1947. The "concatenation," as Professor Charles G. Osgood called it in his book on the celebration, began in September with a sermon in the Chapel by the Archbishop of Canterbury and ended with an address by President Truman in front of Nassau Hall at the concluding convocation in June. Intervening were three other convocations, and in between these "gaudy days" were sixteen conferences of scholars and men of affairs, brought together to help recover some of the momentum that had been lost during the war years and to try to chart what lay ahead. President Dodds made three major addresses at the convocations in October, February, and June. During the course of the year, he also conferred honorary degrees on some hundred eminent persons, including Niels Bohr, John von Neumann, Arnold J. Toynbee, Alvar Aalto, Erwin Panofsky, Reinhold Niebuhr, Salvador de Madariaga, Jacques Maritain, Trygvie Lie, General Dwight Eisenhower, Secretary of State George Marshall, and President Truman. *The chief designer of the Bicentennial Conferences was Dean J. Douglas Brown, who directed a series of conferences in the fall;* Professor Whitney J. Oates directed a series in the winter and spring. Most of the conferences were led by Princeton professors and were concerned with broad topics in their several fields of scholarship, e.g., "The Future of Nuclear Science," Eugene P. Wigner; "The Humanistic Tradition in the Century Ahead," Donald A. Stauffer; "The University and Its World Responsibilities," Gordon A. Craig and Cyril E. Black. The conferences were attended by scholars and men and women of affairs from all parts of the world.[52]

Final Bicentennial Convocation (200th Anniversary). Academic procession down Holder Hall steps June, 17 1947. Individuals and year they received an honorary degree are: Ben Moreell, 1947; Walter S. Adams, 1947; Joseph R. Strayer, 1925 and 1980, marshall; John W. Davis, 1924; Albert Einstein, 1921. From the Historical Photograph Collection, Campus Life Series.

---

[52] Leitsch, *A Princeton Companion* (see note 49). (Italics added).

The Industrial Relations Section
During and After WWII

Princeton University's Industrial Relations Section and its staff played an active role in assisting the U.S. government during World War II. Even before America's entry into the war, the director of the section, J. Douglas Brown, was appointed chief of a special government agency, the Priorities Branch of the Office of Production Management's (later the War Labor Board's) Labor Division, whose aim was to work with industry to help make the most efficient use of human and capital resources both in the build-up to a wartime economy and during the war itself, as well as to facilitate the effective allocation of government defense contracts. In his later years, Dean Brown wrote about his experiences in his *The Industrial Relations Section of Princeton University in World War II,* which contains a wealth of material detailing his involvement and those of his colleagues, section graduates and faculty associates Richard A. Lester and Frederick H. Harbison, in wartime activities of national importance.

From this fascinating memoir, one can see not only the high regard in which Princeton University and its Industrial Relations Section were held by America's commercial, military, and political leaders, right up to the president of the United States (a tradition that has evidently been maintained up to the present time, considering the number of section alumni and faculty associates who have been active participants on high-level governmental and presidential commissions over the years), but the crucial influence Brown and his colleagues had in facilitating the country's industrial preparation for the war. A number of passages from Brown's account are particularly illustrative of the section's role in catalyzing preparations for the national war effort, as well as its contributions once that effort was fully underway. For example, early in the memoir, he describes the atmosphere in which the section operated prior to the United States' entry into the war:

> The shift to high gear in the Section's activity is best summarized in the opening paragraph of the Section's annual report for 1939-1940, written in the summer of 1940.

> > With the outbreak of the European War in September, 1939, it soon became apparent that the problems of industrial manpower, group relations, and social security in this country would be fundamentally affected regardless of our position as a neutral state. Production of munitions for France and

England and for our own defense has, with increasing momentum, shifted American industry from a depressed, peace-time basis to an economy in which the effective use of the Nation's human resources is of paramount concern. As a part of a University long sensitive to national problems, the Industrial Relations Section has found itself faced with new and challenging tasks.

At the Section's ninth annual conference at the Graduate College, which began on September 11, 1939, the talk turned constantly to the impact of the war on American industry, despite the announced program of discussions of conventional issues in industrial relations. The membership of the conference included the senior industrial relations officers of a large proportion of the leading American corporations which would be most involved in the defense program and the succeeding war effort, including those in oil, steel, motors, chemicals, electrical manufacturing, aircraft, communications, rubber, machinery, public utilities, and finance.

The purpose of the annual invitation conferences was to help company executives gain a broader perspective on economic and industrial relations issues and problems. The faculty of the conferences included leading academic, industrial, and government representatives. The 1939 sessions, occurring soon after war was declared in Europe, had unusual significance as a catalyst in stimulating further discussion in the executive offices of many leading corporations concerning the problems of manning for defense. They also helped greatly, when combined with previous conferences and the long-continued interchange in the Section's research program, to give the Section an almost unique capability as a clearing house of information and judgment on policies and experience during the mobilization effort.[53]

A little later, Brown goes on to recount a private meeting he had at the recommendation of his former colleague, Ambassador John G. Winant—director of the Geneva-based International Labor Office and the first head of the Social Security Board—with President Roosevelt on the subject of the nation's industrial preparedness for war:

When on that day I arrived at the front gate of the White House, I was immediately cleared and told to go to the portico entrance. There, a secretary told me that the

---

[53] J. Douglas Brown, *The Industrial Relations Section of Princeton University in World War II* (Princeton: Industrial Relations Section, Princeton University, 1976), 10-11. (Hereafter cited as *IRS WWII*.)

President was in bed with a cold but that he wanted to see me upstairs in his bedroom. I was taken up to the family living room and, after a short wait, ushered into the bedroom. The President was in bed, propped up with several pillows, but apparently in good fettle. A great lover of conversation and an expert in drawing people out, Roosevelt, remembering my earlier activities in government, opened our talk with an idea he had picked up about South American social security programs. He soon got down to business, however, and told me that he wanted me, on my own and on an entirely confidential basis, to study the manning problems involved in a rapid expansion of the industries Winant had outlined as crucial to the British war effort. I was not to make any contacts in government. As I found out later, there were only two officers in the defense establishment who could have helped me had I asked, and they were far down the line.[54]

The report that Director Brown eventually compiled for the U.S. President, coming from an unbiased and highly credible academic source, helped to provide important support for the executive branch's quiet planning for America's war mobilization. According to Brown's mesmerizing personal account:

The Bicentennial Medal of 1946 was reissued with new dates for the University's 250th anniversary in 1996.

By early May 1940, after traveling thousands of miles in the United States and Canada, I was ready to report my findings to President Roosevelt. An appointment was arranged for May 9, the day before the Germans invaded Holland. This time I was told to come to the office entrance of the White House. While I was waiting to in to the President, I asked General Watson, the appointments secretary, how I could get a lot of points across to the President without any conventional detours. He said, "Start talking and don't let the Boss talk." When I went in, I talked a blue streak about the serious problems ahead. Roosevelt knew what I was doing and his eyes twinkled over his glasses. I am sure that he got my message that the problems of manning a rapid expansion in the airplane, steel, and machine tool industries needed the immediate attention of the government. The news the next day of the German attack on Holland underlined the message....The main thrust of my report was the need for both corporations and the government to develop quickly the organized capacity to expand executive and supervisory personnel, to recruit skilled labor, and to plan for the dilution of forces with less trained labor in bottleneck industries such as airframes, air engines, and machine tools. I discussed the need for improved wage

---

[54] Ibid., 13-14.

and salary administration to adjust quickly to the need to move labor into such industries and to meet the rapid increase in the cost of living in defense centers. Also, I emphasized the importance of effective arbitration machinery to avoid stoppages where managements were resisting adjustment to change. I urged a positive policy in gaining union-management cooperation in the acceleration of defense production and the encouragement of active participation by labor in national and regional committees to make clear that building for defense was a joint national effort.[55]

Once the U.S. war effort was in full gear, Princeton's Industrial Relations Section staff continued to make important contributions. Working as consultants in the War Department, Director Brown and his section-associated colleagues provided valuable assistance, troubleshooting such problems as dealing with manpower shortages in specific industries and ensuring that contractors' policies on human resource utilization and optimal work hours were reasonable. Among the many critical issues they handled on behalf of the War Department, they were also charged with keeping essential industries and companies from having their key personnel siphoned off through the draft, as well as preventing the over-contracting of particular firms at the expense of wasted manpower at others. As can be seen from the following illuminating example from Dean Brown's memoir, section staff dealt with a range of highly complex and sensitive issues in service to the nation's war effort.

The variety of problems can be illustrated by a particular manpower emergency. The Quartermaster General called our office in desperation: Would the Secretary of War get the Governor of Connecticut off his back and permit a number of small textile companies to allow women to work night shifts despite the restrictions of state laws and the adverse opinion of his Department of Labor? He explained the urgent need for the product. We called the Governor on behalf of the Secretary of War without going into details, but impressing on him that it was in the national interest in the war effort to make an exception in the particular situation. He agreed to do so. The explanation we did not give the Governor was that the plants were making millions of yards of sandfly netting for the North African campaign, which was to begin in November. The Quartermaster General had spread out over many smaller plants the orders for the massive quantity needed to avoid tipping off German Intelligence agents.[56]

---

[55] Brown, *IRS WWII,* 15-16.

[56] Ibid., 68-69.

As significant as the personal endeavors of Director Brown were to the section's participation in the U.S. war effort during the World War II years, it should also be noted that his were not the only significant contributions. In fact, the entire staff of the section was dedicated to the national service during the war years, and in some cases individual members were involved in important research on groundbreaking developments in industrial relations. One such subject area was the entry of large numbers of women into the industrial workforce during the 1940s.

> It had become evident by the fall of 1941 that a very important reservoir of additional workers for war production would be women. The Armed Forces were drawing off men from the civilian labor force at a steadily increasing rate. The British were moving women into war plants and many supporting and defense services with marked success. At the Section, Helen Baker was unusually fitted to study the problem by both research training and earlier experience as a personnel officer in a large department store. In October 1941 she had initiated a study of the employment of women in sixty-two companies, including both those normally using women and those employing them for the first time....The immediate distribution of the report to government officials, cooperating companies, and the general press led to block orders and much correspondence. As the employment of women increased during 1942 and 1943, Helen Baker's advice was sought more and more by the specialists in the War Department. She reviewed a policy statement prepared for use by Army liaison officers issued in the early fall of 1942. She helped plan working conferences of government specialists and industrial executives in preparation for a major use of women workers in rapidly expanding war industries.[57]

Pamphlet issued by the Office of Production Management of the War Department, containing regulations for its four divisions: Production, Priorities, Purchases, and the Bureau of Research and Statistics. The Priorities branch was headed by Princeton Industrial Relations Section's J. Douglas Brown. From <http://www.ibiblio.org/hyperwar/ATO/Admin/OPM/OPM-Duties/index.html>

Throughout the war years, the Industrial Relations Section continued to pursue its program of research, teaching, and annual conferences (with the exception of the years 1942 and 1943), publishing numerous studies, reports, and annotated bibliographies—of which there were over 20, running to more than 135,000 copies, from 1940 to 1945—and carrying out a variety of firsthand research and data-gathering exercises in conjunction with cooperating companies. By and large, these efforts were increasingly dedicated to subjects of importance to the war effort, and the significance of the section's overall involvement in these activities is nicely summarized in the following passage from J. Douglas Brown's war memoir:

[57] Ibid., 67-68.

J. Douglas Brown during his tenure as Chief of the Priorities Division, Office of Production Management, U.S. War Department, c. 1944. Library of Congress, Prints and Photographs Division, FSA/OWI Collection, LC-

After obtaining clearances at Princeton and completing my teaching duties, I started work in Washington on May 12, 1941, on loan from Princeton on a dollar-a-year basis. The plan was that I work five days a week at OPM and return to Princeton for a two-day weekend to continue my supervisory responsibilities at the Industrial Relations Section. While my job with the OPM and its successor, the War Production Board, was as strenuous as any I have ever experienced, the breaks on weekends greatly helped me to keep in contact with the broader flow of information and research available at the Section. Helen Baker was doing a valiant job of studying problems and trends. The Section's library was a constant help. In getting background for administrative decisions in Washington, it was far easier to ask the Section's staff to make a quick survey than to use the ponderous machinery of government agencies. In a very real sense, Princeton was lending the United States government the staff and resources of the Section at a very critical period in the mobilization effort.[58]

In the course of human history, a number of major wars have been lost in no small part due to supply chain disruptions. It is therefore no exaggeration to state that the efforts of Princeton's Industrial Relations Section and its associated personnel were of enormous significance to the United States in winning the "supply-chain war"—an accomplishment that was in itself a major contributing factor in the Allied victory in the Second World War. However, the section's contributions did not end there; at the close of the war and throughout the remainder of the 1940s, it also played an important role in the nation's transition back to a peacetime economy.

After a two-year hiatus due to the War Department's use of Princeton's Graduate College buildings, the Industrial Relations Section finally resumed its series of annual conferences in September 1944. According to Dean Brown:

> The main "Conference Course," the twelfth in a series which commenced in 1931, was centered on the problems of readjustment from war to peace. In the nineteen sessions, the major issues in reconversion and in planning for the future were thoroughly discussed under the leadership of the best men available throughout the country....Those invited to attend the Conference were the senior industrial relations executives of companies cooperating in the year-round work of the Section. Altogether, the Conference group represented 127 companies employing over four million workers.[59]

---

[58] Brown, *IRS WWII,* 26-27.

[59] Ibid., 105-106.

Moreover, section staff published a number of reports on a variety of topics of importance related to the expected postwar demobilization. Among these were *Seniority Problems during Demobilization and Reconversion* (Harbison, 1944) and *The Readjustment of Manpower in Industry during the Transition from War to Peace: an Analysis of Policies and Programs* (Baker and Baldwin, 1944).

Despite its heavy involvement with the war effort, the section also continued to expand its activities and to produce a number of graduates throughout the 1940s, albeit at a slower pace than during the previous or subsequent decades. From the 1940-1941 academic year to the end of the 1949-1950 academic year, 10 graduate students completed their doctoral programs, bringing the total number of Ph.D. economists produced by the section since its founding to 44. The section also increased its staff, and particularly its number of research associates, by more than half to a total of 13 by the 1949-1950 academic year.

In January 1945, section staff began to publish a series of bimonthly annotated bibliographies, focused on topics of contemporary interest in industrial relations, under the title *Selected References*.[60] Then, in the autumn of the same year, Richard A. Lester, who had completed his Ph.D. at the section in 1936 and had assisted J. Douglas Brown so ably in his work at the Office of Production Management (OPM), returned to Princeton from Duke University as a faculty associate of the Industrial Relations Section. Under the guidance of Lester and Helen Baker, a number of advanced graduate students, most of whom were doctoral degree candidates, worked as section research assistants for up to two years, and several of them authored section reports.

During World War II, the Priorities Branch of the War Department's Office of Production Management, headed by Princeton's J. Douglas Brown, played a key role in coordinating the transition from commercial to military production. In this May, 1943 photograph, workers at a converted Connecticut manufacturing plant inspect bullet jackets for defects. Library of Congress, Prints and Photographs Division, FSA/OWI Collection, LC-USW3-034722-C.

More than just increasing the number of people involved in writing research reports, however, there was also a subtle but important shift in the nature of the section's research program in the years following World War II. From 1930 to 1939, Princeton's Industrial Relations Section published 38 reports on a variety of subjects, for a total of 1,317 pages of research. By contrast, from 1940 to 1949, the section published 19 reports for a total of 1,277 pages, reaching nearly the same volume of research as in the previous decade on half the number of reports. Although a rather crude measure, the ratio of pages to reports is striking in that, on average, it suggests a deepening of the section's research coverage per topic. Further insight into the significance of this development can be gleaned from the following words from Lester's historical monograph:

---

[60] This series, which continues in much the same form to the present day, was supplemented in the 1949-1950 academic year with an annual issue devoted to the "Outstanding Books on Industrial Relations" (later, "Noteworthy Books in Industrial Relations and Labor Economics"). In 1988, the section introduced the Richard A. Lester Award for the Outstanding Book in Industrial Relations and Labor Economics, honoring the best book in the field for the preceding year.

Workers produce anti-aircraft artillery shells at a converted Midwestern automobile plant in 1942. Library of Congress, Prints and Photographs Division, FSA/OWI Collection, LC-USE613-D-004467.

Prior to 1945, the printed reports of the Section were largely surveys of company experience with policies, practices, and administrative arrangements. An effort was made to present an early report on a promising industrial relations policy or program. The postwar developments outlined above led the Section to spread its research into additional areas (e.g., wages, labor markets, government programs) and to use additional research methods and materials (e.g., case studies and data from government sources)....Some Section studies combined a broad survey of many companies with selected case studies to provide more detailed analysis and greater depth of understanding.[61]

In fact, the transition of which Lester wrote was consistent with the industrial relations field's overall trend in the 1940s toward greater academic institutionalization, as well as with the growing trend among the new generation of postwar labor economists to place greater emphasis on the analytical study of labor markets and the development of a more robust theoretical framework for labor economics, as opposed to the cataloguing and treatment of industrial case studies related to specific management-labor problems and their solutions (to be discussed in more detail in the next section).

Steel workers make structural changes to a Michigan Ford Lincoln automobile plant being converted to the production of army tanks and jeeps in 1942. Library of Congress, Prints aand Photographs Division, FSA/OWI Collection, LC-USE6-D-003743.

In addition to continuing its annual conference series for industrial relations executives and its five-day seminar in industrial relations for junior industrial relations executives, in 1947 the section expanded its conference program to include an annual Seminar in Labor Relations for Union Research and Staff Personnel. The seminar's sessions covered such topics as the "economic outlook and collective bargaining, job evaluation and wage incentives, pensions and health benefits under collective bargaining, the effects of federal labor regulations on labor relations, the labor movement over the next decade, and union views on research in industrial relations," and featured discussions led by union research directors, government officials, and such noted industrial relations scholars and economists as George W. Taylor, Frederick H. Harbison, John T. Dunlop, Clark Kerr, Douglas M. McGregor, Arhur Schlessinger, Jr., and Jacob Viner. The first annual seminar in 1947 was attended by 22 union representatives, and within five years, participation had grown to a total of 31 unions.[62]

During this time, the section also embarked on a much-needed capital campaign to increase its endowment from the original amounts donated by John D. Rockefeller, Jr.

---

[61] Lester, *Industrial Relations Section,* 10.

[62] Ibid., 12.

and John D. Rockefeller III in the 1920s. To this end, beginning in 1944, grants were solicited from the numerous companies and labor unions that had availed themselves of the section's services over the years free of charge, with the result that over the next eight years, the section's permanent endowment grew to $1 million. This total included more than $550,000 in contributions from 81 companies and eight national trade unions, as well as a gift of $150,000 from the Princeton University Class of 1926 towards the outfitting of the section's new quarters in Firestone Library, which opened in 1948. Writing about the success of Princeton's Industrial Relations Section in his 1941 memoir, Clarence J. Hicks refers to these early and later developments:

> The Section has had a remarkably successful growth: so much so that at the close of the five-year period Mr. Rockefeller was glad to renew his annual contribution for two or three years and then decided to provide as an endowment a sum which the trustees regarded as adequate to finance the annual budget of the Section. A few years later, when annuity income rates were reduced and the budget was in need of further funds, John D. Rockefeller, 3rd, voluntarily supplemented this original endowment gift that had been made by his father. One of the conditions which the trustees accepted in connection with the original gift from Mr. Rockefeller was to the effect that if a new library should ever be built at Princeton it would provide adequate space for the Industrial Relations Section. Funds are now being raised and plans made for the erection of such a new library building, and in accordance with this agreement the plans include space for library, research and administrative activities of an enlarged Industrial Relations Section.[63]

As a final comment on the section's activities during the 1940s, two important points are worth noting. The first relates to the independence and cohesiveness of the team Director Brown led at the Priorities Branch of the Labor Division of the Office of Production Management, which he considered to be critical factors not only in terms of its efficient operation, but also in terms of its ability to deal authoritatively with important constituencies. A good deal of this independence of thought, coupled with a unity of spirit, can be attributed to the culture of Princeton's Industrial Relations Section, several alumni of which formed the core of Brown's team at OPM. In this regard, he states in his memoir:

> Our main thrust soon became the over-all [sic] strategy and tactics of shifting industry to war production, leaving the extensive and detailed field operations of

---

[63] Hicks, *My Life,* 148.

training, labor relations, and employment statistics to other branches. What we needed was a staff of the ablest and most energetic labor economists who could be enticed to come to Washington to work long hours in the battle to shift millions of people from peacetime to wartime production, preferably where they were already working....My first move was to secure the help of Richard A. Lester as Associate Chief of the Branch. Dick had gotten his Ph.D. at Princeton and had worked in the Section before moving to the University of Washington and later to Duke University. I reached him by phone at a beach resort and persuaded him to come to Washington immediately. My second appeal was to Frederick H. Harbison, who had been a Research Assistant at the Section. He had left Princeton the year before for the University of Chicago. He agreed to come. With this nucleus, we persuaded, by telephone, personal interview, or any other appropriate means, twenty-one other economists to join us by the time we were fully manned....Our group was relatively young but full of enthusiasm for the job. We discussed our mission and policies constantly and presented a solid front in our negotiations with the rest of OPM. As academics, we were used to free-wheeling discussion of issues. We gained confidence by the mutual reinforcement of working out strategy among ourselves in a fast-paced seminar as soon as an issue arose in any particular industry. The result was that, as time passed, the Priorities Branch became noted within OPM as speaking with a single voice.[64]

The second point relates to the enormous benefit derived from the section's close cooperation with companies and labor unions across the country. Through the relationships built and nurtured as a result of its series of conferences, as well as its many on-site visits to industrial enterprises, section personnel were often able to obtain access to key business, labor, and government leaders, and to information which would have been extremely difficult to come by otherwise. Time and again, the section's ability to draw on and analyze data gathered firsthand from surveys and case studies of industrial enterprises proved an invaluable source of insight and expertise which it was able to offer to both the United States government and to corporations and labor organizations.

Interestingly, J. Douglas Brown indirectly credits much of the inspiration for this hands-on approach to the Industrial Relations Section's early benefactor, Clarence J. Hicks, when, early in his wartime memoir, he states the following:

---

[64] Brown, *IRS WWII*, 28-29.

In the summer of 1940 I continued to study the manning problems of defense industries throughout the country. A summary of the trips I made that year totals approximately 29,000 miles of travel with 35 nights spent on sleeping cars. Mr. Hicks had long schooled me on the principle that industrial relations was so imbued with intangible variables that we needed to get into the places where men worked and to see and talk to as many people as possible on site. The hundreds of impressions of plants and of people of all kinds and at all levels of responsibility served in good stead when, later, I was involved in the determination of government policy in the War Production Board and the War Department.[65]

In fact, referring back to the program Hicks originally proposed for an Industrial Relations Section at Princeton, one can see that "a traveling-expense budget that would enable members of the staff to visit any part of the country where interesting labor developments are taking place" was one of the key considerations from the section's very beginnings. The weight that Brown gave to the factors mentioned above can be gleaned from the conclusions drawn in his World War II memoir, written from the vantage point of an industrial relations labor economist at the end of a long and fruitful career. Among the points he emphasizes in those conclusions, which continue to have relevance for today's labor economist and industrial relations scholar, are the following:

With independence and an earned reputation for seeking truth rather than support for a predetermined position, a university research unit can develop sources of information, opinion, and advice beyond those available to either government bureaucracies or other parties of interest. To develop such sources, a university research unit must build two-way channels of intercommunication by providing information as well as receiving it and by expressing judgments as well as seeking advice both within the national academic community and with the outside world.... In the broad field of human relations, there is no substitute for the first-hand exposure to the people, the places, and the conditions involved in any issue. Extensive field study and discussion with interested persons are necessary to understanding the complex attitudes and responses which must be recognized in effective policy. Since policies affecting people involve many variables, it is necessary to be inclusive rather than exclusive in the process of weighing the elements which should be considered in coming to a decision. An aid in that process is the interchange of views among a research group rather than dependence upon a single expert, no matter how

---

[65] Brown, *IRS WWII*, 20.

experienced. Unlike that of the single professor working alone, the product of a university research unit is a part of the flow of findings which are supported by the reputation of the unit for quality and integrity. For this reason, the development of findings should involve group consultation.[66]

As shall soon become apparent, while the methodologies and techniques used by the section's labor economists (as well as by labor economists in general) have evolved substantially since the early 1940s, this team-oriented culture and the tradition of credible, empirical primary research emphasized by Brown and his successors have remained important defining characteristics of Princeton's Industrial Relations Section throughout its history.

---

[66] Brown, *IRS WWII,* 110-111.

J. Douglas Brown

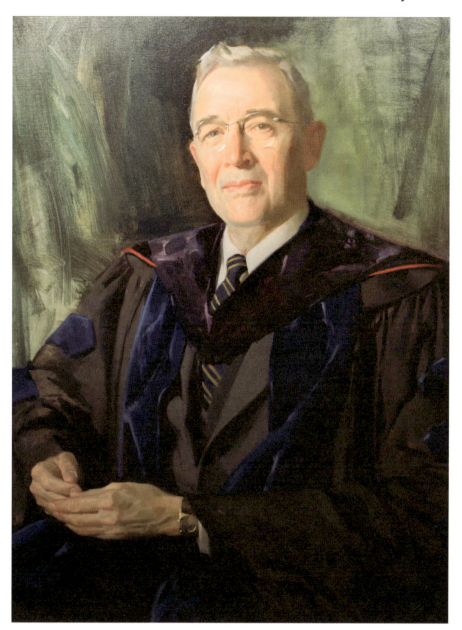

J. Douglas Brown, *an economist, expert in industrial relations and considered "the Father of Social Security," served as director of the Princeton University Industrial Relations Sections from 1926 to 1955 and as a faculty associate from 1955 to 1971. He was a graduate of the Princeton Class of 1915 and earned his Ph.D. from the Graduate School in 1928.*

Portrait of J. Douglas Brown by Robert Oliver Skemp, American, 1910–1984. Oil on canvas
Commissioned by Princeton University, 1969. PP495 Robert Oliver Skemp.
Photograph by David Kelly Crow.

Because of the importance of his many contributions to the Section and to the service of the nation, the following biography from the Princeton University Mudd Manuscript Library is reproduced as a tribute to Dean J. Douglas Brown (Director of the Princeton University Industrial Relations Section from 1926 to 1955, and faculty associate from 1955 to 1971).[67]

J. Douglas Brown (1898-1986) was an economist and Princeton University administrator who was an expert in the field of industrial relations, especially on the topics of Social Security and personnel and manpower issues. He was one of the leaders in the development of the Social Security program and also served in the War Department during World War II on manpower issues.

"James Douglas Brown was born on August 11, 1898 in Somerville, New Jersey to James and Ella M. (Lane) Brown. He began his undergraduate education at Princeton University in 1915, with a focus on pre-med training, but left in 1917 to join the Army. He was a private in the Army Medical Corps in France from 1917 to 1919. Brown then returned to Princeton University and changed his studies from medicine to the field of industrial relations, having acquired an interest in human organization while in the Army. Brown received his A.B. in 1920, although he maintained his membership in the Class of 1919. Brown received his A.M. from Princeton University in 1921. It was during his master's studies that he developed his interest in economics.

"Brown taught as an instructor of economics at Princeton University from 1921 to 1923 and at New York University from 1923 to 1925. He then returned to Princeton University for further graduate work, earning his Ph.D. in 1928. Brown married Dorothy Andrews on June 18, 1923. They had three daughters, Martha Jane (Spencer), Doris Andrews (Miller), and Elizabeth Andrews Brown, and a son, James Douglas Brown, Jr.

---

[67] "J. Douglas Brown Papers, 1910-1978 (bulk 1930-1970)," call number MC155, Princeton University, Mudd Manuscript Library, http://findingaids.princeton.edu/collections/MC155/#description. According to the Mudd Library's website: "The following sources were consulted during the preparation of the biographical note: "Dr. J. Douglas Brown, a Dean and Social Security Architect," by Thomas W. Ennis. The New York Times, January 21, 1986. J(ames) Douglas Brown Profile, Marquis Who's Who on the Web. http://search.marquiswhoswho.com Accessed August 1, 2006. Materials from Series 1: Biographical; J. Douglas Brown Papers; Public Policy Papers, Department of Rare Books and Special Collections, Princeton University Library. Princeton University Class of 1919: Forty Years After, edited by W. E. Studdiford. Progress Publishing Company, Caldwell, New Jersey, 1959."

"Brown's academic career was spent at Princeton University. He was an instructor from 1926 to 1927, assistant professor of economics from 1927 to 1934, and professor of economics from 1934 to 1966. Brown served as director of the Industrial Relations Section at Princeton from 1926 to 1955, as Dean of the Faculty from 1946 to 1966, and as Princeton University's first provost from 1966 until his retirement in 1967. Brown also served as President of the University Store, as a member of the Editorial Board, the Board of Trustees and as Vice President of the Princeton University Press, and as a member of numerous faculty committees. During his career, Brown wrote thirteen books and numerous articles in the field of industrial relations, and on social insurance, labor economics, and education. His works include *The Liberal University; An Institutional Analysis* (1969), *An American Philosophy of Social Security* (1973), *The Human Nature of Organizations* (1974), and *Essays in Social Security* (1977).

"While he was the Dean of the Faculty, Brown was one of Princeton University's chief spokesmen to the academic community and a staunch defender of traditional liberal education. He was also instrumental in strengthening the University's faculty and personnel administration. As the second director of the Industrial Relations Section at Princeton University, Brown was a pioneer in the development of the field of personnel and industrial relations. The Industrial Relations Section was established as part of the Economics Department in 1922 to enhance and extend the knowledge of industrial relations, the first section of its kind. The section serves as a library of documentary materials, a research organization, and an adjunct in undergraduate and graduate instruction. During his tenure, Brown justified establishing the [S]ection on a permanent basis for its value to education and industry, expanded the purpose of the [S]ection to serve industry and other outside groups in addition to Princeton University faculty and students, led an increase in research, and was instrumental in building an endowment for the [S]ection to over $1 million.

"Brown's academic career was interspersed with service to the government at the federal and state levels. His first appointment was as a member of President Herbert Hoover's Emergency Committee for Employment from 1930 to 1931, which was formed to help fight the spread of the Depression.

"Brown's long involvement with Social Security began in 1934. He served on President Roosevelt's Committee on Economic Security from 1934 to 1935, which drafted the original Social Security legislation of 1935. Brown was a leader in the reform and expansion of the Social Security program for the remainder of his career. He was the chairman of the first Federal Advisory Council on Social Security from 1937 to 1938 and served on four subsequent Advisory Councils: 1947 to 1948, 1957 to 1958 as chairman of the drafting committee, 1963 to 1964, and 1969 to 1971. Brown also served as special advisor on Social Security to the Secretary of the Treasury in 1939, and as a consulting economist to the Social Security Board from 1936 to 1950. Brown is often referred to as the "Father of Social Security" for his long and influential role in the original development and continued reform of the Social Security program.

"During World War II, Brown became increasingly involved in government service. He conducted a special study for President Roosevelt in 1940 on the manpower issues the aircraft, machine tool, and steel industries would face if the United States entered the war. Brown was Chief of the Priorities Branch of the Labor Division in the Office of Production Management and the War Production Board from 1941 to 1942, playing a key role in converting the American economy from civilian to wartime production. From 1942 to 1945, he served as a principal consultant on manpower to the Secretary of War and as alternate member for the War Department on the War Manpower Commission. He was also a member of the Advisory Council on Personnel to the General Staff, War Department, from 1946 to 1949.

"After World War II, and throughout the remainder of his career, Brown continued to serve as a consulting economist to various Federal and New Jersey government agencies influencing policies on unemployment relief, Social Security, and manpower planning. He was a member of advisory boards and committees or served as a consultant to a wide variety of agencies, including the Social Security Administration, the Air Force, the Office of Defense Mobilization, the Department of Labor, the National Security Resources Board, the Federal Advisory Council for Employment Security, the New Jersey state government, and the Department of Health, Education and Welfare.

"In addition to his work at Princeton University and with the government, Brown was active in numerous professional organizations. He was a fellow of the American Academy of Arts and Sciences and a member of the Association of American Colleges, the American Management Association, the American Economic Association, the American Statistical Association, and the New Jersey Association of Colleges and Universities. Brown was a founder and president of the Industrial Relations Research Association, and from 1940 to 1942 was an elected member of the Executive Committee of the American Economic Association. He served as a member of executive or advisory committees for the American Association for Labor Legislation, the American Association for Social Security, the Committee for Economic Development, the Institute of Management and Labor Relations at Rutgers University, the Social Science Research Council, the National Science Foundation, the American Council on Education, and the Institute of College and University Administrators. Brown was also a director of

McGraw-Hill Publishing Company and a trustee of the University of Rochester and the Princeton Theological Seminary.

"Brown received honorary degrees from Rutgers University (1947), Kenyon College (1954), Union College (1966), Franklin and Marshall College (1966), and Princeton University (1973). In 1971, he received the Arthur J. Altmeyer Award, the highest award given by the Social Security Administration, for his contributions to the program's success. Brown died on January 19, 1986, at the age of 87."

The Postwar Decades: From "Happy Days" to Revolution

The post-war decades were a period of enormous growth in American society. *In parallel, the 1950s, 1960s, and 1970s are considered "The Golden Age" of industrial relations. Multidisciplinary studies flourished in the field, and many areas of specialization emerged. At Princeton, the Industrial Relations Section continued to grow as more faculty joined and research increasingly focused on empirical analysis of labor markets.*

Photograph from iCLIPART.com.

In contemporary America, it is quite common to remember life in the first two decades after World War II in idyllic terms of economic prosperity, social stability, and political and military ascendancy.

Nostalgia for this period in our nation's history—and in particular for the 1950s and early 1960s—has pervaded popular culture for many years, and has been immortalized in the entertainment media through plays, films, and television series, from *Grease,* "Happy Days," and "The Wonder Years" in the 1970s and 1980s, to *Pleasantville* in the 1990s. In fact, by all accounts, it was a time that

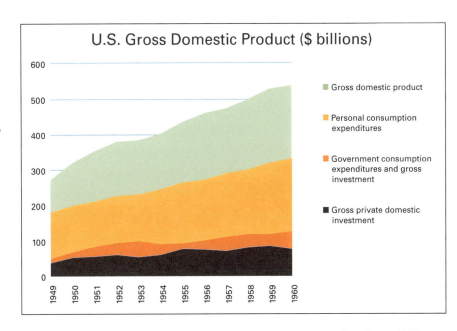

Data Source: U.S. Bureau of Economic Analysis.

ushered in one of the longest periods of economic growth and expansion in U.S. history. However, it was also a period that, in many ways, quietly set the stage for the dramatic social, technological, and economic upheavals of the latter 1960s and the 1970s— changes that have often been described in terms of various revolutions.

In the years immediately following the Second World War, the U.S. experienced a burst of economic growth, fueled in large part by domestic consumption. The release of pent-up demand for manufactured goods, which had been building throughout the war years, caused nominal GDP (which had remained basically flat from 1944 through 1946) to grow suddenly from $222 billion in the year after the war to $267 billion within just a few years, and then nearly to double again to $507 billion by the end of the 1950s. At the same time, the number of private-sector workers grew from roughly 40 million in 1946 to just under 50 million by 1959, while private-sector wages increased from $91.3 billion in 1946 (averaging about $2,265 per employee per year) to $213.9 billion in 1959 (an average annual compensation of about $4,293 per employee). Not surprisingly, with personal income more than doubling between 1946 and 1959, from about $178 billion to $392 billion, personal consumption expenditures grew from

$144 billion to about $318 billion, while personal savings increased from $15.5 billion to over $26 billion. The postwar economy was booming, and the average American was becoming more prosperous.

While the road to America's growth in prosperity was not without its bumps, the postwar economic expansion continued well into the 1960s. In its 1965 annual report, the President's Council of Economic Advisers celebrated the economic achievements of the previous four years with the following words:

As 1965 begins, most Americans are enjoying a degree of prosperity unmatched in their experience, or indeed in the history of their Nation. In 1964, some 70 million of them were at work, producing $622 billion worth of goods and services. The gains of four years of uninterrupted economic expansion had brought fuller pay envelopes, greater sales, larger dividend checks, a higher standard of living, more savings, and a stronger sense of security than ever before. Over that period industrial production grew at an average annual rate of 7 percent, and the total output of all goods and services (valued in constant prices) increased at an average rate of 5 percent....These gains brought jobs to 4 million more persons and raised total consumer income after taxes by 6 percent a year. And all this was accomplished with essentially stable prices....Indeed, in a few months, the duration of this expansion will have surpassed any other on record—except only the prolonged advance before and during World War II.[68]

By the end of the 1960s, however, the specter of higher inflation and questions about the sustainability of the expansion were already significant enough that the same Council of Economic Advisers devoted an entire chapter of its 1968 annual report to the topic of "The Problem of Rising Prices." This was followed in 1969 by an ominous warning, hinting at the subtle beginnings of the problem of stagflation which, exacerbated by the collapse of the Bretton Woods system in 1971, and the global oil shocks of 1973 and 1979, was to plague the country for much of the 1970s:

Since 1965, prices have been rising too rapidly. The history of both the United States and other industrial nations shows that high employment is generally accompanied by inflationary tendencies, and that when prices are reasonably stable, this is at the cost of too many idle men and idle machines. The record of the past poses the

---

[68] Gardner Ackley, Otto Eckstein and Arthur M. Okun, *Annual Report of the Council of Economic Advisers,* January 1965 (Washington: United States Government Printing Office), 35.

critical challenge of the years ahead. Reconciling prosperity at high employment with price stability is the Nation's most important unsolved problem of over-all economic performance. Though the United States has done better than most industrial countries, its record is far from adequate.[69]

Despite governmental policies aimed at controlling runaway inflation, while at the same time stimulating the economy to reduce its growing unemployment, the 1970s remained a turbulent time for both the U.S. and the world economies. As President Jimmy Carter reminded Congress in his 1978 economic report:

The recession of 1974-75 was the worst in 40 years, and the substantial increase in output over the past three years still leaves the economy operating below its productive potential. We cannot be content when almost 6-$\frac{1}{2}$ million people actively seeking jobs cannot find work, when 3-$\frac{1}{4}$ million workers take part-time jobs because they cannot find fulltime employment, and when one million people have stopped looking for a job because they have lost hope of finding one. We cannot be content when a substantial portion of our industrial plant stands idle, as it does today. We cannot be satisfied with an economic recovery that bypasses significant segments of the American people. Unemployment among minorities is more than twice as high as that among whites—and unemployment among minority teenagers is tragically high. Women have fewer satisfying job opportunities than men, and older Americans often find their access to the job market blocked. Farm incomes have dropped precipitously. We must also address other problems if we are to assure full restoration of prosperity. Inflation is a serious economic concern for all Americans. The inflation rate is too high and must be brought down. Moreover, a residue of unease and caution about the future still pervades the thinking of some of our people. Businesses are still hesitant in their long-term investment planning, and the stock market remains depressed despite the substantial increase in business profits….The problems we face today are more complex and difficult than those of an earlier era. We cannot concentrate just on inflation, or just on unemployment, or just on deficits in the Federal budget or our international payments. Nor can we act in isolation from other countries. We must deal with all of these problems simultaneously and on a worldwide basis.[70]

---

[69] Arthur M. Okun, Merton J. Peck and Warren L. Smith, *Annual Report of the Council of Economic Advisers,* January 1969 (Washington: United States Government Printing Office), 94.

[70] Charles L. Schultze, Lyle E. Gramley and William Nordhaus, *Annual Report of the Council of Economic Advisers, January 1978* (Washington: United States Government Printing Office), 3-4.

Naturally, just as the boom conditions of the immediate postwar years had benefitted the labor movement in many ways, the worsening economic conditions of the latter 1960s and the 1970s proved detrimental to the state of industrial and labor relations. Along with the rapid expansion of the postwar economy, labor unions, whose membership and influence had previously been strengthened by legislation enacted under the New Deal policies of the Roosevelt Administration, had also experienced further growth. By 1953, union membership of roughly 16.5 million people represented a third of the total non-farm workforce—the largest percentage ever in the history of the American labor movement. Ironically, however, just as labor was at the height of its success in mustering and organizing large numbers of workers, unions in the private sector were at the beginning of a long process of steady decline that would persist for decades.

The causes of the declining fortunes of organized labor in the U.S. are too numerous to analyze in detail here; however, there are a few factors that merit a brief mention. For one thing, the 1947 Taft-Hartley Act, as well as a number of legislative and judicial acts that followed soon after it, had the effect of weakening unions' influence and collective bargaining leverage in the private sector. For another, the increasing prosperity of the American middle class, growing perceptions of union corruption and cronyism, and the anti-communist sentiments of Cold War–era McCarthyism dealt significant blows to the public appeal, national reputation, and internal solidarity of labor unions. Meanwhile, the growing willingness of large, private-sector employers to move their production facilities to lower-wage, non-union locations—at first domestically, to the South, and later internationally to developing countries—presented significant challenges to the membership and influence of private-sector labor unions in the U.S., which were to become increasingly apparent in the 1960s and 1970s.

Thus, while it continued to wield significant power in the U.S. throughout the 1950s, 1960s, and even into the early 1970s, greatly influencing wages, benefits, and working conditions across a number of industries, organized labor increasingly came up against the strong opposition of both corporate and political interests as the postwar expansion slowed and economic conditions in the country steadily deteriorated. As national opinion polling suggests that, from a high of 75 percent in the mid-1950s, the public approval rating of labor unions had fallen to 55 percent by the end of the 1970s. At the same time, its disapproval rating, over 33 percent, had climbed to its highest level in more than 40 years.[71]

---

[71] Jeff Jones and Lydia Saad, *Gallup Poll Social Series: Work and Education, Final Topline,* Gallup News Service, Timberline: 927534, Princeton Job #: 10-08-011, August 5-8, 2010.

Of course, the changes that America faced in the postwar decades were not restricted to matters of political or economic policy. Social phenomena such as the civil rights and women's liberation movements—which in many ways traced their roots directly to the manpower mobilization exigencies of the Second World War—raised important questions about the labor market participation of minorities and women, and had a tremendous impact on developments in the industrial relations field, as did the rapid technological advances in engineering, transportation, materials science, electronics, communications, and numerous other fields of scientific endeavor during what became known in the late 1950s and 1960s as the Space Age.

Among the technological innovations of the postwar years that had the greatest impact on American industry were advances in the areas of automation, computing, and information technology. Although they were by no means the only important technological developments of the era, the invention of the transistor and the development of a framework for information theory in 1948, the introduction of the first commercial computer in 1951 (and the rapid progress that was made in developing more powerful and cheaper alternatives in the following decades), and the development of integrated circuits in 1959 laid the foundation for a revolution in industrial production. At the same time, in an age in which the pace of scientific progress was accelerating rapidly, and in which the theoretical underpinnings of numerous academic fields were subjected to ever more rigorous standards and challenges to conventional thinking, these developments had major implications for the field of industrial relations and for labor economics as well.

The Industrial Relations Field in the 1950s, 1960s, and 1970s

The decades immediately following the Second World War have been called the "Golden Age" of industrial relations.[72] In many ways, it was a time of multidisciplinary flowering in the field, in which scholars from areas as diverse as economics, sociology, anthropology, and psychology were drawn to research various aspects of employment relationships. It was also a time in which the ramifications of industrial relations on several newly specialized fields of study (such as human relations, industrial psychology, and organizational behavior) began to be examined and explored.

---

[72] Kaufman, *Origins & Evolution,* 75-102.

During this time, institutional labor economists—one of the field's traditional groups of core constituents—also began to formalize and deepen their own theoretical framework, ultimately making important contributions to the field of economics in general.

One example that has been cited of the multidisciplinary nature of the field of industrial relations during the postwar years is a project called the Inter-University Study of Labor Problems in Economic Development. This long-term project, which was initiated by Frederick H. Harbison while at the University of Chicago, together with the University of California's Clark Kerr, Harvard's John T. Dunlop, and MIT's Charles A. Meyers, was sponsored by grants from the Ford Foundation and, over the course of 20 years, produced a dozen books and numerous academic articles by scholars from several disciplines. An important contribution to the project's body of research was Harbison, Dunlop, Kerr, and Meyer's 1960 book, *Industrialism and Industrial Man,* which (along with the authors' final report, *Industrialism and Industrial Man Reconsidered,* issued under the aegis of Princeton's Industrial Relations Section in 1975) provided one of the first rigorous attempts at an analytical study of labor markets and the effects of industrialization on a cross-section of countries.

It was also during this period, after the publication of John Maynard Keynes' *General Theory of Employment, Interest and Money* and other important theoretical works of the 1930s, in which fundamental notions of the labor markets as conceived by neoclassical economic theory were being challenged (though not without controversy)—and following the experience of institutional intervention during the Great Depression and World War II—that a new breed of institutionally oriented labor economists began to exert its influence. According to industrial relations historian Bruce Kaufman:

After the war, many of the new generation of labor economists began to produce a great volume of research on labor markets and collective bargaining. This research was distinctive in that it represented a willingness and an ability to develop and use economic theory, a focus on the operation of labor markets, a skepticism of the ability of competitive theory to explain labor market outcomes such as wage differentials and weekly hours of work adequately, and a desire to broaden economic analysis of the labor market to include social, psychological, and institutional conditions.[73]

As has been shown by Kaufman, initially these institutional labor economists were largely considered by microeconomic price theorists to be outside of the mainstream

---

[73] Kaufman, *Origins & Evolution,* 87.

of economic thought.[74] It was at least in part their frustrated attempts to incorporate their views—which were considered by the economics establishment of the time (as represented by the American Economics Association) to be unorthodox—into the framework of neoclassical economic theory that prompted men like Richard Lester and others to establish the Industrial Relations Research Association as a forum for alternative perspectives on labor problems and on the economics of the labor markets.

Over time, however, as these labor economists and their successors sought to incorporate their institutional perspective into mainstream economic theory, they increasingly utilized the empirical techniques and methodologies of econometrics, mathematics, and statistical analysis that brought them into ever closer alignment with and greater acceptance by neoclassical economists. As labor economics historian Paul J. McNulty points out:

> In subsequent years, that question—how much difference do unions make?—became a central concern of labor economists, largely as a result of the influence of H. Gregg Lewis and the Labor Workshop at the University of Chicago. The question itself was not new; it was related to John Stuart Mill's recantation in 1869 of the wages fund theory, and Alfred Marshall devoted lengthy passages to the topic. What was new was the growing body of data available to researchers, as well as their increasingly sophisticated statistical and econometric techniques.... Lewis's greatest influence was probably in the redirection of labor economics toward analytical and quantitative work. During his years at the University of Chicago, he played a major role in the development of what Albert Rees has recently termed analytical as distinguished from institutional labor economics....[75]

Throughout the 1960s and 1970s, the environment in which industrial relations had come of age and matured also began to change substantively. The relative importance of the influence of labor unions on the private-sector employment relationship began to be supplanted increasingly by other pressing social issues, such as workplace discrimination and gender equality, in the wake of the civil rights and women's liberation movements and the waning influence of organized labor. Labor economists therefore began to be concerned with a much broader range of employment issues. As Bruce Kaufman writes:

---

[74] Ibid., 89-90.

[75] McNulty, *Origins and Development,* 190-192.

[L]abor-management relations had gone from being front-page news to being back-page news as collective bargaining became institutionalized and routinized and strikes and other attention-getting forms of conflict dropped to the lowest levels since the early years of the Depression…. As labor-management relations receded in newsworthiness and policy concern, other labor-oriented issues took their place, including automation and structural unemployment, discrimination and civil rights, job dissatisfaction and alienation among blue-collar workers, poverty, and manpower training programs. All of these were labor problems and thus fully in the intellectual domain of industrial relations.[76]

While the traditional association between labor economics and industrial relations remained strong, the combination of factors mentioned above caused the former gradually to become more specialized, more closely integrated within the broader discipline of economics, and more distant from its earlier social science antecedents in the industrial relations field. Thus, by 1980, the historian of labor economics was able to make the claim that:

Perhaps the most fundamental point to be made about the current state of labor economics is that at no other time in the history of the field has it been more closely aligned with its parent discipline. The study of labor by economists is generally characterized by the same analytical approach that their colleagues are bringing to bear upon problems in other subdivisions of the field: the formulation of hypotheses based generally on observations consistent with economic theory and empirically tested with econometric techniques applied to such data as are available. Moreover the problems analyzed by labor economists extend over a field conceived of in much broader terms than was true of an earlier era, when, for example, the study of unionism was the dominant item on the research and teaching agenda of labor economists. Edward H. Chamberlin's charge, made in the 1950s, that "the typical university course in 'Labor Problems' is a course in trade unionism with little, if any attention paid to the unorganized sector," could not be made today.[77]

---

[76] Kaufman, *Origins & Evolution,* 131.

[77] McNulty, *Origins and Development,* 200-201.

Princeton University in the Postwar Era: 1950-1979

"As she crosses the threshold of a new and fateful age, Princeton will strive to meet any challenge, to dare any adventure to preserve her integrity and to further her enduring purpose. Proud as we are of our history and grateful for the strength our heritage brings to us, we know that to rest on it can lead only to decay and destruction. We intend to be the progenitors of a stronger Princeton, not merely the beneficiaries of generations that went before us."[78]

With these forward-looking words, Princeton's President Harold W. Dodds addressed the final convocation of the University's bicentennial celebrations in June of 1947—and he was a man who knew about challenges. The preceding decade and a half in which he had presided over the University's life had been fraught with seemingly insurmountable ones—the Great Depression, World War II, and the postwar readjustment—and yet, under his guidance, Princeton had not only endured, but had emerged as an even stronger institution. Indeed, in the decades immediately following the Second World War, the truth of Dodds' words was to be proven over and over again.

The developments at Princeton during the 1950s, 1960s, and 1970s were in many ways a microcosm of the swiftly moving currents within the larger society. First there was a welcome return to postwar normalcy, accompanied by a period of rapid growth and expansion of the traditional bases of academic and social life. Later, these developments were roiled by a number of significant changes in the University's student composition, academic programs, and even some of its administrative structures, reflecting the wider changes taking place within the nation as a whole. While these developments are too numerous to treat here in detail, a few key points bear mentioning.

During the war years, Princeton had thoroughly established its reputation as a leading institution in advanced mathematics, science, and engineering. Throughout the 1950s and into the late 1960s, the University continued to expand its resources and its campus to accommodate the growing needs of the scientific research faculty. In 1951, the trustees purchased an 825-acre tract of land, complete with 16 laboratory buildings, from the Rockefeller Institute for Medical Research a few miles north of the main campus. Initially devoted to research and instruction in aerospace and mechanical

---

[78] From President Harold Willis Dodds' address to the final Convocation of the Princeton University Bicentennial celebrations, June 17, 1947, as quoted in Strayer, "Dodds, Harold Willis" in Leitsch, *A Princeton Companion.*

engineering, the new Forrestal Campus—named in honor of U.S. Secretary of Defense James Forrestal of Princeton's class of 1915—later housed a number of other important research facilities, including Project Matterhorn (later named the Princeton Plasma Physics Laboratory), the Princeton-Pennsylvania Accelerator (which operated from 1957 to 1972), and the National Oceanic and Atmospheric Administration's Geophysical Fluid Dynamics Laboratory.

The physical sciences were by no means the only areas to benefit from this effort to reinforce and expand the University's research and teaching resources; a number of important faculty and program additions were also made in the social sciences as well. For example, by the end of World War II, a number of professors of the then-unified Department of Economics and Social Institutions had retired and had not been replaced. At the same time, student interest in these academic fields experienced enormous growth during the postwar period, and the University was faced with the challenge of increasing both the quantity and the quality of its instruction.

In order to meet the demand, many new faculty members were recruited, including such noted economists as William J. Baumol, Fritz Machlup, Jacob Viner, Albert Rees, and others. The department was also divided in 1960 into the separate Departments of Economics and Sociology, to allow for greater focus on each subject matter. In addition, following the generous gift of an alumnus in 1961,[79] the graduate program and the faculty and research resources of the Woodrow Wilson School of Public and International Affairs (where the Industrial Relations Section's William G. Bowen and Richard A. Lester both served as directors of the graduate program) were greatly expanded, and a new building permanently housing the school was dedicated in 1966.

To better appreciate Princeton's growth during the first few decades after the war, it is helpful to consider the following statistics: in the 1949-1950 academic year, there were about 3,755 undergraduate and graduate students enrolled at the University, taught by just over 400 faculty members and administered by about 60 staff members, all on an operating budget of a little less than $9 million. Thirty years later, in the 1979-1980 academic year, there were almost 5,900 undergraduate and graduate students enrolled and being taught by 789 faculty. The University's administrative staff had grown to 567, and the annual operating budget was over $165 million. Moreover, from virtually nil at the close of World War II, by the end of the 1970s, nearly a third of the student body was comprised of women and about 15 percent was made up of minority students.

---

[79] According to Leitsch, *A Princeton Companion,* the gift of $35 million from Mr. and Mrs. Charles S. Robertson ('26) was originally intended to remain anonymous; however the benefactors finally agreed in 1973 to make the source of the donation public.

The rapid increase in the University's population and activities during the 1960s and 1970s also called for a further expansion of its physical plant. Describing these developments in the period from the late 1950s to the early 1970s, one historian of the University put it this way:

> Some twenty-five new buildings were constructed on the main campus, still others at the Graduate College and Forrestal. All told, if measured in terms of square footage under roof, the physical plant increased by 80 percent. In addition, many of the older buildings were renovated to provide more useful space for instructional departments. Among the more important additions were the Art Museum, the Woolworth Center of Musical Studies, the Architecture Building, the Woodrow Wilson School, the Engineering Quadrangle, the Jadwin Gymnasium, the Computer Center, and the complex of Peyton, Fine, and Jadwin Halls constructed for the mathematical and physical sciences in the area immediately adjacent to Palmer Stadium. All of these buildings housed expanded educational programs.[80]

During the 1960s, the social changes that were to transform the nation as a result of the civil rights and women's liberation movements also began to reshape the demographics of Princeton's student body. While the first African-American students had been admitted to the college as early as the beginning of the 1940s, it was in the 1960s that an active policy of increasing diversity on campus resulted in the admission of increasing numbers of African-American and other minority students. Likewise, it was during the 1960s that women made their greatest strides as part of the Princeton academic community.

Although women had been employed in staff positions at Princeton for a number of decades already, it was in the early 1960s that the first women graduate students were admitted, resulting in the first female Ph.D. recipient in 1964; and the first woman faculty member was granted tenure, in 1968. After studying the issue of coeducation for a number of years, in the fall semester of the 1969-1970 academic year, under its 16th president, Robert F. Goheen (and during the tenure of the section's William G. Bowen as provost), the University admitted the first female undergraduates to the Class of 1973.

While these developments were clearly a reflection of the pressures within the larger society during the period, they were also in many ways part of a move by the University's administration to relieve that pressure and maintain the peace by allowing students a greater say in Princeton's governance in the face of increasingly turbulent student protests in the late 1960s. One of the major outcomes of the University's response to the turmoil

---

[80] W. Frank Craven, "Goheen, Robert Francis" in Leitsch, *A Princeton Companion.*

of those years was the creation in 1969 of the innovative Council of the Princeton University Community. The so-called CPUC, or U-Council, was "composed of students, faculty, staff and alumni," and meeting regularly throughout the academic year, "its committees would, among other things, advise on the University's annual budget (Priorities Committee), develop rules of conduct on campus (Rights and Rules), consider stockholder questions (Resources) and assist in honorary degree selection (Governance)."[81]

Finally, over the course of the period from 1950 to 1979, a number of faculty associates of Princeton's Industrial Relations Section made notable contributions to the administration of the University as a whole. For example, the section's longtime director, J. Douglas Brown, served as Princeton's dean of the faculty—the University's oldest and highest-ranking deanship, which "shared with the president increasing responsibility for oversight of departments of instruction and concern for the well-being of the faculty"[82]—from 1946 until 1967, and was succeeded in that position by Richard A. Lester from 1968 to 1973. Several section faculty associates (including J. Douglas Brown from 1966 to 1967, William G. Bowen from 1967 to 1972, and Albert Rees from 1975 to 1977), also served in the capacity of University provost, acting "as general deputy to the president, giving particular attention to the overall academic development of the University, and, in the president's absence or disability, exercises the presidential power and duties relating to the general supervision of the University, if no acting president has been appointed."[83] And, as mentioned earlier, beginning in 1972, William G. Bowen served as the University's 17th president, until 1988.

The Industrial Relations Section in the 1950s, 1960s, and 1970s

Just as the U.S. economy as a whole, in the first two decades following the Second World War, Princeton's Industrial Relations Section experienced a return to normalcy and an extended period of development and growth. There was a steady increase in the number of graduate students and research assistants, the complement of faculty associates grew and visiting scholars from a number of U.S. and foreign universities were attracted to the section, the library expanded its resources and its breadth of

---

[81] Oberdorfer, *Princeton University,* 204.

[82] Leitsch, *A Princeton Companion.*

[83] Ibid.

coverage, and there was an impressive array of research activities covering a variety of subjects and geographic locations. And likewise, as if reflecting the social, economic, and technological currents of change that surrounded it, by the end of the 1970s, the Industrial Relations Section had undergone a subtle but profound transformation, which would shape its future.

The 1950s and 1960s

From the 1950-1951 academic year to the end of the 1959-60 academic year, 21 students completed Ph.D. programs, including five graduates in the Class of 1952—the largest contingent in the section's history up to that time. Among the economists to graduate during this decade were such notable figures as W. Michael Blumenthal (U.S. Secretary of the Treasury under President Jimmy Carter, former Chairman and CEO of Unisys Corporation, and Princeton University trustee emeritus) in 1956, and William G. Bowen (former President of Princeton University) in 1958.

An ad from *The Daily Princeton.* Courtesy of *The Daily Princetonian.*

As Richard Lester points out in his historical monograph, by the 1952-1953 academic year, there were five members of the section's research staff teaching undergraduate and graduate courses, and supervising senior and doctoral theses. At the same time, as many as 150 undergraduate students were taking labor or industrial relations courses in the economics department and the Woodrow Wilson School, of whom two dozen from several academic departments were writing theses on industrial relations.

In 1955, after leading the Industrial Relations Section for nearly 30 years, J. Douglas Brown was succeeded by Frederick H. Harbison, who had returned to Princeton from his position as an associate professor of economics at the University of Chicago. As the section's director from 1955 to 1968, Harbison expanded the research program into three areas: the relationship between management development and economic growth (or the study of problems in "human capital" as it was then called), the human problems of American companies operating abroad, and the comparative study of management practices related to labor problems in industrialized and developing countries. He also brought with him from the University of Chicago the multi-year research project, "Inter-University Study of Labor Problems in Economic Development," which he had initiated with Clark Kerr, John T. Dunlop, and Charles A. Myers under a grant

The Woodrow Wilson School of Public and International Affair's Robertson Hall was designed by architect Minoru Yamasaki and dedicated by President Lyndon Johnson in 1966. Photograph courtesy of the Princeton University Archives. Historical Photograph Collection Additions (AC340): Box AD29, F. 18.

Coeducation at Princeton

PRINCETON'S COEDS - FOR - A - WEEK gave the campus a taste of what coeducation will be like as 800 enthusiastic young women arrived in mid-February to brighten the gloom of New Jersey winter.

Photo by Joe Lincoln

Goheen leads college towards coeducation

By LUTHER MUNFORD

Robert F. Goheen '40, president of Princeton University, has a tough job. On Jan. 11, 1969, the day the trustees announced coeducation at Princeton, that job became a lot tougher.

The trustees called their decision "the largest single decision that has faced Princeton in this century"; they might well have called the implementation of that decision the largest single task that any Princeton president has faced in this century.

Two weeks ago, when the president announced his special coeducation committee, the chairman was Goheen himself, and rightly so.

Attacking financial problems

Rightly so for two reasons. First, because during his eleven years as Princeton's president, he has walked the tightrope—between expectation and feasibility, between student hopes and university finances—that has again appeared as a risky path to university change.

Secondly, as the president who has led the most successful capital campaign in campus history—netting $61 million in three years (1958-61), $7.6 million over the drive's goal—Goheen has demonstrated his considerable talents at raising money, the main obstacle in Princeton's path to coeducation.

"It takes guts to look a man in the eye and ask him for a million dollars," a university fund raiser once said. "President Goheen has that kind of guts."

And it's going to take guts to overcome what Goheen calls the "very real financial problems" standing in the way of coeducation—especially if his committee can find a way to get a "substantial number" of coeds on campus next fall.

Cost cut to a fourth

At least the obstacles aren't as great as had been expected. When Goheen told The Princetonian on May 16, 1967, that coeducation at Princeton was "inevitable," he estimated the cost of putting 1,000 girls on campus at $80 million.

When the Patterson committee, appointed by the June, 1967, meeting of the board of trustees, reported back a year later, the financial estimate was so low—roughly $25 million—that the trustees asked an outside foundation to check the figure.

The reply came back affirmative, and last January the trustees announced their decision—approval "in principle."

Since then the president has been making short-range decisions—such as sending the admission blanks to all women who had asked

(Continued on page thirteen)

Coeds and clubs

Jaynes and Diamond foresee alterations in clubs, expansion of 'college system' when women arrive

By STEPHEN L. DREYFUSS

Coeducation and the clubs? For some, they are conflicts in terms. Others expect girls to bring desperately needed vitality to Prospect Street, thereby saving the system from impotence.

Julian Jaynes, master of Wilson College, favors the college system as ideal for the integration of women into the Princeton social system.

"Should the clubs bicker girls," he noted, "capacity limitations" would mean cutting down section size to admit a section of girls. The clubs would be far more homogeneous, magnifying the whole fault of the club system.

"The kind of sub-unit must be much larger than a club can provide."

Jaynes suggests a college of between 300-400 members, with one dorm reserved for girls, who would be provided with a separate common room and lounge. "Girls at college need a place where they can get away from guys for awhile," he said.

The psychology lecturer, who serves on the committee on social alternatives chaired by Dean Rudenstine, added that the university is "seeking all kinds of advice and fanning out all over the United States."

Many alumni have charged in letters to the Alumni Weekly that the university is engaged in a determined effort to cause the death of the club system.

According to Jaynes, "As a way of organizing undergraduate life, the club system is already dead. It belongs to the 19th century and it should be left there."

He hastened to add, however, that "there are some very good clubs, and some fine things clubs can give to some undergraduates."

The university doesn't want to kill the clubs, nor do I."

Jaynes continued that some students were being "intellectually maimed in that they perceive individuals on the basis of Prospect Street principles—the Bicker mentality." He added that this orientation persists after graduation.

Jaynes, who will leave Princeton at the end of the academic year, concluded that "now we can really

(Continued on page ten)

Funding coeds' $25 million: 'tough, but we're optimistic'

By RAY OLLWERTHER

In order to finance the expansion of facilities for the admission of 1,000 women undergraduates, the university must raise somewhat over $24.3 million.

"It will be tough, but we're optimistic," commented Ricardo A. Mestres '31, financial vice-president.

Both Mestres and provost William G. Bowen emphasized their belief that "though it's never easy to raise money," coeducation raises no unique problems.

"However, we've got to get out and sell this program," Mestres said. "The urgency is paramount."

"We're betting on the fact that, educationally, coeducation is good for Princeton, and on alumni belief in this institution."

The vice-president predicted that once those alumni who oppose coeducation can be persuaded it is "not just social or superficial, but a sound educational idea, 99 per cent" of the 33,000 former Princetonians will support the plan.

In explaining this "persuasion" movement, Bowen said, "Many of us have been talking to alumni groups last fall, and we will continue speaking with them."

Coeducation is "certainly of the highest priority" in fund-raising, Mestres noted.

Bowen added that, though Princeton's ability to provide a good education for its women depends on other projects being carried out, such as expanding the library, "the president has made it clear that this is the most important single plan."

The financial vice-president con-

(Continued on page ten)

The Daily PRINCETONIAN

Admission office prepares for girls

By BILL HIGHBERGER

"We're in business — finally," John T. Osander '57, Princeton's admission director, boasted when asked about accepting women.

Actually, Osander and his staff can only accept application forms —not girls—pending the trustees' final decision—probably April 19—on the timing of coeducation.

Girls on campus will also affect male admissions crucially, since it should solidify Princeton's softening competitive position for top candidates—Group I's, in admission office jargon.

As most everyone knows by now, Princeton saw a three per cent drop in applications last year—a dangerous trend—and the main reason given by those passing up Old Nassau has been its lack of coeducation, according to the extensive Patterson Committee report.

In brief the report states, "There is, in the words of the director of admission 'a marked difference between those men we admit early in the admissions meetings and those with whom we fill the class...'

"Moreover, too many of the students who apply, whom we admit and whom we would most like to have at Princeton, go elsewhere."

The approach being used this year in the admission office to fe-

male applications for next year will be radically different from the intended procedures. This year, pressed for time and stymied by trustee indecision, Osander and his staff have to shorten the admission procedure.

Because the admission staff is already busy chipping away at male admissions for the class of 1973, they will have no time to conduct on campus interviews or process alumni interviews of women.

"As a result we might end up with a totally ugly class," Osander joked.

(Continued on page ten)

Rudenstine investigates coeducation's first stages

By RICHARD BALFOUR

The jump from Elizabethan poetry to the chairmanship of a maze of committees concerned with contemporary student problems is an improbable one. But according to the man who made it, it has been a rewarding one.

One year after becoming Dean of Students, Neil L. Rudenstine '66 is on top of the most important campus issues: coeducation, the role of black students at Princeton, parietals and discipline, the place of ROTC on campus and the social alternatives.

In an interview with The Princetonian, the paisley-tied, long-haired, outspoken dean outlined his role in current changes and looked ahead into the future.

The future at Princeton will soon be coeducational, and according to Rudenstine, who has taught all-male, all-female and mixed classes, the best way to run a school is coeducationally.

"Women will make an enormous difference in the classroom," he stated. "There is a great need for intellectual crosscurrents here."

The first two stages

One of the numerous committees which Rudenstine heads, the Faculty Social Facilities Committee, is currently planning the first two stages of coeducation, the establishment of living and social facilities for 400 to 600 girls.

Dean Rudenstine's role in the planning has included correspondence with Cornell, Harvard and Yale and investigatory road trips to Stanford and Michigan.

Impressed with the "tremendous number of different kinds of living and social facilities" at Stanford, Rudenstine expressed the hope that the variety of the west coast school could be at least partially adapted to Princeton.

All dormitory units at Stanford are identical physically so that no students choose their room on the basis of its inherent attractiveness. They choose instead on the living arrangement: unisexual or coeducational, restricted to one class or open to all academic years.

Princetonians, Rudenstine maintained, "are too attached to their rooms. Choosing on the basis of

(Continued on page fourteen)

Dean Neil Rudenstine
On top of coeducation planning

This special Alumni Day issue of *The Daily Princetonian* in February of 1969 was dedicated largely to the subject of coeducation, following the University's decision to admit women to the Class of 1973. Courtesy of *The Daily Princetonian*.

from the Ford Foundation, and whose final report, *Industrialism and Industrial Man Reconsidered,* was published under the section's aegis in 1975.

Under Harbison's leadership, several noteworthy developments occurred that began a process of modernization of the section's activities in a variety of areas. For example, the number of faculty associates increased significantly, from three in 1955 to eight by the end of his term in 1968. During this period, the section also made increasing use of visiting faculty from both American and foreign universities as research associates. Furthermore, in no small part due to his interest in management and labor issues connected with economic growth in both industrialized and developing countries, the number of doctoral candidates working on their dissertations during Harbison's tenure as director more than doubled from five in the 1957-1958 academic year to 11 in the 1963-1964 academic year. Finally, in order to redeploy its resources more efficiently, the section also discontinued its annual seminar course for junior executives and its annual seminar, Labor Relations for Union Research and Staff Personnel, and restructured its annual conference for senior executives into a series of theme-based symposia.

From its founding in 1922, the Industrial Relations Section's library had always been an integral part of the unit's identity, and as the section grew and developed in the 1950s and 1960s, so did its library. For example, in keeping with Director Harbison's interest in the impact of human resources management issues on economic development, the library expanded its coverage of that area. According to Richard Lester:

A 1952 news article commemorates the Industrial Relations Section's 30th anniversary. Image courtesy of *The Daily Princetonian.*

The Section published in 1958 a ninety-three-page annotated bibliography: *Manpower Problems in Economic Development: A Selected Bibliography,* by Keith Simpson and Hazel Benjamin [Section librarian from 1939 to 1968]. The project was undertaken for the Ford Foundation, which commissioned the Section to keep it up to date and to serve as a central clearing point for material on the subject of human resources in economic development.[84]

With the expanded research interest in new subject matters and geographical areas, Princeton students and foreign researchers alike increasingly turned to the section's library resources for reference assistance and guidance in writing research reports and degree theses. By the 1964-1965 academic

Group on Industrial Relations Holds Anniversary Celebration

The Industrial Relations Section of Princeton's Department of Economics and Social Institutions celebrated its thirtieth anniversary at a dinner held in Procter Hall of the Graduate College September 16.

Now under the direction of Dean of the Faculty Dr. J. Douglas Brown '19, the Section has broadened considerably with its volume and scope since its beginning in 1922.

One of the chief purposes of the Section is to maintain a special library, now containing 300,000 entries, consisting of interviews, plans and policies, which is available to research students and trade unions.

In addition the organization aids in the University's educational program, provides a consulting service and holds conferences and seminars. Its findings of research studies have been published both in the form of printed reports and full-length books.

During the past year publications prepared by the section have been sent to 24 foreign countries, while the current list totals 84 items.

This work is made possible by a recently completed endowment program which now stands at $1,000,000 and which has been contributed by corporations, trade unions and the Rockefeller family.

The Section came into existence

Dean of the Faculty Dr. J. Douglas Brown '19 who directs Industrial Relations Group.

when Clarence J. Hicks, then executive assistant to the Standard Oil Company (New Jersey), persuaded John D. Rockefeller Jr. to finance the project for a trial period. Since then over 20 bureaus of a similar nature have been established.

Dean Brown took over his position from Robert F. Foerster, the first director, in 1926.

---

[84] Lester, *Industrial Relations Section,* 15.

The Industrial Relations Section's librarian and associate director, and the first woman to achieve the rank of associate professor at Princeton University, Helen Baker, is memorialized in a 1955 newspaper article. Photograph courtesy of the Princeton University Library. Article courtesy of *The Daily Princetonian.*

Service Pays Respects To Helen Baker

A memorial service for Miss Helen Baker, associate director of Princeton's Industrial Relations Section, was held yesterday afternoon in the University Chapel. Miss Baker, 55, died here Monday after a short illness.

She was the first female associate professor in Princeton's history, accorded that rank by special action of the University's Board of Trustees in 1948. She would have completed 25 years of service here in June. Dean of the Faculty and Director of the Industrial Relations Section, J. Douglas Brown '19, pays her the following tribute: "There is no question but what she was one of the outstanding experts in the field of industrial relations in the country. One of the few women in the field, she has contributed to its progress for the past quarter century."

Renowned and Respected

Professor Richard A. Lester, chairman of the department of Economics and Social Institutions, acclaims Miss Baker as having been "the most widely-known and respected woman in the field of corporation policy concerning personnel relations. More than anyone else she is responsible for the development at Princeton of a collection of industrial relations material that is unequalled anywhere in the country."

A graduate of Radcliffe in 1921, Miss Baker received her Master of Arts degree from Carnegie Institute of Technology two years later. After serving as a training consultant in private industry, she joined the Princeton faculty in 1930.

She wrote or co-authored twenty reports published by the Section during her career here.

year, the library was fielding requests for assistance from 13 countries, and was being used by 215 undergraduate and graduate students. In that same year, it acquired 3,280 items, including nearly 1,500 company documents and publications from around the world.

The 1950s and 1960s were a period of extraordinary development in the Industrial Relations Section's research activities. As Richard Lester points out:

> By 1958-1959 the Section staff included ten research associates and four research assistants. Seven of the research associates were members of the Princeton faculty and two were professors at other universities, one of them from England. The research projects and programs on which the Section staff was engaged varied widely in subject and in country coverage....Section researchers during the sixteen years from 1956 through 1971 wrote thirty-five books.[85]

In fact, between 1950 and 1959 alone, section staff published 18 reports running to 1,767 pages, in addition to four books running to 1,132 pages that were published at Princeton or elsewhere, and a number of articles in academic journals that were issued as reprints under the section's cover—a research volume of more than double that of the previous decade.

These publications covered a range of traditional industrial relations topics, from studies of various management and union policies and practices under collective bargaining and arbitration arrangements, to investigations into employee benefit and pension programs and research on manpower development and utilization issues. But they also delved into relatively new areas for the section—labor relations, management practices and union issues outside of the United States, e.g., in England, Germany, and Sweden; economic development and human resource management issues in industrializing countries, such as Egypt; and high-talent manpower development in the emerging science- and technology-related industries.

The corresponding figures for the decade from 1960 to 1969 are even more striking. During this period, section staff published 17 research reports running to 2,534 pages,[86] in addition to 10 books published at Princeton or elsewhere running to 3,502 pages, and a total of 25 journal articles issued as reprints under the section's cover, more than doubling again the volume of research produced over that of the previous decade. More

---

[85] Ibid.

[86] The section research report figures for the period include three conference reports (1965, 1966 and 1968) of the Industrial Relations Section's *Princeton Manpower Symposium* series, totaling 617 pages.

than just an increase in volume, however, an examination of the topics covered (and in the case of reprints, the nature of the academic journals in which the articles were published), also underscores the broadening and the deepening of the section's research activities taking place at the time.

For example, publications by section staff during the 1960s covered a variety of new countries, including Brazil, South Africa, Mexico, Nigeria, and Columbia, and new subjects such as education, public health regulation, and labor market participation by urban minorities. Moreover, consistent with the trend in labor economics described earlier, there was a notable increase during this period in the number of publications by section faculty and research staff that emphasized the empirical analysis of labor markets, and also an increase in the number of section-associated articles that appeared in the more mainstream economic journals of the day.

Industrial Relations Section "Conference Course" seminar for industry practitioners, 1953. Princeton University Library.

Among the numerous examples of publications that were part of this trend are several journal articles and books, including:

— Bowen, W.G., "Cost Inflation versus Demand Inflation: A Useful Distinction," *Southern Economic Journal* (1960);

— Lester, R.A., "The Economic Significance of Unemployment Compensation, 1948-1959," *Review of Economics and Statistics* (1960);

— Bowen, W.G. and T.A. Finegan, "Educational Attainment and Labor Force Participation," *American Economic Review* (1966);

— Mooney, J.D., "Urban Poverty and Labor Force Participation," *American Economic Review* (1967);

— Ashenfelter, O. and J.D. Mooney, "Graduate Education, Ability and Earnings," *Review of Economics and Statistics* (1967);

— Rees, A., "Spatial Wage Differentials in a Large City Labor Market," *IRRA 21st Annual Proceedings* (1968);

— Ashenfelter, O. and G.E. Johnson, "Bargaining Theory, Trade Unions, and Industrial Strike Activity," *American Economic Review* (1969);

— Bowen, W.G., *The Wage-Price Issue: A Theoretical Analysis*. Princeton, N.J.: Princeton University Press (1960); and

— Bowen, W.G. and T.A. Finegan, *The Economics of Labor Force Participation*. Princeton, NJ: Princeton University Press (1969).

The developments highlighted above are not isolated occurrences, but were part of a more fundamental transition that took place within the Industrial Relations Section in the 1950s and 1960s, and which gained further momentum in the 1970s. To begin with, in 1960, Princeton's Department of Economics and Social Institutions, under whose aegis the Industrial Relations Section operated, was separated into two discrete departments, economics and sociology. The section remained affiliated with the economics department, and as a result, although there were still a number of sociologists associated with the section for quite some time afterwards, and research was still being done in areas more closely connected with that field, the section gradually became more focused on labor economics.

Sees Nasser 'Genuinely Neutral'
Harbison to Aid Egyptian Growth

By DONALD W. KRAMER

Princeton Economics Professor Frederick H. Harbison '34 left for Egypt Friday to help out on a program of economic development in a country he predicts will be "genuinely neutral" in the East-West cold war.

The director of the Industrial Relations Section of the Department of Economics will aid representatives of the Nasser government, business and labor in establishing an institute for executive training at Cairo.

While stating that Nasser is the "most powerful force" in the Mid-East and that he runs an "authoritarian government—as have been all previous Egyptian governments"—he says Nas-

ser is not anti-American.

"The only extent that Egypt is anti-Western," Harbison says, "is in consequence of economics and political policies pursued by the West in recent years that have driven Egypt against her will into the Russian camp."

He praised the regime as "representing a genuine revolution" and as the "most honest and aggressive in modern times." It is, therefore, "the most troublesome in the eyes of the West," he added.

The professor remarked, "if I didn't think he would remain genuinely neutral I wouldn't go."

Making his sixth trip to Egypt, Harbison will work with the Inter-University Study of Labor Prob-

(Continued on page five)

Frederick H. Harbison '34

Under the leadership of Frederick Harbison from 1955 to 1968, the Industrial Relations Section broadened its research to include developing economies. Image courtesy of *The Daily Princetonian*.

For another thing, throughout this period, a number of faculty and research staff additions were made which influenced the section's research programs in a variety of ways—for example, sociologist Wilbert E. Moore (president of the American Sociological Association, 1966-1967) researched the impact of industrialization on social change as a faculty associate in the section from 1962 to 1964, during which time he published *The Conduct of the Corporation* (1962); and economist T. Aldrich Finegan of Vanderbilt University was a research associate from 1962 to 1964, and again from 1967 to 1968, when he worked with William G. Bowen on their 897-page book, *The Economics of Labor Force Participation*.

Likewise, in 1963, Herman M. "Red" Somers, Professor of Politics and Public Affairs of the Woodrow Wilson School, joined the section as a faculty associate, authoring or co-editing a number of studies on social insurance and health benefits, including the symposium volume, *The American System of Social Insurance* (1968), in honor of former section director J. Douglas Brown. The following year, 1964, his wife, Anne R. Somers, also joined the section as a research associate, focusing her attention on public policy regarding healthcare and hospital regulation, and publishing her book, *Hospital Regulation: The Dilemma of Public Policy,* as a section report. During the mid-1960s, Herman Somers was also a member of President Johnson's Advisory Council on Social Security along with J. Douglas Brown, and both he and Anne Somers assisted U.S. Secretary of Health, Education and Welfare Wilbur J. Cohen in researching and shaping Medicare legislation.

However, one of the most consequential additions to the section's team of faculty associates was made in 1966, when Albert Rees—a former colleague of Frederick Harbison's at the University of Chicago—joined the Princeton Industrial Relations Section. Rees has been called an influential transitional figure in the section's history by several current and former faculty associates, and for this reason it is worth emphasizing the importance of his legacy in some detail.

The director of Princeton's Industrial Relations Section from 1968 to 1971, and provost of the University from 1975 to 1979, Rees had received both his master's and doctorate at the University of Chicago. He became a full professor there in 1961, and spent four years as chairman of the economics department before leaving to join the faculty at Princeton.[87] As such, he was a contemporary of such noted Chicago economists as Frank Knight, George J. Stigler, Milton Friedman, and H. Gregg Lewis.

As a labor economist with a deep interest in wage and price stability, and on the economic impact of labor unions, Rees was heavily influenced by Lewis, about whom he authored a telling tribute upon the latter's retirement from the University of Chicago. Writing in 1976 about Lewis's contributions to the field of labor economics, Rees describes the difference between what he calls "analytical labor economics" and the more traditional form of "institutional labor economics":

> I use the term analytical labor economics, in contrast to institutional labor economics, to mean the application of economic theory and econometrics to problems of the formation of human capital, the allocation of time between market and nonmarket activities, the allocation of labor among alternative uses, and the compensation of labor. Some of these problems are, of course, also addressed by institutional labor economics. There are, however, clear differences in methodology and scope between the two approaches to the field.[88]

In fact, it was precisely because of this more quantitative style of labor economics that Rees brought with him from Chicago that he was invited by Frederick Harbison, William Bowen, and others to join Princeton's economics department as a faculty associate in the Industrial Relations Section in 1966.

Despite his credentials as a bona fide member of the "Chicago School of Economics" (which was more often than not in opposition to the institutional labor economics

Somers Given Wilson School Professorship

Dr. Herman Miles Somers, a leading authority on political processes and on social welfare activities, will join Princeton's faculty next fall as professor of politics and public affairs, President Goheen announced yesterday.

Somers will take an active part in the development of the new graduate program of the Woodrow Wilson School of Public and International Affairs to which he is the seventh faculty appointment.

"Professor Somers combines high competence in political science and economics with wide experience in

Herman Miles Somers

governmental affairs," President Goheen commented. "He will add great strength to both the Woodrow Wilson School and the Department of Politics."

Coming to Princeton from Haverford College, Somers has formerly taught at Harvard, the University of California and Columbia University.

Service in Washington

Prior to teaching, he served on the staff of the Office of War Mobilization and Reconversion and the National Resources Planning Board in Washington.

Somers is presently associated with the International Labor Organization at Geneva and is working on problems of instituting social welfare programs in the under-developed areas. He has also been a member of the President's Commission on National Goals and the President's Committee on Veterans' Pensions.

DeSapio Speaks

Carmine De Sapio, former Democratic party leader of New York City, will address the General Assembly of Whig-Clio tonight at 8 on the subject "The Individual and Politics in a Democracy."

Once head of Tammany Hall, De Sapio controlled New York City politics until he was deposed in the 1961 Democratic primary.

In that election he was opposed by a reform group headed by Robert F. Wagner, incumbent mayor of New York, Mrs. Franklin D. Roosevelt and Herbert Lehmen, former governor of New York.

Herman Miles "Red" Somers. Courtesy of *The Daily Princetonian.*

---

[87] While at the University of Chicago, Rees served as a member of the U.S. President's Council of Economic Advisers and of the Committee to Appraise Employment and Unemployment Statistics. While at Princeton, he also served from 1974 to 1975 as chairman of President Ford's newly created Council on Wage and Price Stability.

[88] Albert Rees, "H. Gregg Lewis and the Development of Analytical Labor Economics," *Journal of Political Economy,* 1976, vol. 84, no.4, pt. 2.

Albert Rees and William G. Bowen. Courtesy of *The Daily Princetonian.*

school of thought), as section alumni and former director, Orley Ashenfelter (Ph.D., 1970; section director from 1971-1995, 1998-2001, 2007-2008 [acting director], and 2010-2011 [acting director]) and John H. Pencavel (Ph.D., 1969) have pointed out, "his role was perhaps distinctive in that group." Ashenfelter and Pencavel's views, expounded upon in their 2006 essay on Rees (section working paper #506), help to put his fit within the Industrial Relations Section's team of faculty associates into context.

The study of unionism was Rees's lifelong interest and his fundamental views about American unionism appear to have changed little from his early scholastic days to his later years. He tended to regard the economic effects of unionism as largely undesirable....Yet he immediately proceeds to describe this judgment as "narrow" if offered as a complete assessment of unionism. He wrote (1950, p. 257) in an early review of a wide-ranging denunciation of unions, "The least that can be said for unions is that their noneconomic activities are, by and large, highly beneficial. Through grievance procedure, seniority, and control of the speed and conditions of work, unions have given the industrial worker a new sense of dignity, individual worth, and participation in the process of production." Rees saw "a strong union movement [as] the best guaranty against movements which might lead workers to demand the exchange of our democratic freedoms for the 'security' of a police state" (1950, p.261-2). In appraising unionism, Rees was ready to accept the basic framework of economic reasoning, but also recognized that a full evaluation required a broader perspective.[89]

Another important aspect of Rees's legacy within the section was his role as a teacher and an adviser. According to Ashenfelter and Pencavel:

> Rees's scholarship centered on Labor Economics and his contributions ranged from theoretical modeling to resourceful empirical research to the careful construction of original data. The public policy ramifications of this work were never far from his research. He was a very conscientious and courteous adviser of many students. Teaching was important to him and, in the 1970s, he authored the major textbook at that time in Labor Economics (1973). His gracious manner made him a popular

---

[89] Orley C. Ashenfelter and John H. Pencavel, "Albert Rees and the 'Chicago School of Economics'," in *The Elgar Companion to the Chicago School of Economics,* Ross B. Emmett, ed. (Cheltenham, Glos, UK and Northampton, MA: Edward Elgar, 2010), 311-314.

teacher and colleague. He served as editor of the Journal of Political Economy for a number of years.[90]

One example of Rees's involvement with the section's research programs and his influence on its graduate students is a project undertaken in 1967, entitled "Systems Analysis of Labor Markets in the U.S." The project, contracted to Princeton's Industrial Relations Section by the U.S. Department of Labor's Office of Manpower Policy, Evaluation and Research, had the goal of "developing a series of models that would (a) enable analysts and policymakers to trace the effects of both external pressures and alternative manpower policies on the American system of labor markets and (b) provide training and research experience for graduate students in labor market analysis."[91]

According to Richard Lester, five of the section's doctoral students wrote their Ph.D. dissertations on topics connected with, or closely related to the project, and the project ultimately resulted in the publication of 13 working papers, in addition to the final report for the Department of Labor. Several section faculty and research associates, as well as other Princeton faculty members—including Stanley Black (the project's director for the first year), William Branson, Ray Fair, Daniel Hamermesh, Harry Kelejian, Joseph Mooney, Wallace Oates, and Orley Ashenfelter (the project's director for the second year)—and at least one visiting faculty associate, George E. Johnson of the University of Michigan, participated in the project at various times. Albert Rees served as the chairman of the project's advisory committee.[92]

From a review of some of the project's earliest working papers (e.g. the April 1967 paper, "A Study of the U.S. Labor Market: A Report on Work in Progress" by S. Black, W. Branson, H. Kelejian, J. Mooney, and W. Oates) it becomes obvious that this research project—with its heavy reliance on neoclassical economic theoretical underpinnings, and on the use of mathematical and econometric computational models designed to be programmed into a computer and applied to large sets of statistical data—represents one example of the significant departure that was being made from the research methodologies utilized in the institutionally oriented labor economics studies of the section's past. Nevertheless, at the core of these new research methodologies was an essential characteristic that had long been a tradition of Princeton's Industrial Relations Section, and which was a defining trait of Albert Rees, as well—that is, a keen focus on careful empirical analysis. In this regard, Ashenfelter and Pencavel write that:

---

[90] Ibid.

[91] Lester, *Industrial Relations Section,* 16.

[92] Ibid., 16. Lester singles out "A Macro Model of the U.S. Labor Market" by S. Black and H. Kelejian (*Econometrica,* 1970) as one of the main papers that resulted from this project.

[A]s a scholar, Rees was above all an empiricist. Even his papers that focused on theoretical models are infused with data. He constructed (1961a) the definitive series on real wages in manufacturing industry in the 25 years before the First World War and, in committee reports with others, he advised (1961b, 1962, 1979) on the government's methods of measuring prices, unemployment, and productivity. With George Schultz, he led (1970c) a major empirical project examining Chicago's labor markets which involved the collection of large bodies of data on wages, employment, and many other aspects of labor markets. Later (1974), he was a principal investigator in the New Jersey/Pennsylvania Income Maintenance Experiment whose purpose was to determine the response of low income people to different terms of welfare benefits. He collaborated (1991) on a survey and analysis on faculty retirement behavior designed to anticipate the effects of the ending of mandatory retirement in universities. This uninterrupted commitment to careful measurement informed by public policy issues and by the precepts of economic theory is the type of scholarship that has the hallmark of the best Labor Economics research which is why so many of today's researchers think of Rees as their intellectual paragon.[93]

As has been shown above, in parallel with the nation, as well as with the field of industrial relations in general, and with Princeton University as a whole, the number of changes experienced by the Industrial Relations Section in the 1960s was significant. In the decade between the 1960-1961 and the 1969-1970 academic years, a further 24 graduates (including Orley Ashenfelter) completed their Ph.D. programs, bringing the total number of economists trained by the section since its inception to 89. Several scholars, whose academic interests broadened and deepened the section's research activities, joined the team of faculty associates and left their mark on a new generation of students.

The section gradually discontinued its series of annual conferences, which had been held with few interruptions since 1931 (the last invitation-only *Princeton Manpower Symposium* was held in 1969 on the subject of "Research on Poverty"); and in 1966, J. Douglas Brown retired from his position as dean of the faculty, a position he had held since 1946, and became the University's first provost for one year before formally retiring in 1967[94] (although he continued on for many more years as an associate of

---

[93] Ashenfelter and Pencavel, *Albert Rees,* 314.

[94] He was succeeded as provost by the section's own William G. Bowen, who subsequently went on to become Princeton University's 17th president.

the section). By 1970, beginning from its original annual budget of about $12,000, the market value of the section's endowment exceeded $5 million.

Indeed, it can be said that, by the beginning of the 1970s, the Industrial Relations Section stood on the threshold of a new era. And when he succeeded Albert Rees as director in 1971, it was the section's own Orley Ashenfelter who took the helm in leading it into what would prove to be the uncharted waters of a new age in labor economics.

The 1970s

The widening and deepening of the Industrial Relations Section's research activities that began in earnest in the 1960s—with its pronounced trend towards the increasingly empirical analysis of various aspects of labor markets—gained further momentum in the 1970s. Over the course of the decade, 14 new faculty associates joined the section's research staff, most of whom stayed for a period of one to two years.[95] Several, however, including Farrell E. Bloch, James N. Brown (acting director, 1984 to 1985), George Cave, Roger Gordon, Daniel S. Hamermesh (acting director, 1972-1973), Cordelia W. Reimers (acting director, 1980-1981), Harvey S. Rosen (chairman of Princeton's economics department from 1993 to 1996, and member of the President's Council of Economic Advisers in 2003, 2004, and its chairman in 2005), and Anne Somers were associated with the section for a term of four years or more.

During the 1970s, the section held a number of research seminars each year, at which graduate students, faculty members, or visiting researchers would present working papers on the subjects of their current research. There were also several academic conferences during this period, which were either sponsored or co-sponsored by the section, and which resulted in the publication of books such as *Discrimination in Labor Markets,* edited by Orley Ashenfelter and Albert Rees (1971); *Labor in the Public and Nonprofit Sectors,* edited by Daniel S. Hamermesh (1975); *Evaluating the Labor Market Effects of Social Programs,* edited by Orley Ashenfelter and James Blum (1976); and *Evaluating Manpower Training Programs,* edited by Farrell E. Bloch (1979).

During this time, a number of visiting professors from both U.S. and foreign universities also held appointments on the section's research staff, while on sabbatical from their home institutions.[96] Several of them contributed papers to the section's series

---

[95] For a complete list of the Industrial Relations Section's faculty associates, including their years of association, see Appendix.

[96] For a complete list of visiting faculty and their years of association, see page 219.

Excerpts from a 1967 Industrial Relations Section working paper, showing an emphasis on neo-classical economic theory coupled with the authors' emerging model of the U.S. labor market. Courtesy of the Industrial Relations Section.

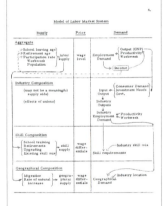

of working papers, and even published articles in academic journals based on research performed or revised while at Princeton. In addition, advanced graduate students also contributed to the section's research activities, often publishing articles related to the subject matter of their doctoral dissertations in academic journals.

Over the course of the 1970s, the section published only nine reports in its research report series (half the number of the previous decade) totaling some 1,361 pages.[97] However, 13 books by section staff, running to 3,688 pages, were published at Princeton or elsewhere, and no fewer than 88 articles were published in various academic journals. Among these were such well-received titles as Sharon P. Smith's *Equal Pay in the Public Sector: Fact or Fantasy,* and Daniel S. Hamermesh's *Labor in the Public and Non-Profit Sectors.* Writing about the section's activities during this time, Richard Lester points out that:

> [R]esearch projects of the Section and training of graduate students tended to emphasize methodological advances that were being applied throughout the social sciences. Much of the Section's research in this period involved the use of quantitative and econometric methods of analysis.[98]

Still, however significant the use of quantitative and econometric methods was, it was only one part of what distinguished the Industrial Relations Section's research during the 1970s from that of prior decades. There were two other factors that, in combination with the use of robust statistical methods, created a sea change in the way in which economics research in general, and labor economics research in particular, was done at Princeton and other institutions active in labor economics. The first was the advent of the modern computer as a truly effective computational tool, and its increasingly widespread availability on university campuses. The second was access to micro-level data from government statistical sources, which had never before been available to academic economists. The significance of these developments is underscored by the fact that the Industrial Relations Section quickly became one of the principal users of the University's Computer Center under Judith Rowe, who worked extensively with Orley Ashenfelter and other faculty, as well as with the section's graduate students, to identify and analyze valuable datasets.

According to Orley Ashenfelter, it was the confluence of these three factors—the use of computers, the sudden availability of micro-level data, and the rapid

---

[97] This total includes one book, Orley Ashenfelter and James Blum, eds., *Evaluating the Labor Market Effects of Social Programs* (Princeton: Industrial Relations Section, Princeton University, 1976), which was a compendium of papers presented at a section-sponsored conference.

[98] Lester, *Industrial Relations Section,* 21.

spread of statistical methods—that caused what some have called the quantitative revolution, and which in a matter of years completely changed the way in which labor economics research was done:

Dean J. Douglas Brown, circa his retirement in 1976. Courtesy of *The Daily Princetonian*.

> The U.S. Labor department started to make their data—the actual micro-data—available anonymously, starting in the 1970s, and that was just an unbelievable breakthrough. The 1960 census was the first one that was available to us in micro-data form, and that made a huge difference in what kind of research you could do. So you had the computer, and you had the data, and then I think the training in statistical methods was very important. I was lucky enough to be here when that revolution—all three things—happened at once. As a result I was one of the first people in our field that used all three of those things. If I had been trained even five years before, I probably would have had a different training background altogether. Everything changed, though most of us, we stuck with the old topics. My dissertation was on labor market discrimination—just a classic subject—but I was using quantitative methods.[99]

Fortuitous timing aside, Ashenfelter's personal ingenuity and creativity undoubtedly played a significant role in prompting him to seize the opportunities presented by this quantitative revolution and to turn them into groundbreaking research pathways, as discussed further below; however, there were perhaps three other elements which also contributed to the section's being one of the first academic units in its field to apply this new range of quantitative tools and methods to research in labor economics.

First, though the techniques were different, from its earliest days the Industrial Relations Section had a longstanding tradition of utilizing empirical data—often in the form of original surveys of various companies and labor unions with which it cooperated—in its research on industrial programs and policies in regard to the problems of labor and the deployment of human capital. Second, several senior faculty associates of the section had an appreciation for and interest in the use of quantitative methods. For example, Frederick Harbison and Albert Rees had both been associated in the past with the University of Chicago, which had long been a leader in the use of quantitative methods in economics research; and William Bowen, who by the late 1960s had already begun to move into important administrative roles within the University, was a strong proponent for quantitative research (having, in fact, been influential in bringing Rees from Chicago in the mid-1960s for the purpose of reinforcing the

Helen Fairbanks, Industrial Relations Section librarian and research associate from 1968 to 1978, originally joined the Princeton University staff in 1947. Courtesy of *The Daily Princetonian*.

---

[99] Orley Ashenfelter, Princeton University Industrial Relations Section, in an unpublished interview with the author, June 12, 2012.

section's quantitative capabilities). And third, there was at Princeton an atmosphere that encouraged innovation and allowed both faculty and graduate students the freedom to explore new avenues of research. As Ashenfelter puts it:

> They always gave you an umbrella to do what you wanted, and they didn't ever try to make you do less quantitative work. That was a very important thing. That wasn't the same everywhere. We want our students to do unusual things and we try to give them a lot of freedom. And so, because there is no resistance, we move pretty quickly.[100]

Early calculator used by the Industrial Relations Section's economists.

As shown above, even before the quantitative revolution of the 1970s, empirical, quantitative, and econometric methodologies were already in use in economics research by many notable economists. However, due to the aggregate nature of the data being used, there were often significant biases that skewed the results of the research. This phenomenon is referenced directly in a 1979 section working paper by visiting faculty associates Charles Mulvey and John M. Abowd, who wrote:

> Prior to the availability of micro-data sets for the U.S. which indicated the union or non-union status of individuals, almost all estimates of the conditional average union/non-union wage differential, given union membership, were made using mean average wages from a sample of industries or occupations....We show below that this incomplete data method has produced biassed [sic] estimates of the union/non-union wage differential when applied to data from the U.K....It is worthwhile stressing at this point that we are not referring to (potentially) biassed [sic] estimates of the structural effect of unionism on wages but rather to (observably) biassed [sic] estimates of the conditional effect of unionism on wages. Before U.S. estimates based on individual data became available, there was some consensus that the average differential was between 20 and 30 per cent. Micro-data estimates now put the U.S. figure at around 12%.[101]

Furthermore, in many areas of economics, quantitative and econometric work was done in modeling hypotheses based on economic theory, and aggregate empirical data that fit the hypotheses were then used as supporting evidence, often without a clear distinction between correlation and causality in the underlying data.

---

[100] Ashenfelter, unpublished interview.

[101] Charles Mulvey and John M. Abowd, "Estimating the Union/Non-Union Wage Differential: A Statistical Issue," *Working Paper 108A, Industrial Relations Section,* Princeton University, June 1979.

Among the enduring fundamental contributions made by the Industrial Relations Section to the field of labor economics (as well as to many other areas of economics, and even to other academic disciplines) from the 1970s onward, has been an emphasis on the careful (and frequently innovative) gathering of relevant primary data, the use of credible, transparent quantitative techniques with which to analyze that data, and the design of unbiased experimental methods to help determine causal relationships in the areas being studied—what some have called the "credibility revolution." As pointed out by section alumnus and longtime faculty associate David E. Card:

Orley Ashenfelter

> Under the guidance of Orley [Ashenfelter]…and others, labor economics has been an engine of growth for the development and application of important techniques and ideas that are now spreading to other fields in economics and to the other social sciences. Economists and other social scientists look to labor economics as a role model for credible, evidence-based research on controversial and difficult problems.[102]

Much of the approach described above, which has become fairly standard today, is due to the enormous influence of the early work done by Orley Ashenfelter, as well as that of the students he inspired. According to the 2003 award statement of the prestigious IZA Prize in Labor Economics:

> Ashenfelter's intellectual work stands out due to his ingenuity in devising clever ways to derive and test hypotheses of economic models, his exceptional creativity in using and collecting data, and his originality in pioneering the natural experiment methodology. Setting off the development of methods for empirical tests of labor market models Ashenfelter's scholarly contributions have fundamentally transformed the analysis of labor markets. In a number of seminal articles he has broken new ground in various core areas of labor economics including research on trade unions, wages and employment, the analysis of labor supply, and the study of discrimination, education and training.[103]

From 1972 to 1973, while on a one-year leave of absence from his position as director of the Industrial Relations Section, Ashenfelter worked as the director of the U.S. Department of Labor's Office of Evaluation. The research he began as a result of his

---

[102] David E. Card, from "Laudation for Orley Ashenfelter, Recipient of the 2003 IZA Prize in Labor Economics," an unpublished speech delivered on September 22, 2003 at the IZA Prize award ceremony in Bonn, Germany.

[103] Institute for the Study of Labor (Institut zur Zukunft der Arbeit), *IZA Prize Award Statement* (Bonn: IZA, 2003).

experience there not only opened up an entirely new direction in the study of labor markets, but inspired a generation of young labor economists to follow in his footsteps. In the words of the official statement of the IZA prize committee:

> Serving as the Director of the Office of Evaluation of the U.S. Department of Labor in 1972, Ashenfelter became the founding father of what has by today developed into the separate field of quantitative social program evaluation. His conviction that empirical analyses have to be credible and simple in order to trigger changes in the social system was the impetus for a rigorous development of econometric tools for quantitative evaluation of social programs. This is reflected in two landmark contributions to the literature on the evaluation of government retraining programs, the 1978 and 1985 Review of Economics and Statistics articles. These papers developed methods for longitudinal program evaluation that have become known as the "difference-in-differences" approach. The earlier article pioneered the exploitation of natural variation produced by the social system to investigate important social questions by elaborating the idea of using a comparison group to assess the effect of training. It also identified the bias in the estimation of the effects of training on program participants that is caused by a drop in earnings of trainees relative to the comparison group, which has become known in the economics literature as "Ashenfelter's dip." The later paper, which is co-authored with David Card, advanced the natural experiment methodology to partly make up for the lack of experimental data. Apart from expounding new econometric techniques, Ashenfelter has also been a leader in the creative collection of data that are suitable to conclusively answer important economic questions.[104]

As a leading figure in the Industrial Relations Section, Ashenfelter not only pioneered the use of new quantitative and empirical methods in labor economics research, but helped to inspire and train a generation of new labor economists in innovative ways of thinking about labor markets. In the decade between the 1970-1971 and the 1979-1980 academic years, the Industrial Relations Section produced 27 graduates—including such figures as James J. Heckman GS'71, winner of the Nobel Prize in Economics in 2000; Elizabeth E. Bailey GS'72, the first woman to receive a Ph.D. in economics from Princeton; and Henry S. Farber GS'77, who would later become a longtime faculty associate of the section—a number of whom were trained by Ashenfelter.

[104] Ibid.

By the end of the 1970s, the faculty composition of the section had changed dramatically. Although he continued on as an associate for several years after his 1967 retirement, J. Douglas Brown's involvement with the section was drastically reduced after the early 1970s, and Richard A. Lester and Frederick Harbison also both retired by the middle of the decade (the former in 1974 and the latter in 1976). William Bowen, who had replaced Brown as the University's provost in 1967, went on to become the president of Princeton University in 1972; and after spending a year in Washington, D.C. heading President Gerald Ford's Council on Wage and Price Stability from 1974 to 1975, Albert Rees returned to Princeton for four years to become the University's provost, before leaving again in 1979 to become president of the private Alfred P. Sloan Foundation in New York.

Thus, just 10 years after completing his Ph.D. in the Industrial Relations Section, Orley Ashenfelter was for a time the only tenured professor of economics who remained on the section's staff. Over the course of the next several years, he set about rebuilding the section's team of faculty associates, which, as shall be shown in the next section, he accomplished with impressive results.

The 1980s and Beyond, or Back to the Future

President Ronald Reagan explains his tax reduction plan in a nationally televised speech from the Oval Office on July 27, 1981.

The shape of industrial relations scholarship has shifted in recent decades, *pointing to specialized disciplines like human resources management and organizational behavior. The Princeton Industrial Relations Section has continued to have a profound impact on the field, leading the way in bringing methodological rigor and precision in labor economics, expanding its output of publications, and by staff members like Alan Krueger and Cecilia Rouse continuing to influence public policy.*

The 1980s and Beyond, or Back to the Future

At the macroeconomic level, the 1980s were in many ways a turbulent time for the U.S. labor market. The decade started out with back-to-back recessions in 1980 and 1981-1982, and saw high unemployment (as much as 10.8 percent in 1982, falling to under 6 percent by 1989), a tripling of the national debt (from roughly $930 billion at the start of the decade to $2.6 trillion near its end), a widening trade deficit (from $19.4 billion in 1980 to as much as $151.7 billion in 1987, before falling to $93.1 billion by 1989),[105] and the savings and loan crisis of the late 1980s. On the other hand, inflation, which had been in the double digits for much of the 1970s, was brought under control, falling to 3 percent by 1983, and the economy gradually recovered from the recessions and grew at a modest pace through the end of the decade.

Workers protest at a Professional Air Traffic Controllers Organization (PATCO) Solidarity Strike in Houston, Texas, on August 24, 1981. PATCO V_11_08, Professional Air Traffic Controllers Organization Records (electronic version), L1986-45, Southern Labor Archives, Special Collections and Archives, Georgia State University, Atlanta.

During this period of supply-side economics, the administration of President Ronald Reagan, and later that of President George H.W. Bush, pursued policies designed to encourage private initiative and business investment.[106] At the same time, the American economy was characterized by several significant trends that had an enormous impact on the labor markets. These included an accelerating shift from a domestic economy dominated by manufacturing jobs to a more service-oriented domestic economy, an increase in the pace and scope of the industrial deregulation which had begun during the previous decade, a growing liberalization of international trade and globalization, and the rapid disintermediation of organized labor.

Many studies in recent decades have analyzed the causes for the gradual weakening of private-sector labor unions during the 1960s, 1970s, and beyond. What is clear is that, over the course of the 1980s, the negative pressures on private-sector unions only increased. According to a Gallup poll taken in August of 1981, public sentiment against organized labor was at its all-time high, with a disapproval rating of 35 percent.[107]

---

[105] U.S. Census Bureau, Foreign Trade Division.

[106] Ronald W. Reagan, *Economic Report of the President* (Washington: United States Government Printing Office, 1983), 3.

[107] Jones and Saad, *Gallup Poll Social Series.*

Meanwhile, in order to escape the higher labor costs of unionized plants, many manufacturers began relocating their operations to cheaper, non-unionized locations within the United States, and increasingly, overseas.

According to some researchers, these adverse currents for organized labor were exacerbated by a conservative political environment and an administration that pledged "to strengthen economic incentives, reduce burdensome regulations, increase capital formation...."[108] For example, as economist and industrial relations historian Bruce Kaufman writes:

> The political environment in the 1980s also turned hostile to the New Deal IR system. The election of Ronald Reagan to the presidency in 1980 precipitated a significant turn toward political conservatism with respect to government labor policy. Reagan was an outspoken champion of free markets and of minimalist role for government, a philosophical belief that was at direct odds with the ILE policy program erected over the previous half-century. Over the next decade the Reagan administration, and to a lesser degree that of George Bush, implemented several policy initiatives that struck at the heart of the New Deal system. The organizing ability and bargaining power of labor unions, for example, were heavily circumscribed by adverse changes in the interpretation of law and precedent by the National Labor Relations Board. Similarly, Reagan's decision to fire the air traffic controllers when they went on strike in 1981 was widely interpreted as sending a signal to private sector employers that it was alright to play hardball with unions. Reagan and Bush also sought to eliminate or soften numerous workplace regulations or protections, such as the minimum wage and occupational safety and health laws.[109]

The devastating effects of such an environment on the U.S. labor unions are further described by Kaufman:

> Between 1979 and 1989, unions lost almost 5 million members and saw the proportion of the organized work force shrink from 23 to 17 percent. More ominously, by the late 1980s, unions were able to win fewer than 100,000 new members through the NLRB representation election process, while many times that number were lost through decertifications, plant closing, layoffs, and striker

---

[108] Reagan, *Economic Report of the President,* 3.

[109] Kaufman, *Origins & Evolution,* 141.

replacement. In effect, the organized labor movement was slowly being bled to death....Not since the 1920s had the prospects for organized labor looked so bleak.[110]

Nevertheless, as pointed out by the Princeton Industrial Relations Section's Henry S. Farber, the most significant factors in the decline of union membership during this period were structural ones. In particular, in a study on the decline of private-sector unions co-authored with Princeton's Bruce Western (section working paper #437), Farber states:

Overall, this is a very pessimistic analysis from the perspective of the union movement. It is clear that labor unions in the private sector are caught between the proverbial rock and hard place. On one side, employment growth rates are much lower (even negative) in the union sector relative to the nonunion sector. On the other side, unions have not been able to muster a meaningful amount of new-organizing activity....Notwithstanding recent changes in labor law, the causes of the divergence in employment growth rates between the union and nonunion sectors are fundamentally related to the structure of the U.S. economy. Employment has shifted away from the sectors in which unions were strongest such as manufacturing, transportation, and communications. In manufacturing, the opening of the U.S. economy to global competition undoubtedly has played a role. Capital is extremely mobile, and it is unlikely that owners of capital are willing or able to pay a wage premium that union workers might command. In transportation and communication, there has been substantial deregulation that has made it harder for firms to pass along the union wage premium (e.g., Rose, 1987). This is at least part of the reason why nonunion workers have become less likely to demand union representation (Farber, 1990; Farber and Krueger, 1993), making it harder to organize. It is also part of the reason why new manufacturing capacity is disproportionately located in regions of the country which have historically not been friendly to labor unions.[111]

Princeton's Henry S. Farber (right), along with fellow Labor and Employment Relations Association Academic Fellows Sanford M. Jacoby, UCLA Anderson School of Management (left), and David B. Lipsky, Cornell University Scheinman Institute on Conflict Resolution (center), are presented with plaques in a 2010 LERA awards ceremony. Photo courtesy of LERA. From <http://www.lera.uiuc.edu/awards/Fellows/index.html>

---

[110] Ibid., 143.

[111] Henry S. Farber and Bruce Western, "Accounting for the Decline of Unions in the Private Sector, 1973-1998," *Journal of Labor Research,* Summer 2001: 459-485.

During the last years of the 1980s, the U.S. economy experienced a period of economic malaise, which by July of 1990 had turned into a full-fledged recession. Between 1990 and 1991, roughly 1.5 million net jobs were lost in the private sector. Then, in what is considered to be the longest expansion on record, the U.S. economy entered into a period of sustained economic growth that lasted from March of 1991 to March of 2001. GDP grew from just under $6.0 trillion in the second quarter of 1991 to $10.3 trillion by the second quarter of 2001. Moreover, driven largely by growth in the technology and service sectors, as well as by further trade liberalization and deregulation in the financial, communications, and other sectors under President Bill Clinton, a net 16 million new jobs were created between 1990 and 1999,[112] while unemployment—which had reached as much as 7.8 percent in mid-1992—fell to just over 4 percent by the end of the decade.

Throughout the 1990s, the influence of private-sector labor unions, which had already been weakened significantly, continued to be eroded. Although total union membership remained relatively flat, at about 16.5 million members by 1999 (representing 13.9 percent of the workforce) versus 16.7 million in 1990 (representing 16.1 percent of the workforce), private-sector union membership fell by more than a million (to about 9.4 million members). Moreover, from 1990 to 2000, private-sector unions' share of total private employment fell from 12 percent to 9.4 percent—the lowest level since the 1930s. This negative trend continued largely unabated through the first decade of the 21st century, so that by 2009, the number of private-sector union members fell below that of public-sector unions for the first time.

According to the National Bureau of Economic Research, after an unprecedented 10 years of economic expansion, the U.S. economy began to contract in March of 2001. The downturn followed closely after a tightening of monetary policy (between June of 1999 and May of 2000, the Federal Reserve raised the benchmark Fed Funds rate six times to a level of 6.50 percent[113]), and the bursting of the so-called dot-com bubble, from March of 2000 through early 2001, when investors decided that a slew of NASDAQ-listed internet service companies (many of which were hit with a liquidity crunch in the wake of rising interest rates) were overvalued. However, a series of other events, such as the liquidity crises in Asia and Russia in the late 1990s, and fears over the so-called Y2K bug (a concern that the change in date from 1999 to 2000 would cause widespread computer system failures), had also contributed to a degree of economic uncertainty in the years between 1998 and 2000.

---

[112] U.S. Commerce Department, Bureau of Economic Analysis, Table 6.5C Full-Time Equivalent Employees by Industry (Last revised: August 20, 2009).

[113] Board of Governors of the Federal Reserve System, *Open Market Archive* (http://www.federalreserve.gov/monetarypolicy/openmarket_archive.htm#2000)

In the autumn of that same year, the economy was shaken by a combination of two major events—the Wall Street crash that followed the terrorist attacks of September 11, 2001, and the Enron accounting scandal, which came to light soon afterwards. Gross private domestic investment, which had exceeded $1.8 trillion by the second quarter of 2000, fell to below $1.6 trillion by the fourth quarter of 2001 and did not regain its 2000 high for another two years.[114] Nevertheless, fueled in part by growth in personal consumption (spurred largely by rising home values), and in part by a significant increase in government expenditures (notably due to the Iraq War), the economy recovered relatively quickly and continued to grow until the start of the global financial crisis in the fourth quarter of 2007.

While a detailed discussion of the causes of the recent financial crisis is outside of the scope of this history, a few observations may be made about some of its effects. At the end of 2006, the official unemployment rate in the United States stood at 4.4 percent. As a result of the so-called Great Recession of 2007-2009, by October of 2009 official unemployment was at 10.0—a level last seen in June of 1983. In addition to massive job losses, persistently high unemployment in the years immediately following the recession introduced the term "long-term unemployment" into the national social and political debate. In the words of the section's Henry S. Farber:

> The Great Recession from December 2007 to June 2009 is associated with a dramatic weakening of the labor market from which it is now only slowly recovering. The unemployment remains stubbornly high, and durations of unemployment are unprecedentedly long….An important concern in the aftermath of the Great Recession is the high unemployment rate, which remained at 9.6 percent in the fourth quarter of 2010, more than one full year after the 'official' end of the recession in June 2009….A related concern are the unprecedentedly long durations of unemployment….It is clear that the dynamics of unemployment in the Great Recession are fundamentally different from unemployment dynamics in earlier recessions.[115]

Further on, Farber compares the labor market effects of the 2007-2009 recession with the recession of the early 1980s, and observes that:

---

[114] U.S. Bureau of Economic Analysis, Table 1.1.5 Gross Domestic Product, Last Revised: July 27, 2012.

[115] Henry S. Farber, "Job Loss in the Great Recession: Historial Perspective from the Displaced Workers Survey, 1984-2010," Working Paper #564 (Princeton: Industrial Relations Section, Princeton University, 2011), 1-2.

Both unemployment and job-loss rates were very high in the two most serious recessionary periods (1981-83 and 2007-09...). While the unemployment rates were comparable in 1983 and 2009 (9.6 percent vs. 9.3 percent), the job loss rate was much higher in the 2007-2009 period than in the 1981-83 period (16.0 percent vs. 12.8 percent). This suggests that the Great Recession was associated with a much higher job loss rate than the norm, which makes it of particular interest to study the consequences of job loss in the most recent period.[116]

Based on his analysis of data from 1984 to 2010, Farber concludes that "the re-employment experience of job losers is substantially worse for those who lost jobs in the Great Recession than in any earlier period in the last thirty years," and that "[m]ost importantly, job losers in the Great Recession have been much less successful at finding new jobs (particularly full-time jobs) than in the aftermath of earlier recessions."[117] As Farber points out, it is too soon to know what the consequences of the situation described above will be for the labor market in the long run; however, recent studies have also linked the 2007-2009 recession to what they cite as a longer-term trend of the disappearance of mid-wage, mid-skilled jobs in favor of low-paying, low-skilled jobs and an increase in wage disparity in the United States. If proven correct, these trends highlight the issue of job quality, in addition to job availability, in a post-Great Recession recovery.[118]

The Industrial Relations Field in the 1980s and Beyond

As previously shown, from its beginnings in the 1920s, industrial relations was largely conceived of as a multidisciplinary field whose principal concern was the dynamic relationship between capital and labor. Indeed, if there was one subject matter that could unify such diverse interests as economics, sociology, industrial psychology, and law, it was the study of the employment relationship in all its complexity. By the 1980s, however, the situation had changed significantly.

---

[116] Ibid., 5-6.

[117] Ibid., 9 and 28.

[118] See, for example, Nir Jaimovich and Henry E. Siu, "The Trend is the Cycle: Job Polarization and Jobless Recoveries," Working Paper No. 18334 (Washington: National Bureau of Economic Research, August 2012); and the National Employment Law Project's "The Low-Wage Recovery and Growing Inequality," August 2012.

In his historical monograph on the Industrial Relations Section published in 1986, Richard Lester makes reference to the changes taking place in the field of industrial relations at the time. Discussing the section's financial resources, he states:

With the substantial changes taking place in industrial relations in much of the economy, flexibility in the use of these resources is a real advantage for research.... Pressed by the recession of 1982, many organized and non-union firms have made significant changes in their industrial relations policies and practices, often in order to adjust to global and domestic pressures of competition. Companies have been experimenting with participatory management and workplace practices similar to those in large Japanese companies. Such marked changes can lead to a new era in American industrial relations.[119]

Thus by the mid-1980s it was already clear to many in the field that great changes were occurring in the contours of industrial relations. What was perhaps not as clear at the time was the direction in which those changes would take an academic discipline that had been one of the preeminent areas of study in the social sciences for a number of decades. Indeed, evidence suggests that by the time Lester wrote those words, the former multidisciplinary nature of industrial relations—as a rather large academic pavilion, so to speak, containing any number of social sciences interested in various aspects of the labor relationship—had already entered into a period of decline, and a process of branching out into the field's numerous, specialized constituent disciplines was well under way.

In a chapter entitled "Industrial Relations in Decline" in his history of the field's development in the United States, Bruce Kaufman writes:

While the quality and quantity of scholarly research in industrial relations improved, this "plus" was outweighed by several "negatives" that clearly signaled an overall decline in the intellectual and organizational vitality of the field. These developments included a dramatic decade-long decline in union membership and union power, significant attrition in the number of extant IR institutes and degree programs, a marked shift in student demand from IR to HR courses, a widespread perception among both academics and practitioners that IR had lost much of its relevance as an agent for change and innovation in employment practice and

[119] Lester, *Industrial Relations Section*, 25-26.

policy, and a marked stagnation in membership and participation in the Industrial Relations Research Association.[120]

According to Kaufman, the number of academic programs specializing in employment-related subjects grew significantly during the 1980s. Increasingly, however, those programs focused on such disciplines as human resources management and organizational development and behavior, rather than on the previously more traditional area of industrial relations. Furthermore, many academic industrial relations programs changed their names and the content of their curricula to emphasize human resources or employment relations, while still others were subsumed under business faculties or closed down altogether. Thus:

> For all intents and purposes, the creation of free-standing, degree-granting IR units with multidisciplinary faculties came to a halt....The creation of IR degree programs and majors also slowed to a trickle. Herman's surveys of IR and HR programs (1984) reveal that of the net increase of forty-three master's degree programs between 1974 and 1984, only eight included one or more of the terms industrial relations, labor relations, labor studies, or employee relations in their titles, while the remainder included one or more of the terms personnel, human resource (or human relations), organization, or management. In some cases these new programs were multidisciplinary in character, but more often they were housed in a department of management or a graduate school of business and provided a largely behavioral science, nonunion perspective on employee relations. Finally, even as the birth of new IR units was coming to a standstill, a simultaneous increase in the "death" or downsizing of existing units was occurring. Some universities, such as Columbia, Chicago, and Pace, chose to eliminate their programs altogether. Other schools, such as Michigan, Berkeley, and Massachusetts, reduced the operating budgets and/or the number of faculty positions of their IR units significantly.[121]

In other words, the declining vitality of industrial relations as an academic field decried by Kaufman was at heart a displacement caused by a number of developments that stimulated the rapid growth of more specialized, but related fields such as human resources management and organizational behavior.

---

[120] Kaufman, *Origins & Evolution,* 137-138.

[121] Ibid., 147-148.

In their 1986 book, *The Transformation of American Industrial Relations,* MIT's Thomas A. Kochan, Harry C. Katz, and Robert B. McKersie described the situation:

The history of U.S. industrial relations should caution anyone from making bold predictions about the future based on the trends of the recent past. We have documented how over the course of the past half century union and nonunion systems traded positions as the innovative force in industrial relations. Moreover, the points at which a transition in leader/follower relations occurred could never have been predicted based on previous trends. The union sector recaptured the lead in the 1930s as a result of the New Deal legislation, the explosion of industrial unionism, and an abrupt change in the economic, political, and social environment that undermined the confidence and trust American society had placed in the business community. The stability provided by the new labor legislation and its subsequent enforcement, along with the favorable economic environment, allowed unions to strengthen their leadership position by gradually improving wages, benefits, and working conditions through collective bargaining. No one foresaw the rise of an alternative human resource management system that, over the course of the 1960s and 1970s, gradually overtook collective bargaining and emerged as the pacesetter by emphasizing high employee involvement and commitment and flexibility....[122]

Among the developments that influenced this branching out process were the previously discussed decline in the power of private-sector trade unions and the concomitant growth of the nonunion labor force, as well as the turning of the tide of public opinion against labor unions (with negative repercussions for the academic fields associated with them); however they were not the only ones. Other factors— for example, the rapid expansion in federal employment legislation and job training programs in the 1970s and 1980s, following the civil rights and women's liberation movements of the 1960s and 1970s, and the increase in litigation that accompanied them, which required ever more sophisticated specialists within corporations to ensure compliance with the growing body of regulations—added to the momentum. Some of those factors also played a significant role in the type of research that was done in the field of labor economics in the 1980s and beyond, further differentiating it from its industrial relations antecedents.

---

[122] Thomas A. Kochan, Harry Charles Katz, and Robert B. McKersie, *The Transformation of American Industrial Relations* (New York: Basic Books, 1986), 226.

The de facto segmentation of the field of industrial relations into its more specialized constituent disciplines continued throughout the 1980s and 1990s, and into the 21st century, with the result that, by 2004, even the field's principal academic organization, the Industrial Relations Research Association (IRRA), had made the telling decision to change its name to its current Labor and Employment Relations Association (LERA). Indeed, by 2012, of the 103 universities in the United States and Canada which responded to the LERA's survey on IR/HR degree programs, 90 offered a specialization or advanced degree program in human resources management, organizational behavior, or a derivation thereof. More than 61 percent of the respondent programs were part of a business school, or a school or department of management, while nearly 14 percent were part of a school or department of human resources (not specifically considered part of a business school). Many of these schools and programs in fact considered their disciplines to represent an unbroken line of succession from the original and more antiquated field of industrial relations.

What is perhaps also not surprising, considering the general trend described above, is that only 11 of the 103 schools responding to the survey (five of which were in Canada) contained industrial relations in the name of the department or program concerned; and only 22 of them (including those in which an industrial relations program was offered in conjunction with a specialization or degree program in human resources management) offered a specialization or an advanced degree in industrial relations or some other area such as collective bargaining, which has been more traditionally associated with industrial relations over the years. Moreover, most of the schools that offered such programs were situated in geographic regions where a fairly significant level of private-sector labor union activity remained. At the same time, just 11 of the responding schools offered a specialization or advanced degree in economics, of which only five—including Princeton—had a specialization in labor economics.

From the above observations, a clear sense emerges of the increasingly distinct identities of the old, multidisciplinary industrial relations field of the 1940s, 1950s, and 1960s, and of the more specialized human resources management, organizational behavior, and labor economics fields of the 1980s, 1990s, and 2000s. While the study of the employment relationship, and in particular the relationship between labor and capital, and of the related policy implications, whether at the level of the individual firm or of public institutions, remains a strong common bond between these disciplines, ever since the mid-1970s, there has been an increasingly divergent path taken in terms of the specific problems analyzed, and the methodological and theoretical frameworks used by each of them.

Thus, in regard to labor economics, Stanford University economic historian Gavin Wright was able to declare in a 1987 book:

Labor economists, on the other hand, are interested in the effects of policies and behavior on economic performance: wages, unemployment, productivity, etc. They are specialists. Many labor economists are careful to differentiate their field from industrial relations in terms of interests and subject matter rather than doctrine: broad issues of labor markets and resource allocation versus a narrower specialty in collective bargaining. Certainly the differences in underlying interests are real and substantial, and it would be folly to propose that these disciplines should be amalgamated into "one big union."[123]

Nevertheless, despite the increased specialization in the field, there remain many labor economists who have maintained their traditional association with the field of industrial relations up to the present time (as in the case of Princeton University's Industrial Relations Section, for example). And, methodological differences aside, when one considers some of the theoretical and empirical work done in the 1950s and 1960s by institutional economists like John Dunlop, Clark Kerr, Richard Lester, Frederick Harbison, and others like them, there is a strong case to be made that the labor economics research of recent decades would not be unfamiliar to them. Thus, while recognizing the centrifugal effects of the developments of the last 30 years on these fields of study, one must also recognize the many commonalities they still possess. Perhaps, therefore, it might also turn out to be something of a folly to draw too sharp or too indelible a line between the closely related and long-intertwined disciplines of industrial relations and labor economics.

Princeton University in the 1980s, 1990s, and the 21st Century

As Princeton entered the 1980s, the period of unprecedented change that had accompanied the previous two decades gradually began to relent. Growth continued, to be sure, but at a more manageable pace. For example, the size of the student body, which had ballooned by nearly one-third during the 1970s (largely as a result of the

---

[123] Gavin Wright, "Labor History and Labor Economics," in Alexander Field, ed., *The Future of Economic History* (Boston: Kluwer-Nijhoff Publishing, 1987).

decision in the 1960s to actively recruit students from underrepresented groups, and to admit women to the college), grew by only about 7.5 percent to more than 6,300 undergraduates and graduate students by the end of the 1980s. By the end of the decade, the size of the faculty, which had increased rapidly since the 1950s, finally surpassed 1,000 and the University's operating budget had increased by 2.5 times to $414 million. Meanwhile, another major milestone was achieved when, through a series of highly successful fundraising operations, the University's endowment, which had stood at over $600 million at the beginning of the 1970s, was increased to over $2 billion by the end of the decade.

At the beginning of the 1980s, the social turmoil of the 1960s and 1970s had long since ended; however, the legacy of the changes the University experienced during those years presented its own unique set of challenges. One of the greatest of these was the quality of student life, particularly for freshmen and sophomores—two groups of undergraduate students for whom residential life on campus had never been particularly well organized, even going back to the presidency of Woodrow Wilson. As early as 1906, Wilson had unsuccessfully attempted to do away with the private eating clubs and introduce a residential quadrangle plan; by the late 1970s, the pressures of a greatly expanded student body comprised of a mix of both men and women had only exacerbated the problem to a critical degree. The issue, as described by one historian of the University, boiled down to the following:

> For most of the 20th century, virtually all undergraduates lived in dormitory rooms unconnected to their dining facilities. Most freshmen and sophomores ate their meals in Commons, the five Gothic dining halls erected in the immediate post-Wilson era, and socialized in a variety of piecemeal and makeshift arrangements until joining Prospect Avenue clubs in the second semester of sophomore year. Juniors and seniors ate their meals and attended parties in the eating clubs, which, as private institutions, were a frequent source of tension with the university. There was no serious connection between any of these facilities and academic advising or the scholarly life of the university. In the 1960s Commons became extremely crowded due to the gradual expansion of the undergraduate body. When enrollment jumped by another one-third in the 1970s because of coeducation, the old system for feeding freshmen and sophomores became inadequate, leading to a patchwork of supplemental arrangements. At the same time, as costs increased and

membership in the upperclass eating clubs declined, some clubs folded and others were going broke.[124]

By the late 1970s the problem had come to a head, even giving rise to a large student demonstration in the winter of 1978 and prompting then President William Bowen to establish a Committee on Undergraduate Residential Life (CURL), tasked with analyzing and making recommendations concerning the University's dining and social options. The result of the committee's work was a plan to create a system initially consisting of five new residential colleges—Butler, Forbes, Mathey, Rockefeller, and Wilson—for freshmen and sophomores, which was officially implemented in 1982 after a highly successful fundraising drive. Since their establishment in the mid-1980s, the residential colleges have become a centerpiece of Princeton campus life—not only as a focal point for dining and housing, but also as an important source of student education, entertainment, and involvement in the University community.

During the 1990s, during the tenure of Princeton's President Harold T. Shapiro, a number of other important initiatives and their associated milestones were realized. For example, after a number of successful fundraising drives, the University's endowment was increased fourfold to over $8 billion by the end of the decade. Throughout the course of the decade, outreach efforts to improve the University's diversity profile and to increase opportunities for students from lower- and middle-income families were increased, and a number of undergraduate teaching initiatives and new academic programs were implemented. During this time, Princeton also undertook a major program of building and renovation, which increased the number of buildings on campus to 324 by the turn of the century. And finally, in 1996, Princeton held its 250th anniversary celebrations and changed its unofficial motto from "Princeton in the Nation's Service" to "Princeton in the Nation's Service and in the Service of All Nations."

Harkening back to the words of President Harold W. Dodds—that "[p]roud as we are of our history and grateful for the strength our heritage brings to us, we know that to rest on it can lead only to decay and destruction. We intend to be the progenitors of a stronger Princeton, not merely the beneficiaries of generations that went before us"— one can conclude that the pace of growth enjoyed by Princeton in earlier decades has not been found wanting in recent years. From the centennial celebration of the Graduate School in 2000, to the establishment of a large number of new academic and research

[124] Oberdorfer, *Princeton University,* 234-235.

programs and facilities,[125] to the transition of the undergraduate residential college system to a full four-year experience, the first decade of the 21st century has certainly been an active and productive one for the University.

In addition to his many contributions in the field of labor economics, the Industrial Relations Section's Orley Ashenfelter was a pioneer in the study of the economics of wine, which he discussed with participants at this 1992 wine-tasting event. Photo by Ken Vastola.

Among the many consequential developments of recent years, however, one in particular merits particular mention due to its enormous impact on a large cross-section of the student body—the no-loan financial aid policy initiated by Princeton's 19th president, Shirley M. Tilghman. This policy, implemented shortly after President Tilghman's appointment in 2001, has vastly improved access to the benefits of a Princeton University education for thousands of students from lower- and middle-income backgrounds over the past decade, and stands out as one of the hallmark achievements in educational equality of any university in the country this century. Indeed, it reinforces the essential characteristic of Princeton University as more than just an institution of higher education, but also as a philanthropic organization that lives up to its long-cherished ideal of public service not only in word, but also in deed. It further underscores the intellectual freedom that comes along with the University's judicious use of the vast resources at its disposal—a theme that resonates deeply with the story of Princeton's Industrial Relations Section, as has previously been shown.

The Industrial Relations Section in the 1980s and Beyond

By the beginning of the 1980s, the faculty of Princeton's Industrial Relations Section consisted of one professor of economics (Orley Ashenfelter); an associate professor of economics (Harvey Rosen); two or three assistant professors of economics (including Cordelia W. Reimers and James N. Brown); a handful of research associates (including Anne Somers on a part-time basis), overlapping at various points in time; and a couple of emeritus faculty associates (including Richard Lester and Herman Somers), who spent part of their time on section-related activities. Over the course of the decade, a number of important additions were made to strengthen the team of faculty associates.

---

[125] Including, among others: the Lewis-Sigler Institute for Integrative Genomics (established in 2003), the Princeton Neuroscience Institute, Princeton Center for Theoretical Science and the Keller Center for Innovation in Engineering Education (established in 2005), the Peter B. Lewis Center for the Arts, and the University's Office of Sustainability (established in 2006).

Orley Ashenfelter receives the IZA Prize in Labor Economics in 2003.

The IZA Prize in Labor Economics 2003 is awarded to one of the leading labor economists, Orley C. Ashenfelter, for his outstanding contributions to the field. IZA Director Klaus F. Zimmermann announced the decision of the IZA Prize Committee in Bonn on August 21, 2003. Among the members of the Committee are Nobel laureates George A. Akerlof, Gary S. Becker and James J. Heckman.

The official award ceremony will take place in Berlin on September 22, 2003, with a number of high-ranking guests from Germany and abroad. The Prize will be presented by Klaus Zumwinkel, CEO of Deutsche Post World Net and President of IZA.

Orley Ashenfelter is Professor of Economics at Princeton University, New Jersey. His intellectual work stands out due to his ingenuity in devising clever ways to derive and test hypotheses of economic models, his exceptional creativity in using and collecting data, and his originality in pioneering the natural experiment methodology. Ashenfelter's scholarly contributions have fundamentally transformed the analysis of labor markets. In a number of seminal articles he has broken new ground in various core areas of labor economics including research on trade unions, wages and employment, the analysis of labor supply, and the study of discrimination, education and training.

Serving as the Director of the Office of Evaluation of the U.S. Department of Labor in 1972, Ashenfelter became the founding father of what has by today developed into the separate field of quantitative social program evaluation. During that time he pioneered a field of research that has become ever more important since the effects of government-sponsored labor market programs are increasingly called into question.

Ashenfelter's influence on the development of economic science has been tremendous. Having served the labor economics community as former editor of the American Economic Review and co-editor of the Handbook of Labor Economics, Ashenfelter continues to take on important service responsibilities. Currently he is the President of the Society of Labor Economists (SOLE) and editor of the American Law and Economics Review. His scholarly contributions have made Orley Ashenfelter one of the most influential architects of modern labor economics. The IZA Prize in Labor Economics 2003 honors the work of an exceptional scholar who greatly shaped the advance of empirical labor market research.

Photograph and text courtesy of IZA.

These included section graduate David E. Card GS'83, who later directed the section from 1989 to 1990; Rebecca Blank (MIT, 1983); and Alan B. Krueger (Harvard, 1987), who also later directed the section from 2001 to 2006.

During this time, the section also hosted several visiting faculty and research associates, many of whom had completed their Ph.D. programs at Princeton earlier. Among this latter group were the following economists, in alphabetical order, along with the year(s) of their visit: Yale University's Joseph G. Altonji GS'81, 1984-1985; University of Maryland's John C. Ham GS'80, 1984-1986; University of Arizona's Ronald L. Oaxaca GS'71, fall of 1982; Brigham Young University's Michael R. Ransom GS'83, spring of 1985; and Colby College's Clifford E. Reid GS'73, spring of 1983. In addition, between the 1980-1981 and the 1989-1990 academic years, the Industrial Relations Section produced 32 Ph.D. graduates, including its largest-ever contingent of nine in the Class of 1983. Many from among this group of accomplished economists made significant contributions during their time as either faculty or research associates of the section, including such figures as David Card GS'83, Robert J. LaLonde GS'85, and Joshua D. Angrist GS'89.

Over the course of the 1980s, faculty and research associates produced roughly 70 papers under the section's series of research reports and working papers, 78 articles in academic journals, 19 chapters in books, and seven books authored or edited elsewhere. In addition, visiting faculty who were alumni of the section also authored a dozen papers under the section's research or working paper series, as well as four journal articles related to research done while visiting the section.

Following a trend established earlier in the 1970s, the majority of these publications treated classical labor economics topics, albeit using—and in some cases either introducing or elaborating on—increasingly more sophisticated econometric, statistical, and experimental methods. The clear aim of these refinements in methodology, which are evident throughout the body of work that was done in the section during this time (as well as in subsequent decades), was to be able to isolate and measure, with ever greater empirical precision, the cause and effect relationship between a given set of changes in economic policy (or conditions) and the economic outcome for (or behavior of) a selected group of labor market participants. Section researchers were interested in removing, to the maximum extent possible, specification and selection biases from their econometric analyses, in order to achieve credible, transparent and convincing results.

Numerous examples abound of the scientific (and increasingly experimental) orientation that prevailed in the section during the 1980s, as well as of the persistent and incremental process of innovative methodological refinements and advances that were being made. An early one is the September 1982 working paper (#155) by Orley Ashenfelter and then doctoral candidate Gary R. Solon (1983), entitled "Longitudinal Labor Market Data: Sources, Uses, and Limitations," in which the authors state:

> Until recently, most research on labor force behavior and experience analyzed cross-section data, which pertain to a population sample at a single point in time....[C]onvincing research on a number of public policy issues requires longitudinal data. Indeed, without longitudinal data, some important research issues cannot be addressed at all.... Still other issues previously addressed with cross-section data can be treated with more reliable research methods when longitudinal information is available [126]

In another such example—the October 1984 working paper (#174) by Orley Ashenfelter and David Card, entitled "Using the Longitudinal Structure of Earnings to Estimate the Effect of Training Programs"—the authors state:

> The rise and fall of subsequent federal training programs underscores the need for credible and continuous evaluation of these programs. Yet, apart from the results of one genuine experiment, these training programs must still be analyzed by non-experimental methods, even some two decades after they were first initiated. Any evaluation must therefore bring to bear statistical methods for untangling the actual effect of these programs from other factors that would have influenced trainee earnings even if no training had taken place.... Nevertheless, this particular aspect of trainee earnings introduces considerable ambiguity into the determination of whether observed post-training earnings increases are a result of training or merely of the way in which workers are selected into the program.... In this paper we set out some methods that utilize the longitudinal structure of earnings of the trainee group and of a comparison group to estimate the effect of training....As we shall see, this method is no substitute for a properly designed experimental test of the effectiveness of training, but it does provide some evidence on the empirical consistency of the estimated program effects. In the absence of experimental methods, there seems to be no alternative to the adoption of this or similar methods of program evaluation, since we find that small differences in

---

[126] Orley C. Ashenfelter and Gary R. Solon, "Longitudinal Labor Market Data: Sources, Uses, and Limitations" in *What's Happening to American Labor Force and Productivity Measurements?*, National Council on Employment Policy, 1982; revised as Industrial Relations Section Working Paper No. 155, September 1982.

model specification can lead to remarkable differences in the estimated impact of training. Hopefully, the accuracy of these methods may eventually be the subject of experimental testing.[127]

Indeed, the "one genuine experiment" referenced in the paper by Ashenfelter and Card was the subject of yet another influential working paper (#183) written in November of 1984 by Bob LaLonde. In his paper, entitled "Evaluating the Econometric Evaluations of Training Programs with Experimental Data," the then doctoral candidate convincingly demonstrates the weaknesses of non-experimental methods of evaluating the impact of training programs by comparing the estimates produced by those methods to actual results produced in a randomized experiment. In particular:

> MDRC's experimental data offer labor economists the opportunity to test the non-experimental methods of program evaluation. Since MDRC's programs use random assignment, an unbiased estimate of the training effect is known. Therefore one can investigate whether any commonly used model of earnings and program participation would have yielded the same estimated training effect as the experimental data.... If the econometric model is specified correctly, the estimated training effect will be the same as the effect computed from the experimental data.... Based on the evidence presented in these chapters, an econometrician using the non-experimental methods of program evaluation could have chosen a training effect from a considerably large range of estimates....The results in this paper are likely to diminish our confidence in the precision of previous non-experimental evaluations of government training programs. What is clearer, however, is that training effects estimated from non-experimental data are no substitute for experimental results.[128]

Commenting later on LaLonde's conclusions, in a January 1986 working paper (#203) entitled "The Case for Evaluating Training Programs with Randomized Trials," Orley Ashenfelter offers his views on this methodological advance by stating:

> I have come to conclude that the evaluation of the economic benefits of training programs will be greatly enhanced by the use of classical experimental methods. In particular, I am convinced that some of these training programs should be operated so that control and experimental groups are selected by random assignment

---

[127] Orley C. Ashenfelter and David E. Card, "Using the Longitudinal Structure of Earnings to Estimate the Effect of Training Programs," Review of Economics and Statistics, vol. 67, no. 4, 1985: 648-60.

[128] Robert J. LaLonde, "Evaluating the Econometric Evaluations of Training Programs with Experimental Data," American Economic Review 76 (September 1986): 604-20.

(randomized trials). It follows that a simple comparison of earnings, employment, and other outcomes as between control and experimental groups subsequent to participation in the experimental program will provide a simple and credible estimate of program success (or failure). The principal reason why randomized trials should be used in this field is that too much of the non-experimental estimation of the effects of training programs seems dependent on elements of model specification that cannot be subjected to powerful statistical tests. As most of us who do econometric work know, it is rarely classical sampling error that makes us uncertain about our inferences. More typically, it is the possibility that some alternative, reasonable model specification will lend [sic] us to a different conclusion that makes us uncertain about our inferences. In the field of training program evaluation I believe this model uncertainty can now be documented.[129]

Ashenfelter then concludes his paper with an interesting historical note, referencing the views he had expressed on the same subject 11 years earlier, at the annual winter meeting of the Industrial Relations Research Association in December of 1974:

"Manpower training programs have not been run as if they were experiments in the past, and there is a great deal of difficulty and resistance in changing past practices. The argument against experimentation is usually shrouded in the rhetoric of morality....There is, of course, no reason why this policy could not be continued in an experimental environment so long as the basis of the selection criteria were known and measurable, in which case the selection criteria could be controlled statistically. No doubt there would be resistance to requiring the practice of using explicit and objective criteria for entrance to the programs, but such a practice might be desirable on grounds of fairness even in the absence of an experimental environment."[130] I wrote the above words over ten years ago and, since that time, some progress has been made as LaLonde's work shows. Further progress will have been made if randomized trials are used again in the evaluation of training programs. Without at least some use of randomized trials in this area we will never know whether our non-experimental evaluation methods are leading us to correct inferences or whether the programs we design are effective.[131]

---

[129] Orley Ashenfelter, "The Case for Evaluating Training Programs with Randomized Trials," *Economics of Education Review,* vol. 6, no. 4, 1987: 333-338.

[130] Quoted from *Proceedings of the twenty-seventh annual winter meeting, December 28-29, 1974* of the Industrial Relations Research Association, Madison, WI, 1975, pp. 252-260.

[131] Ashenfelter, "Case for Evaluating Training Programs," pp. 337-338.

As can be seen from the papers highlighted above (as well as from numerous other examples which can be gleaned from the section's hefty volume of working papers, research reports, journal articles, and other publications produced during the course of the decade on this and other topics of interest to labor economists), throughout the 1980s an evolution of thought and of methodological rigor and precision was taking place within labor economics—starting from within Princeton's Industrial Relations Section—which had, and continues to have, a profound impact on the entire field. Speaking of the developments of this time period, section alumnus and faculty associate Alexandre Mas (Ph.D. 2004) points out their relevance, not only for labor economics, but for other disciplines, as well:

> If we go back to the innovations of the '70s, '80s, and '90s, which in large part were methodological, I think you can trace forward to a lot of the tools and the research designs that we use now. The way we think about data, the way we think about bringing data to bear on economic problems stems from that era. But I think it goes beyond labor economics. If you look at other fields, many have drawn from deep innovations in the labor [economics] approach. So, development [economics], corporate finance, public finance, and other fields—a lot of their methodology at least can be traced back to those periods. We are still seeing methodological innovations that will have a broad and lasting impact, such as the more recent work on regression-discontinuity designs.[132]

What is also clear is that these developments can be traced back to the earlier work done by Ashenfelter and others in the section throughout the 1970s (and may in fact even have antecedents that go further back, especially to the late 1960s, in the context of the "Systems Analysis of Labor Markets in the U.S." project), and in particular to Ashenfelter's work on program evaluation, following his 1972 to 1973 stint in Washington, D.C. as director of the U.S. Labor Department's Office of Evaluation. For an example of some of the early section research containing the germ of an experimental methodological approach, one can look to such works as Orley Ashenfelter and his fellow section alumnus James J. Heckman's 1974 working paper (#52), entitled "Measuring the Effect of an Anti-Discrimination Program."

In this paper, which develops a framework for the measurement and evaluation of the effects of a government affirmative action program, the authors offer a detailed

---

[132] Alexandre Mas, Princeton University Industrial Relations Section, in an unpublished interview with the author, May 17, 2012.

discussion of their research design and an analysis of the randomness of the sample used in the study. In explaining their analytical framework, and in particular the question of what is, and is not, measurable in the context of their study, they write:

> Before discussing specific indices, it is clarifying to consider a problem that plagues this and other studies that seek to measure the effect of a program on its target population. Since we have a (two point) time series, a natural method for assessing the effectiveness of a program is to measure the change in a suitable index for target firms relative to the change in the index for the remaining firms. The basic problem is the absence of a control group in the presence of a program with economy-wide impact. Although a program may directly affect one group of firms, it also indirectly affects the remaining group of firms as well. Accordingly, comparisons of changes in the relative status of blacks in target and nontarget [sic] firms cannot be measured relative to what might have been in the absence of the program since that state is not observed. Thus, we cannot measure the contribution of the Executive Order to improvements in the aggregate relative status of blacks, as compared to the hypothetical situation that would exist in the complete absence of the program. Nonetheless, we can measure whether or not the contract compliance program has had any differential impact on the two types of firms, and this is presumably some evidence on the more general question.[133]

Council of Economic Advisers Chair Christina Romer (right) and Cecilia Rouse, a member of the Council of Economic Advisers, watch as President Barack Obama signs the Economic Report of the President in the Oval Office, Feb. 11, 2010. (Official White House Photo by Pete Souza)

The evolution of thought and of methodological refinement discussed above was, therefore, not restricted to the 1980s, but was rather an endemic characteristic of the Industrial Relations Section's team of labor economists, grounded in Ashenfelter's insistence on credible and transparent empirical research. In fact, this evolution—or credibility revolution, as it was often called within the section—continued into the 1990s, and beyond into the 21st century, in important ways that were foreshadowed in Ashenfelter's previously mentioned 1986 working paper (#203) on "The Case for Evaluating Training Programs with Randomized Trials."

For example, in referencing the experimental findings of a particular national training program, Ashenfelter makes the following observations:

> Apparently some types of employment and training programs are very effective. The above results are provocative and, when presented to most groups of

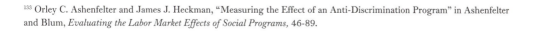

---

[133] Orley C. Ashenfelter and James J. Heckman, "Measuring the Effect of an Anti-Discrimination Program" in Ashenfelter and Blum, *Evaluating the Labor Market Effects of Social Programs,* 46-89.

economists, it is my experience that the discussion turns almost immediately to substantive, as opposed to methodological, matters. The reason substantive matters get discussed is because the methods used to obtain the results are not only simple, they are credible. This is clearly the benefit of the experimental method. On the other hand, there is a cost. These experiments were considerably more costly to monitor and evaluate than any simple non-experimental analysis would be. This raises a fundamental question: Is it possible to obtain the benefits of the credibility of studies that use randomized trials by the use of non-experimental (that is, econometric) methods? It also raises the issue of whether it is possible to implement evaluations by randomized trials that are less expensive than those implemented thus far. The promise, of course, of econometric methods is the delivery of the information benefits associated with experimentation without the heavy costs. In the normal course of events it is impossible to determine whether the econometric results have produced these benefits because to do so would require a comparison of the results of the non-experimental econometric analysis with the results of an analysis of data from randomized trials. The former would generally never be completed if the latter were feasible. In the evaluation of training programs, however, we now have a remarkably careful study by Robert LaLonde (of the University of Chicago) that carries through analyses of both experimental and non-experimental data so just this comparison can be made.[134]

U.S. Department of Labor Chief Economist Alexandre Mas testifying before a hearing of the Senate Finance Subcommittee on December 9, 2009.

Later, in discussing the relative merits of alternative approaches to selecting an estimate of the training effect, Ashenfelter suggests the following:

A second approach is to allow the data, by themselves, to tell us which is the appropriate estimate to select. This is accomplished by applying a series of tests of model specification. The most natural test to apply here would be a test of whether the regression-adjusted differences in earning between the trainees and proposed comparison group is negligible in the pre-training period. This is a backcasting [sic] test, much like the forecasting tests proposed by many econometricians....
It appears that this example is a telling practical demonstration of the principle that specification tests are merely necessary and not sufficient for purely empirical reasoning....In sum, it appears that in the area of the analysis of training programs

---

[134] Ashenfelter, "Case for Evaluating Training Programs," pp. 333-335.

the econometric methods available may not be able to deliver the benefits that randomized trials offer. At a minimum, therefore, it appears that some experimental evaluation of these programs using randomized trials is desirable, if only to provide the occasional check on how well the non-experimental methods are working.[135]

In other words, Ashenfelter considered rigorous experimental methods utilizing randomized trials to be desirable, first, because of their credibility, and, second, because of their ability to aid in the construction and refinement of less costly (and potentially more adaptable) econometric models, and thereby to represent a powerful tool for enhancing the evaluation of program effects. The drawback, however, was that they were not always feasible. The solution to this dilemma—and the next step along the path of methodological evolution that the Industrial Relations Section pioneered in the late 1980s and early 1990s—came in the form of natural experiments.

In many areas of life or public policy, actual experiments can be extremely difficult (and costly) to organize—and they may even be completely impossible or inappropriate for logistical or ethical reasons. Occasionally, however, situations can arise in which real-life events arguably approximate a randomized trial, potentially including both test and control groups. These situations can be studied, and their outcome data used to test economic models. The main benefit of this approach is a transparent methodology, whose range of predicted outcomes can be objectively stipulated in advance based on the experiment-like conditions.

Natural experiments (and the associated delineation of instrumental variables within certain areas of these experiments) were thus used to great effect by section faculty associates and advanced graduate students at the end of the 1980s and throughout the 1990s. For example, in one of the earliest demonstrations of the effectiveness of this technique—a 1989 working paper (# 251) entitled "Lifetime Earnings and the Vietnam Era Draft Lottery: Evidence from Social Security Administration Records"—Josh Angrist writes:

In this paper, an estimation strategy is employed that enables measurement of the effects of veteran status while controlling for differences in other personal characteristics related to earnings. The randomly assigned risk of induction generated by the Vietnam era draft lottery is used to construct instrumental variables that are correlated with earnings solely by virtue of their correlation with veteran status....The estimates suggest that the effect of Vietnam era military service on white veterans is equivalent to a loss of two years of civilian labor market

---

[135] Ashenfelter, "Case for Evaluating Training Programs," p. 337.

experience....The research reported in this paper is distinguished from previous work by the use of the draft lottery to set up a natural experiment that enables measurement of the veteran effect without selection bias. In the experimental design generated by the draft lottery, inferences about the effects of military service can be made as if veterans [sic] status itself had been determined on the basis of random assignment.[136]

Likewise, in an influential working paper (#253) from May of the same year, "The Impact of the Mariel Boatlift on the Miami Labor Market," David Card used a natural experiment to study the effects of a sudden influx of immigrant labor on wages and unemployment rates of less-skilled workers in the Miami labor market between 1979 and 1985. As he explains it:

Despite the strong presumption that an influx of unskilled immigrants will depress the wages of less-skilled natives, existing empirical studies suggest that immigration has only a small effect on the wages of natives. There are two main explanations for this finding....These considerations illustrate the difficulty of using the inter-city correlation between wages and immigrant densities to measure the effect of immigration on the labor market opportunities of natives. They also underscore the value of a natural experiment that corresponds more closely to an exogenous increase in the supply of immigrants to a particular labor market. The experiences of the Miami labor market in the aftermath of the Mariel Boatlift form one such natural experiment.[137]

Other such natural experiments were used by section researchers throughout the 1990s and 2000s. For example, Angrist and Alan Krueger, in 1990 and 1991 working papers (#273 and #290, respectively),[138] exploited natural experiments to estimate both the impact of compulsory schooling laws, and the return to education and the veteran premium; and, in a 1997 working paper (#376) with Harvard's Claudia Goldin, entitled "Orchestrating Impartiality: The Impact of 'Blind' Auditions on Female Musicians," Cecilia E. Rouse utilized natural experiment methodologies in an individual

---

[136] Joshua D. Angrist, "Lifetime Earnings and the Vietnam Era Draft Lottery: Evidence from Social Security Administration Records," *American Economic Review,* June 1990.

[137] David E. Card, "The Impact of the Mariel Boatlift on the Miami Labor Market," *Industrial and Labor Relations Review* 43 (January 1990).

[138] Joshua D. Angrist and Alan B. Krueger, "Does Compulsory School Attendance Affect Schooling and Earnings?", *Quarterly Journal of Economics,* November 1991; and Angrist and Krueger, "Estimating the Payoff to Schooling Using the Vietnam-era Draft Lottery," Working Paper #290 (Princeton: Industrial Relations Section, Princeton University, August, 1991).

fixed-effects framework to study sex bias in the hiring practices of symphony orchestras. In a 2009 working paper (#546), Henry S. Farber used natural experiments to examine the potential effectiveness of a national holiday in increasing voter turnout.

However, perhaps among the best known and most impactful examples of the research of this period utilizing the methodology of natural experimentation in innovative ways to address questions of perennial concern to labor economists (and indeed economists in general) are presented in Orley Ashenfelter's classic 1991 study entitled "How Convincing is the Evidence Linking Education and Income?" (working paper #292), and David Card and Alan Krueger's groundbreaking 1993 paper entitled "Minimum Wages and Employment: A Case Study of the Fast Food Industry in New Jersey and Pennsylvania" (working paper #315). In the first case, Orley Ashenfelter used the combination of an ingenious natural experiment and an innovative data collection technique to analyze the correlation between income and educational attainment, by obtaining original survey data on both of these variables from identical twins at one of the country's largest annual twins festivals. In his words:

Is the correlation between income and educational attainment a result of the payoff to investments in schooling? Since the experiment of randomly selecting individuals to go to school cannot be performed, non-experimental methods must be used to estimate the economic returns to schooling. This paper reviews new studies that measure the effect of schooling on income (1) by using the comparison of brothers, fathers and sons, and twins and (2) that focus on natural experiments. These studies provide very credible evidence that schooling does increase incomes and that earlier studies may have underestimated the role of schooling in determining incomes....The recent research on the link between schooling and income provides a fascinating example of the new emphasis on credibility in empirical economics. This new research style began with the study of problems in the labor market, but it has also influenced other social scientists and even some policy makers. As we shall see, this research style emphasizes the importance of collecting new data and of finding and creating actual or natural experiments that will permit us to make more credible inferences about the effect of public policy changes.[139]

In the second case, through their research utilizing a real-time natural experiment that evaluated the effects of a legislative change, Card and Krueger caused no small amount of controversy by demonstrating convincingly that a widely held notion among economists, with significant public policy implications—that an increase in

---

[139] Orley Ashenfelter, "How Convincing is the Evidence Linking Education and Income," *Labour Economics and Productivity,* vol. 6, (1994): 1-12.

President Barack Obama and Alan Krueger leave the Oval Office before a statement in the Rose Garden of the White House, August 29, 2011. The president announced Krueger as his nominee to lead the Council of Economic Advisers. (Official White House Photo by Pete Souza).

the level of the minimum wage would necessarily result in higher unemployment—did not hold up to experimental scrutiny. Specifically:

> This paper presents new evidence on the effect of minimum wage legislation on establishment-level employment decisions. The evidence is based on the experiences of 410 fast food restaurants in New Jersey and Pennsylvania following the April 1992 increase in New Jersey's minimum wage from $4.25 per hour to $5.05 per hour. Comparisons of employment, wages and prices at stores in New Jersey (the treatment group) and Pennsylvania (the control group) before and after the rise in the New Jersey minimum present a simple method for evaluating the effects of a rise in the minimum wage. Comparisons within New Jersey between initially high-wage stores (those paying more than the new minimum rate prior to its effective date) and other stores provide a further contrast for studying the impact of the law. The quasi-experimental design of our empirical analysis provides simple robust estimates of the effect of the increase in New Jersey's minimum wage.[140]

President Barack Obama meets with advisers in the Oval Office, August 10, 2012. Pictured, from left, are: Mike Froman, Deputy National Security Advisor for International Economic Affairs; Senior Advisor David Plouffe; Chief of Staff Jack Lew; National Economic Council Director Gene Sperling; and Council of Economic Advisers Chair Alan Krueger. (Official White House Photo by Pete Souza).

Thus the approach first used in Princeton University's Industrial Relations Section in the 1980s, involving natural experiments and other methodological refinements in order to isolate and specify causal relationships in the evaluation of the effects of programs (and other changes in economic conditions) on target groups, continued throughout the 1990s and into the twenty-first century. And, although not completely without controversy at times, the credibility of these methods has had an enormous impact on economics (as well as on other areas of the social sciences), with many of the techniques introduced or elaborated upon by the section's associates having quickly become accepted tools of the labor economics trade.

As a final testimony to the critical role Princeton University's Industrial Relations Section has played in the developments outlined above, it is worth considering an excerpt from the statement of the 2006 IZA Award, conferred upon two of the section's most noteworthy scions, Berkeley's David Card and Princeton's Alan Krueger. According to the award committee:

---

[140] David E. Card and Alan B. Krueger, "Minimum Wages and Employment: A Case Study of the Fast Food Industry in New Jersey and Pennsylvania," *American Economic Review* 84, September, 1994.

Their work has crucially shaped the research agenda in labor economics and has certainly raised the standards for empirical research in applied economics. Their studies are directed towards the analysis of policy-relevant issues, and their research findings continue to have a substantial impact on the debate of labor market policy and education policy around the globe....With a remarkable sense for using the appropriate dose of sophisticated econometric techniques, they have unearthed intriguing facts from existing data or from appropriate natural experiments that would have otherwise remained in obscurity.[141]

Orley Ashenfelter mentoring Economics graduate students. Princeton University Library.

Throughout the remainder of the 1990s and 2000s, the Industrial Relations Section continued to grow and to expand its base of activities and resources. Going from just one tenured professor of economics (Ashenfelter) at the beginning of the 1980s to four (Ashenfelter, Rosen, Card, and Krueger) by the end of the decade, the section was further reinforced when it added alumnus Henry S. Farber GS'77 and Cecilia E. Rouse (Harvard, 1992) to its team of faculty associates in 1991 and 1992, respectively. Thus, with a cohort of five to six tenured faculty associates for most of the 1990s (David Card left Princeton in 1998 to head the Labor Studies program at the University of California, Berkeley), as well as three to four assistant professors overlapping as research associates at any given time, the section went through a remarkable period of research and publication.

For example, in the 10 years between 1990 and 1999, section faculty associates and visiting scholars produced 204 journal articles, 257 working papers, 62 chapters in books edited by others, eight books either authored or edited, and 35 reviews and miscellaneous publications. Likewise, in the period between 2000 and 2011, section-associated faculty and visiting faculty produced 239 journal articles, 264 working papers, 66 chapters in books edited by others, 14 books either authored or edited, and 57 reviews and miscellaneous publications.

The ability of the Industrial Relations Section to expand its research output during this period was facilitated in part by significant new developments in its resources. For example, as Bobray Bordelon—Princeton's economics and finance librarian and head of data and statistical services, who has worked closely with the section since the early 1990s—points out, when budget cuts threatened the data and statistical services

[141] Institute for the Study of Labor (Institut zur Zukunft der Arbeit), IZA Prize Award Statement (Bonn: IZA, 2006).

David Card (second from right) and Alan Krueger (second from left) receive the IZA Prize in Labor Economics in 2006

The IZA Prize in Labor Economics 2006 is awarded to the outstanding and highly productive U.S. labor economists David Card (University of California, Berkeley) and Alan Krueger (Princeton University). Their work has crucially shaped the research agenda in labor economics and has certainly raised the standards for empirical research in applied economics. Their studies are directed towards the analysis of policy-relevant issues, and their research findings continue to have a substantial impact on the debate of labor market policy and education policy around the globe. David Card and Alan Krueger have become a leading authority with regard to policy advice based on sound econometric research. Card and Krueger share an instinct for finding the right kind of exogenous

variation and collecting the relevant data from which reliable inferences can be drawn. With a remarkable sense for using the appropriate dose of sophisticated econometric techniques, they have unearthed intriguing facts from existing data or from appropriate natural experiments that would have otherwise remained in obscurity. Many of their findings spurred substantial debates and inspired much subsequent work. Often challenging the conventional views of the profession, their surprising new results were at times received with skepticism and critical distance. But David Card and Alan Krueger convinced many skeptics by their in-depth analyses that are based on carefully designed research strategies and reflect their expert knowledge on the details of the data they use. Card and Krueger's work abounds with key methodological contributions on instrumental variable estimation, measurement error, regression-discontinuity methods, or the use of "natural experiments". Card and Krueger have greatly promoted the quasi-experimental approach to causal modeling as a transparent scientific methodology. Their studies, which contain several brilliant examples of "natural experiments," have fueled the quest for and the use of natural experiments in a large economics literature that followed….As is true for most of their work, their studies on the effects of the minimum wage have inspired much subsequent research that has eventually led to a better understanding of the functioning of labor markets. In a sequence of studies, which are collected in their book *Myth and Measurement: The New Economics of the Minimum Wage,* they assembled empirical evidence from various labor markets, different periods, and different states showing no indication that higher minimum wages – contrary to the predictions of the traditional labor market model – reduce employment in the US. In one of their most famous joint studies, they surveyed 410 fast-food restaurants in New Jersey and Pennsylvania before and after the minimum wage was raised by about 20 percent in New Jersey, but not in its neighboring state. By comparing outcomes before and after the policy change within and across states, they evaluate the effects of the minimum wage change. This excellent example of using "natural experiments" to make causal inferences illustrates the power of the quasi-experimental approach as a transparent empirical strategy in labor economics. This has inspired original data collection and the search for exogenous variation generated by natural experiments in a large economics literature that followed. The influence of Card and Krueger's work is also felt in many other fields of economic science. Their style of doing empirical research has become a role model for research methodology across the economics profession. The IZA Prize 2006 honors the work of two scholars who have given great momentum and research spirit to the field.

Photograph and text courtesy of IZA.

department (which had previously been housed in the computing and information technology building) in 1996, the Industrial Relations Section teamed up with the economics department, the Woodrow Wilson School, and Firestone Library to help fund its relocation to the Social Science Resource Center. In addition to preserving the 30-year-old statistical support service and data library—which was reported to have been an early model for similar services at a number of universities around the world[142]—the move also benefited the section in one very important respect: it increased efficiency by bringing the specialized electronic data resources of the data and statistical services unit, of which the Industrial Relations Section was one of the heaviest users, into close proximity and coordination with the industrial relations library's print resources and research staff. But there were other important developments as well.

As noted earlier, in keeping with its emphasis on credible measurement and the rigorous analysis of data from natural and "quasi-natural" experiments, the section had long been at the forefront of labor economics in terms of its innovative primary data collection techniques. Capitalizing on these strengths, in 1992 the section's Alan Krueger led the establishment of the independent Princeton University Survey Research Center, of which he continues to serve as director. The aim of the center was to provide a resource to Princeton students, faculty, and administration for consultation, education, and management of surveys for research purposes. Since its founding, the Survey Research Center has completed well over 100 faculty-funded survey projects (including more than two dozen projects on behalf of the Industrial Relations Section), and has advised thousands of students in regard to research for their undergraduate theses and graduate dissertations.

Krueger was also instrumental in the section's initiation in 2007 of the Princeton Data Improvement Initiative—a two-year joint effort involving economists and researchers from Princeton University, Cornell University, the Universities of Chicago and Minnesota, the U.S. Census Bureau, U.S. Bureau of Labor Statistics, U.S. Bureau of Economic Analysis, Educational Testing Service, and Westat, a major private research and statistical survey organization. The initiative—the first of its kind sponsored by an academic institution—focused on identifying and mitigating gaps in data sets of critical interest to labor economists and econometricians, as well as on generally improving core data collection methodologies used in the field.

Yet another area in which the section expanded its resources during this period was in regard to education. Labor economics research on topics related to education

---

[142] Andrea Cohn, "Cuts force two departments to move from CIT building," *The Daily Princetonian,* Volume 120, Number 70, 12 September 1996, p.1.

has a rich history within the Industrial Relations Section. For example, among Orley Ashenfelter's extensive body of groundbreaking research, one of the best-known pieces is his previously referenced seminal work on the link between education and income, using the comparative study of the education and income levels of identical twins as a natural experiment. Between 1971 to 2001 the section produced 64 working papers with the keywords "education," "schooling," "academic," "college," "university," "class," or "student" in their titles, authored or co-authored by no fewer than 44 researchers. Among the faculty associates most actively involved in research on education-related topics during this time was Cecilia Rouse, who authored or co-authored at least 15 working papers involving some aspect of the labor economics of education in the almost nine years between January of 1993 and November of 2001 (in addition to her many publications on the economics of education within the last decade). Rouse explains the significance of this research area from a public policy perspective:

> The issue of the relevance of modern-day research in education to economics came up during a keynote address I gave when I was in Washington....I was discussing my work in education and randomized evaluations, and somebody stood up and asked, "Why is this economics?" In other words, why is research on the impact of technology on educational attainment, for example, related to economics?... [T]he answer is that if you go back to the Solow growth model which lays out the foundations of growth, you see that education is a big component—it's one of the underlying factors of growth. And really it's a big component because it has to do with the productivity of labor, which is key to output. And output is the result of a production function which involves capital and labor. So a natural question is then, "What makes labor more productive?" Well, education—and the question that's constantly on the minds of policymakers is, how do we make our educational investments more effective?...[P]eople ask, "We're making all of these investments in education, but is that actually improving our "L" in the production function?" That is, are [investments in education] having the desired outcomes in improving the productivity of our workers? If not, what do we need to do in order to make them more effective?[143]

Following on this research interest, in the fall 2002, Rouse led the foundation of Princeton University's Education Research Section (ERS), as an interdisciplinary unit within the Industrial Relations Section and the Woodrow Wilson School of Public and

---

[143] Cecilia E. Rouse, Industrial Relations Section, Princeton University, in an unpublished interview with the author, June 7, 2012.

International Affairs. The primary mission of the ERS, which is co-located with the Industrial Relations Section, was to bring together faculty from diverse backgrounds (including economics, psychology, sociology, and demography) to promote and conduct high-quality education research using experimental and quasi-experimental research designs, and to disseminate its results to educators, policy-makers, and the public. In addition to Cecilia Rouse (the ERS's founder), other section faculty associates who have also been associated with the unit since its inception are Orley Ashenfelter and Alan Krueger.

Along with the expansion of staff and other resources mentioned above, the number of section-affiliated doctoral students completing their Ph.D. programs also increased during this period. Between the 1990-1991 and 1999-2000 academic years, the section produced 38 graduates, including David S. Lee, provost since 2013. In the decade between the 2000-2001 and 2009-2010 academic years, an additional 36 graduates completed their Ph.D. programs at the section, to which were added three more graduates in the first two academic years of the present decade. Thus, by the end of the 2014-2015 academic year, the total number of Ph.D. economists produced by the Industrial Relations Section since its inception in 1922 amounted to 235 graduates.

In 1997, the section awarded its first Albert Rees Prize of the Outstanding Princeton Ph.D. Dissertation in Labor Economics. The biannual prize—which commemorates the great contributions of Albert Rees to labor economics at Princeton, in the words of the prize committee, "as a scholar, teacher, mentor, colleague, and friend"—was inaugurated to honor the Princeton Ph.D. dissertation, completed within the previous six years, judged to have made the greatest contribution to labor economics. The first winner of the prize was Dartmouth's Patricia M. Anderson GS'91, for her dissertation, "Incentive Effects of the U.S. Unemployment Insurance System."[144]

Other winners of the prize (with the year of their award) have included Cornell University's Kevin F. Hallock GS'95, 1999; Brown University's Kenneth Y. Chay GS'98, 2003; University of California, San Diego's Gordon B. Dahl GS'98, 2003; the Federal Reserve Bank of Chicago's Luojia Hu GS'00, 2005; University of California, Santa Barbara's Olivier Deschenes GS'01, 2007; Harvard's Erica Field GS'03, 2007; Case Western's Mark Votruba GS'03, 2009; Princeton Industrial Relations Section's Alexandre Mas GS'04, 2009; and Collegio Carlo Alberti (Turin, Italy)'s Giovanni Mastrobuoni GS'06, 2011. Princeton University Industrial Relations Section's current director, David Lee GS'99 was also a recipient of the Rees Prize in 2005 for his work on

---

[144] Patricia M. Anderson, "Empirical Analysis of the Incentive Effects of the U.S. Unemployment Insurance System," Ph.D. dissertation, (Princeton: Seeley G. Mudd Library, Princeton University, June, 1991).

"An Empirical Analysis of Changes in Wage Inequality in the United States during the 1980s."[145]

The most recent additions to the Industrial Relations Sections team of faculty associates, bringing it up to its current complement of seven professors of economics, also happen to be Princeton Ph.D. graduates and former students of the section: David Lee, who joined the section in 2007 (becoming its director in 2009); and Alexandre Mas, who joined in 2009. In a very real sense, the work being done by these young labor economists represents the next phase in the continuation of the Princeton Industrial Relations Section's legacy of careful empirical research and a commitment to methodological refinement and innovation, married to a tradition of interest in the classical questions of labor economics and a strong public policy orientation.

For example, in their joint January 2009 working paper (#547), "Long-Run Impacts of Unions on Firms: New Evidence from Financial Markets, 1961-1999,"[146] Lee and Mas use "quasi-experimental" econometric methodologies, such as regression discontinuity designs, to determine the economic effect of unions on firms by examining the impact on corporate share prices of new unionization events. Similarly, in research with Berkeley's David Card and Jesse Rothstein (both section alumni), Alexandre Mas used regression discontinuity models to examine the dynamics of racial tipping in integrated neighborhoods—a phenomenon with significant public policy implications. In fact, along with the strength of its scientific approach to economics research and its highly collaborative team atmosphere, this public policy component is one of the factors that drew both Lee and Mas to the Industrial Relations Section from the start.

Besides the close ties that have always existed between the Industrial Relations Section and Princeton's Woodrow Wilson School of Public and International Affairs, over the years a number of the section's faculty associates have also held influential positions in government policymaking circles. For example, as mentioned earlier, Orley Ashenfelter was director of the U.S. Labor Department's Office of Evaluation in the early 1970s, while J. Douglas Brown, Richard Lester, Frederick Harbison, and Albert Rees all held important advisory positions within the U.S. government from the 1930s through the 1960s.

More recently, Alan Krueger held positions as the chief economist of the U.S. Department of Labor (1994-1995) and the Treasury Department (2009-2010), as well as serving as the Treasury's Assistant Secretary for Economic Policy (2009-2010),

---

[145] David S. Lee, "An Empirical Analysis of Changes in Wage Inequality in the United States during the 1980s," Ph.D. dissertation (Princeton: Seeley G. Mudd Library, Princeton University, June, 1999).

[146] David S. Lee and Alexandre Mas, "Long-Run Impacts of Unions on Firms: New Evidence from Financial Markets, 1961-1999," *Quarterly Journal of Economics,* 2012, 127(1).

before becoming chairman of the President's Council of Economic Advisers in 2011. Cecilia Rouse—recently named as dean of the Woodrow Wilson School—likewise served on the President's Council of Economic Advisers under President Barack Obama from 2009 to 2011, and, prior to that, on President Bill Clinton's National Economic Council in the late 1990s. And finally, Alexandre Mas served as the chief economist of the U.S. Department of Labor (2009-2010) and of the President's Office of Management and Budget (2010-2011).

Thus it can certainly be said that a strong public policy orientation—or what might otherwise be called a clear appreciation for the public policy implications not only of the conditions and phenomena which affect labor markets and institutions, but also of the way in which those conditions and phenomena are researched, interpreted, and communicated, and the resulting effect on how public policy is shaped—has long been a hallmark of the Industrial Relations Section of Princeton University, and of the economists associated with it, going all the way back to the section's founding in 1922. Indeed, it is one of the characteristics that has kept the Industrial Relations Section true to Princeton University's informal motto, "Princeton in the Nation's Service, and in the Service of All Nations."

Princeton University's Industrial Relations Section in Historical Perspective

Members of the Industrial Relations Section *in front of Firestone Library in spring 2013. They are, left to right, Henry S. Farber, Alexander Mas, Orley Ashenfelter, Cecilia Elena Rouse, Alan B Krueger, and David S. Lee.* Photograph by David Kelly Crow.

On August 16, 2012, an ongoing labor dispute at a South African diamond mine erupted into violence, ending in the deaths (allegedly at the hands of the police) of at least 34 miners and the wounding of 78 more.[147]

While half a world away and a hundred years removed from similar incidents in the coal mines of West Virginia and Colorado, the steel yards of Pennsylvania, and dozens of other industries across the United States in the last decades of the 19th and the first decades of the 20th centuries, this event and others like it are a grim reminder of the conditions that led to the birth of the field of industrial relations in this country in the early 1920s. They also help to put the significance of Princeton University's Industrial Relations Section into historical perspective.

The early 1900s was a time of rapid industrialization in America. It was also a time in which the relationship between capital and labor was frequently mistrustful, sometimes antagonistic, and occasionally openly hostile, and in which the specter of anarchic violence and class warfare inspired by socialist movements in Europe and communist revolution in Russia was never very far away from the minds of business owners and civil authorities. There was, as yet, no rule book governing the dynamics of the employment relationship, and no social safety net to protect workers and their families from such catastrophes as disability, old age, or unemployment.

In this time before the passage of many of the protective labor laws taken for granted today, hours were long, wages barely allowed workers and their families to subsist, and labor disputes were often put down with violent repression. Companies frequently relied on local authorities, including local police and militia units, and sometimes even the National Guard, or on the feared private-detective agencies of Pinkertons or Baldwin-Felts, to ensure that production was not disrupted by striking workers. Sometimes the intervention of federal troops was even required to separate combatants in pitched battles over labor issues and to restore peace.

---

[147] Lydia Polgreen, "In Police Shooting of Miners, South Africa Charges Miners," *The New York Times,* August 30, 2012. Interestingly, the Princeton Industrial Relations Section's Cecilia E. Rouse and Wellesley College's Kristin F. Butcher (a 1993 alumna of the IR Section), in their 2000 working paper (#442) on the "Wage Impacts of Unions and Industrial Councils in South Africa," began their discussion with the ominous words: "Unions played a crucial role in South Africa's historic transition from the apartheid era. Now, however, they are coming under fire as major contributors to inflexibility in the South African labor market."

In that bygone era—punctuated from time to time by the outbreak of deadly labor–related violence, which pitted wealthy capitalists against the complex tapestry that was the emerging organized labor movement—a belief gradually developed within certain circles of industrialists that, in order to preserve the capitalist system, an accommodation between capital and labor had to be found. Among this small but influential group of would-be reformers was one of the world's wealthiest men, John D. Rockefeller, Jr., who had learned from firsthand experience how quickly and unexpectedly an antagonistic relationship between capital and labor could spiral out of control and lead to the tragic loss of life, property and reputation. Together with his close associate, the like-minded Clarence J. Hicks, Rockefeller became a dedicated promoter of the ideal of a collaborative relationship between capital, labor, and the community—an ideal that critics would call welfare capitalism, but which supporters would call industrial relations.

Rockefeller was also a supporter of the notion, spearheaded by Hicks, that, as a neutral and respected third party, the academic community—and, in particular, the nation's top universities—had a unique role to play in promoting the causes of industrial peace. This role was typified by the program that Hicks originally suggested to Princeton's President John G. Hibben in proposing the creation of what he termed an "Industrial Relations Section" in 1922. In essence, from its inception, Hicks envisioned the section (as well as similar units he helped to introduce at several other universities in the United States and Canada) as an independent, unbiased research and teaching facility, whose aim it would be to gather and disseminate information concerning current practices and legislation, not only to students, but to all parties interested in any aspect of the labor relationship, i.e., company management, labor union leaders, and public policymakers.

As he states in his memoirs, which encapsulate the experience of a lifetime spent in shaping the industrial relations field:

> Just as scientific laboratories and engineering technicians have increased the productive capacity of this country many fold, so the wider application of the developing science and art of industrial relations will some day raise the productivity inherent in man-power [sic] to levels little imagined.[148]

In other words, in Hicks's view, one of the primary purposes of an independent industrial relations unit was to place its unbiased research of all aspects of the labor relationship at the disposal of the public through the contribution of a fact-based assessment of best practices and policies, in the interest of promoting industrial peace and productivity.

---

[148] Hicks, *My Life,* 116.

The contours of the industrial relations field have changed dramatically over the last 90 years since Clarence Hicks's dinner with President Hibben and his "Economics men." However, one of the greatest success stories in regard to the academic industrial relations units he helped to inspire has been Princeton's Industrial Relations Section. According to industrial relations historian and economist Bruce Kaufman, "[o]f the five IR units Hicks created in the United States, the two most successful have been the ones at Princeton and at MIT. They remain in existence and continue to produce noteworthy research."[149] Yet, even as it has evolved significantly over time, in a very real sense Princeton's Industrial Relations Section has maintained a number of the traditions that have defined it from its foundation.

For one thing, it has maintained its active role in public service, as reflected throughout its history in the work of many of its associates. From the contributions of one of its founding fathers, Dean J. Douglas Brown, to the formulation of the Social Security legislation that has enriched the lives of many millions of Americans over the decades since it was first adopted in 1935, to the work of another of its prime movers of more recent decades, Orley Ashenfelter, in modeling the effects of workplace discrimination and in developing innovative techniques with which to evaluate the efficacy of government job training programs, and to the policy-oriented research of the recently named dean of the Woodrow Wilson School of Public and International Affairs, Cecilia Rouse, on the economics of education, Princeton's Industrial Relations Section has helped to define the terms of the national public policy dialogue in regard to labor and the economics of labor.

Indeed, long after the construction of an institutional framework for collective bargaining and the various components of a social safety net—a framework that has endured for many decades, and to which men such as J. Douglas Brown, Richard Lester, Frederick Harbison, and their institutional labor economist counterparts at a number of other universities, made significant contributions during their lifetimes—the section's labor economists have continued to contribute to the shaping of public policy. One of the ways they have done this is through their service in various public agencies and commissions in a variety of capacities over the years.

As mentioned previously, many of the section's faculty associates and alumni have served as federal government officials (including a Treasury Secretary and several members of the President's Council of Economic Advisors, among other roles); and, in fact, nearly all of the section's current cohort of faculty associates have done so at one time or another (several even holding their appointments simultaneously). As the section's Orley Ashenfelter puts it:

---

[149] Kaufman, *Origins & Evolution,* 211-212 (note 5 to chapter 3).

There has always been a history of public policy here: Alan Krueger is the chairman of President Obama's Council of Economic Advisers. Cecilia Rouse was on the Council. Alex Mas was the chief economist in the Labor department. I was in the Department of Labor in 1972-1973 as the director of the Office of Program Evaluation. Everybody has been there at one time or another. It's just the style that changed from the days of J. Douglas Brown. I mean, it's more quantitative—that's the way economics went—but the topics, and the interest in public service, are very similar.[150]

Near the end of his career, J. Douglas Brown outlined what he considered to be "the most precious attribute[s]" of a university research unit "in assisting in the determination of policy." Several of these are worth mentioning, in that, in some very fundamental ways, they still encapsulate the unspoken values of Princeton's Industrial Relations Section. In Brown's view, these precious attributes, or values, included the following:

– [T]he freedom of the members of a university research unit to preserve their independence. In a field in which big government, big industry, and big unions promote conformity within their own organizations and exercise powerful persuasion upon those who would influence policy, independence is a critical source of strength. With independence and an earned reputation for seeking truth rather than support for a predetermined position, a university research unit can develop sources of information, opinion, and advice beyond those available to either government bureaucracies or other parties of interest. With independence and an earned reputation for seeking truth rather than support for a predetermined position, a university research unit can develop sources of information, opinion, and advice beyond those available to either government bureaucracies or other parties of interest.

– In the broad field of human relations, there is no substitute for first-hand exposure to the people, the places, and the conditions involved in any issue. Extensive field study and discussion with interested persons are necessary to understanding the complex attitudes and responses which must be recognized in effective policy.

– Since policies affecting people involve many variables, it is necessary to be inclusive rather than exclusive in the process of weighing the elements which should be considered in coming to a decision. An aid in that process is the interchange

---

[150] Ashenfelter, unpublished interview, June 12, 2012.

of views among a research group rather than dependence upon a single expert, no matter how experienced....Unlike that of the single professor working alone, the product of a university research unit is a part of the flow of findings which are supported by the reputation of the unit for quality and integrity. For this reason, the development of findings should involve group consultation.[151]

In considering how Princeton's Industrial Relations Section has measured up against these values over the course of its history, among the first things to consider is that, while its research methodologies and econometric techniques have advanced substantially over time, in keeping with the words of Dean Brown, the section has successfully preserved its independence of thought and the unbiased nature of its careful empirical research. There are many examples of this, but perhaps one of the best in recent decades is the previously mentioned groundbreaking research done by David Card and Alan Krueger on the effect of minimum wage legislation on establishment-level employment decisions in the fast food industry in New Jersey and Pennsylvania in the early to mid-1990s.

The results of this work—which obtained unbiased empirical evidence through the use of a natural experiment—challenged the notion, long held within the mainstream economics establishment, that an increase in the minimum wage would necessarily lead to a decrease in employment. In describing the essential driving force behind the Industrial Relations Section's research, Krueger puts it this way:

A unifying theme throughout the Section's history is a mission to do credible research—work that people would view as credible—innovative, insightful, but first and foremost that it would stand up to scrutiny and wasn't predestined to find a particular answer.[152]

The next thing to consider is how the section has continued to emphasize what Brown called "extensive field study" and the "first-hand exposure to the people, the places, and the conditions involved in any issue." Many examples of this approach can be found throughout the section's history, from J. Douglas Brown's work with the Priorities Branch of the War Labor Board during World War II, to Orley Ashenfelter's groundbreaking analysis of the economic returns to education through the difference-in-differences study of the wage histories of identical twins. As Cecilia Rouse explains, referring to some of her earlier work on gender bias in the hiring of musicians:

---

[151] Brown, *IRS WWII*, 110-111.

[152] Alan B. Krueger, Industrial Relations Section, Princeton University, in an unpublished interview with the author, June 9, 2012.

> The symphony orchestra [example] goes back to the case study [approach], because I literally went and sat and talked to the orchestra managers and musicians. I sat in on auditions; I tried to understand the institutions.[153]

One anecdote from the section's Henry S. Farber illustrates the point particularly well. In a June 2012 interview, Farber recounts how, as a young graduate student writing his Ph.D. dissertation at the section in the mid-1970s, he was encouraged by J. Douglas Brown to visit a coal mine.

> When I was in grad school and Doug was emeritus, he would come in every once in a while, and he said, "Son, I'd like to talk to you." I sat down with him—he was probably close to 80 at the time—and he asked, "So what are you working on?" And I explained to him my dissertation idea on wage and employment outcomes of bargaining between the United Mine Workers and the Bituminous Coal Operators Association. He asked, "Have you ever been in a coal mine?" I answered, "No, sir." He said, "Well you can't write about the mine workers unless you've been in a coal mine." And he said—"I'll tell you what," he said. "U.S. Steel owns coal mines. They've been a longtime sponsor of the Industrial Relations Section. You write them a letter and tell them what you're doing, and they'll have you come and visit a coal mine." So I wrote them a letter…and got a letter back saying: "Well, we couldn't possibly let you visit a coal mine….if we let everyone [in] who wanted to visit, we'd never be able to mine any coal." And I showed it to Doug and he said, "This won't do," and he wrote a letter to the president of U.S. Steel invoking the names of several past presidents of U.S. Steel that he knew. The next thing I knew, I had a tour of a coal mine from a vice president! I remember the trip vividly. There were some fascinating economics I learned that day. It was a great day. The point is, that the same sentiment that drove Doug to do that for me drives me to say, "Well, there's some data out there you haven't looked at; you need to go do that. You need to talk to those people about those data—where they came from, what they mean, and so on. It's a very empirical evidence-based approach to how one understands the world we live in."[154]

Another important consideration in regard to any test of the historical integrity of the section's values is that, while enjoying the advantages of a university setting in which

---

[153] Rouse, unpublished interview, June 7, 2012.

[154] Henry S. Farber, Industrial Relations Section, Princeton University, in an unpublished interview with the author, June 11, 2012.

the intellectual freedom and the individual contribution of each scholar are highly prized qualities, the Industrial Relations Section has nevertheless also managed to retain the benefits of a team-oriented and unusually collaborative approach to the work produced by each of its faculty members. This team spirit is demonstrated in a number of ways, from the extraordinary degree of research collaboration between its faculty associates, visiting scholars, graduate students, and alumni (many of whom have continued to publish research papers together over the years), to the frequency of its workshops and seminars, to the close personal relationships between its staff members that has been a mainstay of the section's life for decades—and even to the section's inviting physical environment, which provides a locus for frequent discussion and interaction.

To this point, one of the Industrial Relations Section's former research associates, T. Aldridge Finegan (now an emeritus professor of labor economics at Vanderbilt University) recalls how the section had a daily tea time in the mid-1960s, during which the faculty, staff, and students would get together to exchange views; and even today it is not unusual to find groups of faculty, research associates, and students gathered in the inviting reception area or near the section's famous espresso machine to discuss a research project or to share ideas. Another veteran staff member of the section, former head librarian Kevin Barry, speaking of his experience there from 1978 to 2007, sums it up this way:

> I could not have asked for a more hospitable, enjoyable and stimulating working environment, because there was a lot of sharing that went on. I credit the Section's directors with creating this energy, because somehow year after year they ensured that there was an inevitably good mix of able and friendly scholars on board. It was one of those lively cultures where there was an abundance of informal conversation, listening, and exchange of information happening every day over coffee. That's pretty unusual. That kind of convergence of good will and work product just doesn't occur, that I know of, very often anywhere else. I never saw it elsewhere at Princeton to such a strikingly egalitarian degree, and I do think maybe it was [due to] the combination of being a smaller and more focused unit, where everybody knew and respected each other personally…. Just a tremendously gratifying place to work.[155]

In fact, many of those who are most familiar with the day-to-day operation of the section—including its former director, David S. Lee—consider the ready access between

---

[155] Kevin Barry, Library Director of St. Paul's School, Concord, NH, in an unpublished interview with the author, June 11, 2012.

the faculty and students which is provided by the unit's physical layout to be a key strength. According to Lee:

> I think that this kind of environment—with the suite of offices and the way the students are integrated physically into this sort of laboratory setting—is unique. It's a very good environment for collaborative research, and really promotes intellectual interaction: faculty-faculty, student-student, student-faculty interactions. But, other than at the National Bureau of Economic Research, you don't see it that often. I think perhaps that might have been one of the reasons I came to Princeton. I just felt this very collaborative atmosphere.[156]

The section's Alan B. Krueger, who recently served in Washington, D.C. as the chairman of the President's Council of Economic Advisers, shares this assessment. In his words:

> I think one of the things which makes the Industrial Relations Section unique is that it's a pretty collaborative environment. I moved from Harvard to Princeton 25 years ago and when I was at Harvard I spent most of my time at the National Bureau of Economic Research. The NBER had a similar phone system. At night, the receptionist wasn't there and the phone would ring, and it was up to somebody to answer the phone, find out who was calling and transfer them. At the NBER, the phone would ring all night long because nobody would pick it up; and at the Industrial Relations Section, on the first ring someone would pick it up....[T]hat was kind of Ashenfelter's ethic, David Card's ethic. For me, what really forged my career was Ashenfelter and Card in the first ten years I was at Princeton— getting to work with them, observing the way that they worked, how they advised students, learning from them. And it wasn't just learning economics. It was also learning about their commitment to the Industrial Relations Section.[157]

Finally, another indicator of the Princeton Industrial Relations Section's continuity with its historical roots can be found in the form of its well-known library. As shown earlier, the Industrial Relations Section library, and its role as a clearinghouse for information and empirical data gathering and dissemination in regard to numerous aspects of the employment relationship, was central to the unit's founding in 1922. In fact, the

---

[156] David S. Lee, Industrial Relations Section, Princeton University, in an unpublished interview with the author, June 28, 2012.

[157] Krueger, unpublished interview, June 9, 2012.

library was such a crucial element of the section that its maintenance was one of the conditions of the original endowment funding from John D. Rockefeller, Jr., as well as that from subsequent benefactors.

Throughout the section's history, the library has been instrumental, both in terms of the collection of important original documents—including original research, such as company and labor union surveys, employee handbooks, and other material—and as a research resource for faculty and students alike. The Industrial Relations library and the way in which it operates have certainly evolved over time. Much of its physical book collection has been integrated into the University's larger collection through the Social Science Resource Center, and the once laborious and time-consuming practice of collecting physical documents from companies and trade unions has been abandoned in favor of digitally preserving relevant electronic publications via the internet. Nevertheless, it continues to play an important role in the life of the section.

Today, the Industrial Relations library focuses on three principal duties: preserving the section's unique and valuable historical document collections, acquiring and managing both physical and electronic research materials and relevant digital data sets, and providing extensive support to faculty and student researchers. In regard to the latter, the section's current head librarian, Linda Oppenheim, notes that an important part of the Industrial Relations library's role is now helping to train undergraduate students writing junior papers and senior theses in regard to basic research techniques—that is, understanding what data sets are available, where to get them, what their limitations are, how to use them, and the kinds of questions that can and perhaps cannot be addressed through them—as well as rooting out often obscure and hard-to-find data for researchers. Indeed, although the methods, media, and technology have changed dramatically over the last 90 years, the role that the Industrial Relations library plays in our own times is one that the section's very first librarian, Helen Baker, would have found very familiar.

From the few examples presented above, it is clear that, while its research priorities and methodologies have evolved substantially over the past ninety years, the Princeton University Industrial Relations Section has been successful at maintaining the historical continuity between its underlying values as a research and teaching unit and its founding fathers' vision of actively contributing to the development of public policy. Another way it has made such contributions is through the quality of its basic research into the causes and effects of various labor-related economic conditions, which has both informed and often defined the terms of the public policy debate over significant issues in the labor markets.

In this regard, yet a further measure of its success as a university research and teaching unit is the record of the accomplishments and the contributions of the students it has developed. Here as well, the Industrial Relations Section has proven its worth time and again throughout its history. According to the section's Henry Farber, much of the approach of today's economics (and even of other social sciences) has come from the pioneering work done at the Industrial Relations Section. As he puts it:

The language of a certain kind of very popular empirical work in economics is a language that comes out of Princeton's Industrial Relations Section. This core idea of the natural experiment—which has permeated across fields, not just labor economics, but in public finance, in development economics—has really taken over. Here is one example. Josh Angrist, who is very well known for this, was a student of Orley [Ashenfelter]'s, who worked on the effect of military service on earnings and labor market outcomes of veterans. And then—to show you the ripple effects of that—a student of Josh's is a woman named Esther Duflo, who is one of the highest profile young economists in the country, who does development economics and has founded something at MIT called the Poverty Action Lab that runs actual randomized trials—not natural experiments, but randomized trials—on questions of development in countries all over the world. It's a huge operation, and you can trace a line from her to Josh Angrist to Orley Ashenfelter.[158]

While the accomplishments and contributions of the Industrial Relations Section's intellectual offspring are too numerous to narrate here in detail, the example above does provide a sense of the section's profound influence in the world of economics. And as Orley Ashenfelter notes in a recent interview, it is hard to find a major economics faculty in the country that has not been influenced by Princeton. Describing his path to some of his early, groundbreaking research, he comments:

[A]nd then my students were basically doing the same things. It's much harder now: Our students, basically, are now our competitors. If you go up to MIT, there's one of our guys, or if you go to Yale, there's one of our guys. Go to Stanford, there's one of our guys. Go to Chicago, there's one of our guys. Go to Michigan, Berkeley…I mean, they're all over the place.[159]

---

[158] Farber, unpublished interview, June 11, 2012.

[159] Ashenfelter, unpublished interview, June 12, 2012.

Nevertheless, from his perspective, Ashenfelter sees these kinds of developments as a positive reflection on the unique legacy of Princeton University's Industrial Relations Section. As he puts it in the same interview: "You create your own competitors. They're all good, and the whole subject is now vastly more prestigious."

Bibliography

Anderson, Patricia M. "Empirical Analysis of the Incentive Effects of the U.S. Unemployment Insurance System." Ph.D. diss., Princeton University, 1991.

Angrist, Joshua D. "Lifetime Earnings and the Vietnam Era Draft Lottery: Evidence from Social Security Administration Records." *American Economic Review* (June 1990).
— and Alan B. Krueger. "Estimating the Payoff to Schooling Using the Vietnam-era Draft Lottery." Working Paper #290, Industrial Relations Section, Princeton University, 1991.
— and Alan B. Krueger. "Does Compulsory School Attendance Affect Schooling and Earnings?" *Quarterly Journal of Economics* (November 1991).

Ashenfelter, Orley. "The Case for Evaluating Training Programs with Randomized Trials." *Economics of Education Review 6,* no. 4 (1987): 333-338.
— "How Convincing is the Evidence Linking Education and Income." *Labour Economics and Productivity 6* (1994): 1-12.
— and David E. Card. "Using the Longitudinal Structure of Earnings to Estimate the Effect of Training Programs." *Review of Economics and Statistics 67,* no. 4 (1985): 648-60.
— and James J. Heckman. "Measuring the Effect of an Anti-Discrimination Program." In *Evaluating the Labor Market Effects of Social Programs,* edited by Orley C. Ashenfelter and James Blum. Princeton: Princeton University Press, 1976.
— and J.H. Pencavel. "Albert Rees and the 'Chicago School of Economics'." *The Elgar Companion to the Chicago School of Economics,* edited by Ross B. Emmett. Cheltenham, England and Northampton, Mass.: Edward Elgar (2010): 311-314.
— and Gary R. Solon. "Longitudinal Labor Market Data: Sources, Uses, and Limitations." In *What's Happening to American Labor Force and Productivity Measurements?,* National Council on Employment Policy (1982). Revised as Industrial Relations Section Working Paper No. 155, Industrial Relations Section, Princeton University, 1982.

Bloomfield, Daniel. *Problems in Personnel Management.* New York: H.W. Wilson, 1923.

Brown, J. Douglas. *The Industrial Relations Section of Princeton University in World War II.* Princeton: Industrial Relations Section, Princeton University, 1976.

Card, David E. "The Impact of the Mariel Boatlift on the Miami Labor Market." *Industrial and Labor Relations Review* 43 (January 1990).

— and Alan B. Krueger. "Minimum Wages and Employment: A Case Study of the Fast Food Industry in New Jersey and Pennsylvania." *American Economic Review* 84 (September 1994).

— and Alan B. Krueger. *Myth and Measurement: the New Economics of the Minimum Wage.* Princeton: Princeton University Press, 1995.

Farber, Henry S. "Job Loss in the Great Recession: Historical Perspective from the Displaced Workers Survey, 1984-2010." Working Paper #564, Industrial Relations Section, Princeton University, 2011.

— and Bruce Western. "Accounting for the Decline of Unions in the Private Sector, 1973-1998." *Journal of Labor Research* (Summer 2001): 459-485.

Golden, Claudia and Cecilia E. Rouse. "Orchestrating Impartiality: The Impact Of 'Blind' Auditions On Female Musicians." *American Economic Review* 90 (4 Sept 2000): 715-741.

Heneman, Herbert G., Jr. "Contributions of Current Research." In *The Role of Industrial Relations Centers: Proceedings of a Regional Meeting of the International Industrial Relations Association in Chicago, Illinois,* May 17-18, 1968. Madison, Wis.: International Industrial Relations Association, 1968.

Hicks, Clarence J. *My Life in Industrial Relations: Fifty Years in the Growth of a Profession.* New York and London: Harper & Brothers, 1941.

Industrial Relations Research Association. *Proceedings of the twenty-seventh annual winter meeting, December 28-29, 1974 of the Industrial Relations Research Association.* Madison, Wis.: International Industrial Relations Association, 1975.

Jaimovich, Hir and Henry E. Siu. "The Trend is the Cycle: Job Polarization and Jobless Recoveries." Working Paper No. 18334, Washington: National Bureau of Economic Research (August 2012)

Jones, Jeff and Lydia Saad. *Gallup Poll Social Series: Work and Education, Final Topline.* Gallup News Service (5-8 Aug 2010).

Kaufman, Bruce E. *The Origins & Evolution of the Field of Industrial Relations in the United States.* Ithaca, N.Y.: ILR Press, 1993.
— *The Global Evolution of Industrial Relations: Events, Ideas and the IIRA.* Geneva: International Labour Office, 2004.

Kochan, Thomas A., Harry Charles Katz and Robert B. McKersie. *The Transformation of American Industrial Relations.* New York: Basic Books, 1986.

Krueger, Alan B. and David E. Card. *Myth and Measurement: the New Economics of the Minimum Wage.* Princeton: Princeton University Press, 1995.

Lalonde, Robert J. "Evaluating the Econometric Evaluations of Training Programs with Experimental Data." *American Economic Review* 76 (September 1986): 604-20.

Laurie, Clayton D. "The United States Army and the Return to Normalcy in Labor Dispute Interventions: The Case of the West Virginia Coal Mine Wars, 1920-1921." *West Virginia History* 50 (1991): 1-24.

Lee, David S. "An Empirical Analysis of Changes in Wage Inequality in the United States during the 1980s." Ph.D. diss., Princeton University, 1999.
— and Alexandre Mas. "Long-Run Impacts of Unions on Firms: New Evidence from Financial Markets, 1961-1999." *Quarterly Journal of Economics* 127 (1) (Feb 2012): 333-378.

Leitsch, Alexander, editor. *A Princeton Companion.* Princeton: Princeton University Press, 1978. [Revised 1995 edition published online at http://etcweb.princeton.edu/ CampusWWW/Companion/]

Lester, Richard A. *The Industrial Relations Section of Princeton University, 1922 to 1985.* Princeton: Industrial Relations Section, Princeton University, 1986.

McNulty, Paul J. *The Origins and Development of Labor Economics: A Chapter in the History of Social Thought.* Cambridge: MIT Press, 1980.

Montgomery, David. *The Fall of the House of Labor.* Cambridge: Cambridge University Press, 1987.

Mulvey, Charles and J.M. Abowd. "Estimating the Union/Non-Union Wage Differential: A Statistical Issue." Working Paper #108A, Industrial Relations Section, Princeton University, 1979.

Oberdorfer, Don. *Princeton University: The First 250 Years.* Princeton: Princeton University, 1995.

Rees, Albert. "H. Gregg Lewis and the Development of Analytical Labor Economics." *Journal of Political Economy* 84, no.4 (1976), pt. 2.

Romer, Christina. "Spurious Volatility in Historical Unemployment Data." *The Journal of Political Economy* 91 (1986): 1–37.

Rouse, Cecilia E. and Kristin F. Butcher. "A Study of the Wage Impacts of Unions and Industrial Councils in South Africa." *Industrial and Labor Relations Review* 54, no. 2 (January 2001): 349-374.
— and Claudia Goldin. "Orchestrating Impartiality: The Impact Of 'Blind' Auditions On Female Musicians." *American Economic Review* 90 (4 Sept 2000): 715-741.

Troy, Leo. *Trade Union Membership, 1897-1962.* New York: National Bureau of Economic Research, 1965.

Wright, Gavin. "Labor History and Labor Economics." In *The Future of Economic History,* edited by Alexander Field. Boston: Kluwer-Nijhoff Publishing, 1987.

Faculty Biographies

Orley Ashenfelter is the Joseph Douglas Green 1895 Professor of Economics at Princeton University. He is a member of the faculty steering committee of the Griswold Center for Economic Policy at Princeton University, and a member of the advisory board of Stanford University's Institute for Economic Policy Research. He is a member of the editorial boards of the *Journal of Cultural Economics,* the *Economic and Labour Relations Review,* and the *Australian Bulletin of Labour,* and has served as editor or co-editor of numerous other scholarly journals and publications. Professor Ashenfelter is a former president of the American Economics Association, the American Law and Economics Association, and the Society of Labor Economists, and a former member of the Executive and Supervisory Committee of the Charles University's (Prague, Czech Republic) Center for Economic Research and Graduate Education Economics Institute. In addition to holding various faculty positions in the Department of Economics of Princeton University, he has been a faculty associate of the Industrial Relations Section since 1970, and was its director from 1971 to 1985 and from 1998 to 2001.

As Director of the Office of Evaluation of the U.S. Department of Labor from 1972 to 1973, Professor Ashenfelter began the work that led to the development of what is now widely recognized as the separate field of quantitative social program evaluation. The rigorous methods he developed for the quantitative econometric evaluation of federally funded job retraining and other social programs included the use of randomized trials and longitudinal program evaluation methods, which are now often called the "difference-in-differences" methods.

With his innovative research and data collection techniques spanning a broad array of topics in the economic analysis of labor markets, Professor Ashenfelter is widely regarded as the originator of the use of so-called natural experiments to infer causality about economic relationships. His research using twins to control for genetic factors that may confound the estimation of the payoff to schooling is an example of this approach. He has also used this experimental approach to estimate the impact of arbitration statutes on wages, the end of mandatory retirement rules on the retirement decisions of faculty, and the effects of many other public policies on the labor market.

Professor Ashenfelter's numerous honors and awards include the Karel Englis Honorary Medal of the Academy of Science of the Czech Republic, the

Jacob Mincer Award of the Society of Labor Economists, the IZA Prize in Labor Economics, and the Ragnar Frisch Prize of the Econometric Society. In 2005, he was named a Corresponding Fellow of the Royal Society of Edinburgh, and in 1977 he was named a Fellow of the Econometric Society. He received the degree of Doctor Honoris Causa from the University of Brussels in 2002.

He received his B.A. from Claremont McKenna College in 1964, and his Ph.D. from Princeton University in 1970.

 Will Dobbie is an Assistant Professor of Economics and Public Affairs at Princeton University, and a research fellow at the Education Innovation Laboratory at Harvard University. Professor Dobbie holds a joint appointment in the Department of Economics and the Woodrow Wilson School of Public and International Affairs of Princeton University, and has been a faculty associate of the Industrial Relations Section since 2013.

Professor Dobbie's research interests are primarily in the areas of labor economics and the economics of education. His work has examined the effect of school inputs on student outcomes, the importance of peer effects, the impact of voluntary youth service, and the benefits of the consumer bankruptcy system.

He received his B.A. degree in Economics from Kalamazoo College in 2004, his M.A. degree in economics from the University of Washington in 2007, and his Ph.D. in public policy from Harvard University in 2013.

 Henry S. Farber is the Hughes-Rogers Professor of Economics at Princeton University and Director of the Industrial Relations Section. He is a research associate of the National Bureau of Economic Research and a research fellow of the Institute for the Study of Labor (IZA). Professor Farber is a member of the Executive and Supervisory Committee of the Charles University's (Prague, Czech Republic) Center for Economic Research and Graduate Education as well as a member of Statistics Canada's Labour and Income Statistics Advisory Committee. He has served as a member of the editorial board of the American Economics Review and of the Quarterly Journal of Economics, and as a co-editor of the Industrial and Labor Relations Review.

Since 1991 he has been a faculty associate of the Industrial Relations Section, which he also directed from July to December of 1993, July 1995 to June 1998, July 2003 to June 2004, and July 2013 to June 2017.

From 1977 to 1991, Dr. Farber held faculty appointments at the Massachusetts Institute of Technology, where he was a Professor of Economics from 1986 until 1991.

Professor Farber's primary research interests are in the areas of labor economics, econometrics, law and economics, and industrial relations. His current research involves unemployment, liquidity constraints and labor supply, the economics of labor unions, worker mobility, wage dynamics, the analysis of dispute settlement mechanisms (including arbitration and litigation), and the analysis of voter behavior.

Among the organizations from which Professor Farber has received research grants are the National Science Foundation and the United States Department of Labor. In 1991 he was named an Alfred P. Sloan Foundation Research Fellow. In 2000 and 2012 he was awarded Princeton University's Richard E. Quandt Teaching Prize and in 1984 he (with Max H. Bazerman) received the Edwin E. Ghiselli Award for Research Design of the American Psychological Association. He is a Fellow of the Econometric Society, the Society of Labor Economists, and the Labor and Employment Relations Association. Professor Farber was a Fellow of the Center for Advanced Study in the Behavioral Sciences from 1983 to 1984 and from 1989 to 1990, a Visiting Scholar at the Russell Sage Foundation from 2002 to 2003, and a Member of the School of Social Science at the Institute for Advanced Study from 2006 to 2007.

He received his B.S. in economics from Rensselaer Polytechnic Institute in 1972, his M.S. in industrial and labor relations from the New York State School of Industrial and Labor Relations of Cornell University in 1974, and his Ph.D. in economics from Princeton University in 1977.

 Alan B. Krueger is the Bendheim Professor of Economics and Public Affairs. He holds a joint appointment in the Economics Department and Woodrow Wilson School of International and Public Affairs of Princeton University, and is the founding director of the Princeton University Survey Research Center. He has been a member of the boards of directors of the Russell Sage Foundation, the MacArthur Foundation, and the American Institutes for Research. He has also been a member of the executive committees of the American Economic Association and the International Economic Association, and has served as the Chief Economist for the National Council on Economic Education. Dr. Krueger has been a faculty associate of the Industrial Relations Section since 1987, and was its director from 2001 to 2006.

From November 2011 until resigning to return to Princeton in August of 2013, Professor Krueger served as Chairman of President Barack Obama's Council of Economic Advisers and as a member of the president's cabinet. He also served as Assistant Secretary for Economic Policy and Chief Economist of the U.S. Department of the Treasury from 2009 to 2010, and as Chief Economist at the U.S. Department of Labor from 1994 to 1995.

Professor Krueger has published widely on the economics of education, unemployment, labor demand, income distribution, social insurance, labor market regulation, terrorism and environmental economics. He has also been a member of the editorial board of *Science* magazine, editor of the *Journal of Economic Perspectives,* co-editor of the *Journal of the European Economic Association,* and from 2000 to 2006 was a regular contributor to the "Economic Scene" column in *The New York Times.* Among the books he has authored are *What Makes A Terrorist: Economics and the Roots of Terrorism,* and *Education Matters: A Selection of Essays on Education.* He co-authored *Myth and Measurement: The New Economics of the Minimum Wage* with Professor David E. Card of the University of California at Berkeley, and *Inequality in America: What Role for Human Capital Policies?* with Professor James J. Heckman of the University of Chicago.

Dr. Krueger was elected as a fellow of the Society of Labor Economists in 2005, a fellow of the American Academy of Political and Social Science in 2003, a fellow of the American Academy of Arts and Sciences in 2002, and a fellow of the Econometric Society in 1996. He was named a Sloan Fellow in Economics in 1992, and from 1989 to 1990 was an Olin Fellow of the National Bureau of Economic Research. Among the distinctions he has been awarded are the IZA Prize in Labor Economics (with David Card in 2006), the Mahalanobis Memorial Medal of the Indian Econometric Society (in 2001) and the Kershaw Prize of the Association for Public Policy and Management (in 1997).

He received a B.S. degree (with honors) from Cornell University's School of Industrial & Labor Relations in 1983, an A.M. in economics from Harvard University in 1985, and a Ph.D. in economics from Harvard University in 1987.

 David S. Lee is the Provost of Princeton University, and Professor of Economics and Public Affairs, holding a joint appointment in the Economics Department and Woodrow Wilson School of International and Public Affairs at Princeton University since 2007. He has been a research associate of the National Bureau of Economic Research since 2009, and has been co-editor of the *Review of Economics and Statistics,*

a foreign editor of the *Review of Economic Studies* and associate editor of the *American Economic Journal: Applied Economics* and the *Journal of Business and Economic Statistics.* Professor Lee has been a faculty associate of the Industrial Relations Section since 2007, and was its director from 2009 to 2013.

From 2006 to 2007, Dr. Lee was a professor of economics at Columbia University, and he held faculty positions at the University of California-Berkeley and Harvard University from 1999 to 2006.

Professor Lee's research interests are primarily in the areas of labor economics and econometrics. He has worked on issues of inequality in the labor market, including the differential impact of the federal minimum wage across regions of the United States and the impact of education, race, and job training programs on relative wages. His research has also focused on econometric methodologies used to analyze experiments and quasi-experiments. His work has investigated how economic agents respond to laws, institutional rules, and policy regimes that have the potential to affect the distribution of resources. Some of his work has examined how data from elections can be used to analyze social science phenomena from a quasi-experimental perspective, and has used this framework to study, for example, the impact of unionization on employment, output, productivity, and stock valuations of publicly-traded firms. More recently, his research has examined the impact of unemployment insurance benefits on the duration of unemployment. He has also studied a number of other topics, including congressional voting behavior, as well as the deterrence effect of prison on youth criminal behavior.

Professor Lee has received the Journal of Econometrics Dennis J. Aigner Award, the Labor and Employment Relations Association's John T. Dunlop Outstanding Scholar Award, and Princeton University's Albert Rees Prize. In 2006, he was named a fellow by the Alfred P. Sloan Foundation, and in 2003 by the Center for Advanced Study in the Behavioral Sciences.

He received his A.B. in economics (summa cum laude) from Harvard University in 1993. He received his M.A. in economics in 1996, and his Ph.D. in economics in 1999, both from Princeton University.

 Alexandre Mas is a Professor of Economics and Public Affairs at Princeton University. He is a research fellow at Institute for the Study of Labor (IZA), and a research associate at the National Bureau of Economic Research. He is also co-editor of *American Economic Journals: Applied Economics,* associate editor of the *IZA Journal of Labor Economics,* and serves on the International Advisory Committee of the

British *Journal of Industrial Relations.* Professor Mas has held a joint appointment in the Department of Economics and the Woodrow Wilson School of Public and International Affairs of Princeton University, and has been a faculty associate of the Industrial Relations Section, since 2009.

From 2010 to 2011, Professor Mas served as the Associate Director for Economic Policy and Chief Economist at the Office of Management and Budget in the Executive Office of the President, and as Chief Economist at the U.S. Department of Labor from 2009 to 2010. Previously he held appointments at the Haas School of Business and the Department of Economics of the University of California-Berkeley.

Professor Mas' research has dealt with fairness considerations and norms in the labor market, social interactions, neighborhood segregation, the labor market effects of credit market disruptions, and unions.

He received the IZA Young Labor Economist Award and Princeton University's Albert Rees Prize in 2009, and the Labor and Employment Relations Association's John T. Dunlop Outstanding Scholar Award in 2008. He was named an Alfred P. Sloan Foundation Research Fellow in 2009, and was a National Bureau of Economic Research Faculty Research Fellow from 2006 to 2009.

He received a B.A. degree in economics and mathematics from Macalester College in 1999, and a Ph.D. in economics from Princeton University in 2004; he was acting director of the section in 2014-2015.

 Harvey S. Rosen is the John L. Weinberg Professor of Economics and Business Policy at Princeton University. Rosen has been a member of Princeton's Department of Economics since 1974. He served as chairman of the department from 1993 to 1996, and was co-director of the Center for Economic Policy Studies from 1993 to 2011. From 2007 to 2011 he served as the inaugural master of Princeton's sixth undergraduate residential college, Whitman College. Since 1978, he has been a research associate of the National Bureau of Economic Research, and is a member of the editorial boards of Contemporary Economic Policy and the National Tax Journal. He served as a member of the President's Committee on the National Medal of Science, is a member of the American Council for Capital Formation's Board of Scholars, and also chairs the National Tax Association's Dissertation Prize Committee. Professor Rosen has been a faculty associate of the Industrial Relations Section since 1978.

In 2005, Professor Rosen served in Washington, DC as the chairman of the President's Council of Economic Advisers, where he was also a member from 2003 to 2005. From 1989 to 1991, he served as Deputy Assistant Secretary (Tax Analysis) in the U.S. Department of the Treasury. He has also served as a consultant to the U.S. Treasury's Office of Tax Analysis, the Joint Economic Committee of the United States' Congress, the New York State U.S. Attorney's Office, the Federal Reserve Bank of Philadelphia, the Board of Governors of the Federal Reserve Bank, the Joint Committee on Taxation of the U.S. Congress, and the Small Business Administration.

Professor Rosen's main field of research is public finance. He has published several dozen articles in scholarly journals. He has also authored a popular undergraduate textbook on the subject of public finance and co-authored a textbook on microeconomics, both of which have been translated into numerous languages.

Professor Rosen has received research grants from organizations such as the National Science Foundation, the Robert Wood Johnson Foundation, the Hoover Institution, and the U.S. Department of Labor. He has been awarded numerous academic prizes, including the National Tax Association's Daniel M. Holland Medal for distinguished lifetime contributions to the study and practice of public finance, the President's Distinguished Teaching Award, the National Tax Association's Richard Musgrave Prize, the Richard Quandt Teaching Prize, and the Allyn Young Teaching Prize. In 1986 he was elected a Fellow of the Econometric Society, and in 1969 he was elected a member of the Phi Beta Kappa Society.

He received his bachelor's degree (with high honors) from the University of Michigan in 1970. In 1972 he received his A.M. in economics and in 1974 his Ph.D. in economics, both from Harvard University.

 Cecilia Elena Rouse is the Dean of the Woodrow Wilson School of Public and International Affairs and the Lawrence and Shirley Katzman and Lewis and Anna Ernst Professor in the Economics of Education. She is the founding director of the Princeton University Education Research Section, a member of the National Academy of Education, and a research associate of the National Bureau of Economic Research. Professor Rouse has served as an editor of the *Journal of Labor Economics* and is currently a senior editor of *The Future of Children,* a collaborative initiative of the Woodrow Wilson School of Public and International Affairs at Princeton University and the Brookings Institution. She has been a faculty associate of the Industrial Relations Section of Princeton University since 1992, and was its director from 2006 to 2008.

From 2009 to 2011, Professor Rouse served as a member of the President's Council of Economic Advisers, and from 1998 to 1999 she served as Special Assistant to the President of the United States at the National Economic Council. She is a member of the board of directors of MDRC, a leading public policy research institute, and is an independent director of the T. Rowe Price Equity Mutual Funds and a member of the advisory board of the T. Rowe Price Fixed Income Mutual Funds.

Professor Rouse's primary research and teaching interests are in labor economics with a particular focus on the economics of education. She has studied the economic benefits of community college attendance, evaluated the Milwaukee Parental Choice Program, examined the effects of education inputs on student achievement, tested for the existence of gender bias in the hiring practices of professional symphony orchestras, and studied Florida's school accountability system as well as the impact of the use of computers in schools on student achievement. Her current research is focused on ways of improving persistence in post-secondary education such as with performance-based scholarships.

Among the organizations from which Professor Rouse has received research funding are the Bill and Melinda Gates Foundation, the Carnegie Foundation, the Spencer Foundation, the Smith Richardson Foundation, the Atlantic Philanthropic Services Company, and the National Institutes of Health. In 2002, Professor Rouse received the Minnesota Award for "Orchestrating Impartiality: The Impact of 'Blind' Auditions on Female Musicians," and in 1999 she received the Advancement for Literacy Award from the National Coalition for Literacy.

She received her B.A. in economics from Harvard University in 1986 and her Ph.D. in economics from Harvard University in 1992.

Staff, Visiting Professors, Directors, Dissertation Advisers, Faculty Associates, and Research Associates

The contributions over the years of many of its staff members have made the Industrial Relations Section what it is today. The names of some key staff members and their years of service are presented below. In the interest of brevity, only current staff and those who served for at least five years out of the last 30 are included. The Industrial Relations Section gratefully acknowledges the contributions of the many other former staff members and colleagues whose names do not appear; their efforts will forever be appreciated.

INDUSTRIAL RELATIONS SECTION

Program Managers

Linda Belfield	2001—Present
Barbara Radvany	1988—2001
Irene Rowe	1969—1975; 1976—1988

Administrative and Office Support

Patricia (Patti) Tracey	2010—Present
Joyce Howell	1989—2010
Charlotte Howard	2003—2009
Dorothy Silvester	1966—1997
Cynthia (Cindy) Gessele	1983—1989
Katherine (Sheila) Hall	1983—1988

Computer Support

Eugenia (Jeannie) Moore	2004—Present
Cathleen (Cate) Carroll	2006—2012
Wayne Appleton	1998—2004 (Part-Time)

SOCIAL SCIENCE REFERENCE CENTER

Phebe Dickson	2015—Present
Kevin Barry	1978—1982, 1985—2007, Industrial Relations Librarian
Bobray Bordelon	1993—Present, Economics and Finance Librarian; August 2007—February 2008, Acting Industrial Relations Librarian
Ginger Kou	1999—Present, Special Collections Assistant
Joel Burlingham	2007—2011 (In Memoriam)
Helen Hansen	1989—1997
Alice Kirikian	1968—1982

PAST INDUSTRIAL RELATIONS SECTION LIBRARIANS

Linda Oppenheim	2008—2014
Kevin Barry	1985—2007
Katherine Bagin	1982—1985
Kevin Barry	1978—1982
Helen Fairbanks	1968—1978
Hazel Benjamin	1939—1968
Leahmae Brown	1937—1939
Helen Baker	1928—1937

Visiting Professors

Jessica Pan	2014-15	National University of Singapore
Ian Walker	2014-15	Lancaster University Management School (UK)
Stephen Woodbury	2014-15	Michigan State University
Roland Fryer	2014	Harvard University
Bruce Weinberg	2012-2013	Ohio State University
Giovanni Mastrobuoni	2013	Collegio Carlo Alberto (Italy)
Betsey Stevenson	2011-2012	University of Michigan
Justin Wolfers	2011-2012	University of Michigan
Lara Shore-Sheppard	2011-2012	Williams College
Matthew Freedman	2011-2012	Cornell University
Nancy Qian	2010-2012	Yale University
Ann Morrison-Piehl	2010-2011	Rutgers University
Damon Clark	2009-2011	Cornell University
Jordan Matsudaira	2010-2011	Cornell University
Marco Manacorda	2009-2011	Queen Mary University of London (UK)
Abigail Wozniak	2008-2009	University of Notre Dame
Alexandre Mas	2008-2009	Princeton University
Maria Guadalupe	2008-2009	Columbia Business School
Morris Kleiner	2008-2009	University of Minnesota
Richard Hurd	2008-2009	Cornell University
Gordon B. Dahl	2007-2008	University of California, San Diego
Alfonso Flores-Lagunes	2006-2007	University of Florida
Ian Walker	2006-2007	University of Warwick (UK)
Jonathan Guryan	2006-2007	Northwestern University
Luojia Hu	2006-2007	Federal Reserve Bank of Chicago
Francine D. Blau	2005-2006	Cornell University
Lawrence M. Kahn	2005-2006	Cornell University
Sandra E. Black	2005-2006	University of Texas at Austin
Stefano Della Vigna	2005-2006	University of California, Berkeley

Ann Bartel	2005	Columbia University Business School
Olivier Deschenes	2004-2005	University of California, Santa Barbara
W. Bentley MacLeod	2003-2004	Columbia University
Jose Galdon	2003	Universidad de Navarra, Pamplona (Spain)
Maia Guell	2003	The University of Edinburgh (UK)
Solomon Polachek	2002-2003	State University of New York at Binghamton
Katharine Abraham	2001-2002	Maryland Population Research Center
Rajeev Dehejia	2002	New York University
David E. Card	2000-2001	University of California, Berkeley
Michael R. Ransom	2000-2001	Brigham Young University
David Jaeger	1999-2000	University of Cologne (Germany)
Stephan Jurajda	1999-2000	Center for Economic Research and Graduate Education—Economics Institute (Czech Republic)
Arnaud Lefranc	1998-1999	Université de Cergy-Pontoise (France)
Kenneth Y. Chay	1998-1999	Brown University
Kevin F. Hallock	1998-1999	Cornell University
Sewin Chan	1998-1999	New York University, Robert F. Wagner Graduate School of Public Service
Arie Kapteyn	1997-1998	University of Southern California
Douglas Staiger	1997-1998	Dartmouth College
Kristin Butcher	1997-1998	Wellesley College
Reuben Gronau	1996-1998	Hebrew University of Jerusalem (Israel)
Dwayne Benjamin	1996-1997	University of Toronto (Canada)
Gerald Oettinger	1996-1997	University of Texas at Austin
Daniel Parent	1995-1996	Institute of Applied Economics (Canada)
Alan Manning	1994-1995	London School of Economics and Political Science (UK)
John E. DiNardo	1994-1995	University of Michigan, Gerald Ford School of Public Policy
Caroline Hoxby	1992-1994	Stanford University
Carol Rapaport	1991-1992	Federal Reserve Bank of Chicago
Craig Olson	1990-1992	University of Illinois
Sara de la Rica	1991-1992	Universidad del País Vasco (Spain)
Thomas Lemieux	1991-1992	University of British Columbia (Canada)

Anne Case	1990-1991	Princeton University, Woodrow Wilson School of Public and International Affairs
George Neuman	1990-1991	University of Iowa
James P. Begin	1990-1991	Rutgers University
Daniel G. Sullivan	1989-1990	Federal Reserve Bank of Chicago
Guy Lacroix	1989-1990	Université Laval (Canada)
Mark Killingsworth	1989-1990	Rutgers University
Sharon Smith	1988-1990	University of Pittsburgh
Shelly Lundberg	1989-1990	University of California, Santa Barbara
Bruce Meyer	1988-1989	University of Chicago, Harris School of Business
Robert Gibbons	1988-1989	Massachusetts Institute of Technology, Sloan School of Management
Claudia Goldin	1987-1988	Harvard University
Peter Kuhn	1987-1988	University of California, Santa Barbara
Robert Porter	1987-1988	Northwestern University
Charles Beach	1986-1987	Queen's University (Canada)
John Abowd	1986-1987	ILR School, Cornell University
Mark W. Plant	1986-1987	International Monetary Fund
George Jakubson	1985-1986	Cornell University
Hirschel Kasper	1985-1986	Oberlin College
John Ham	1984-1986	University of Maryland
Vincent P. Crawford	1985-1986	All Souls College, University of Oxford (UK)
Joseph G. Altonji	1984-1985	Yale University
Andrew Oswald	1983-1984	University of Warwick (UK)
Christopher A. Pissarides	1984	London School of Economics and Political Science (UK)
Clifford E. Reid	1982-1983	Colby College
Mark Stewart	1982-1983	University of Warwick (UK)
Ronald L. Oaxaca	1982-1983	University of Arizona
Dante Canlas	1981-1982	University of the Philippines School of Economics (Philippines)
Michael Abbott	1981-1982	Queen's University (Canada)

Stephen J. Nickell	1979	London School of Economics and Political Science (UK)
Charles Mulvey	1978	University of Western Australia (Australia)
Robert C. Vowels	1976-1977	The Atlanta University School of Business
David Metcalf	1975	London School of Economics and Political Science (UK)
H. Gregg Lewis	1974-1975	University of Chicago
Michael L. Wachter	1974	University of Pennsylvania
Walter Y. Oi	1974	University of Rochester
Yoram Weiss	1973-1974	Tel Aviv University (Israel)
Barry R. Chiswick	1973	George Washington University
Burton A. Weisbrod	1973	Northwestern University
Anthony P. Thirlwall	1972	University of Kent (UK)
James A. Hefner	1971-1972	Tennessee State University
T. Aldridge Finegan	1971, 1967-1968	Vanderbilt University

Directors

	Years in section	Years as Director (Academic Years)
Robert F. Foerster	1922-1925	1922-1926
J. Douglas Brown	1926-1971	1926-1955
Frederick H. Harbison	1955-1976	1955-1968
William G. Bowen	1958-1985	1962-1963*
Albert Rees	1966-1979	1968-1971
Orley Ashenfelter	1968-	1971-1995; 1998-2001; 2007-2008*; 2010-2011*
Daniel S. Hamermesh	1969-1973	1972-1973*
Cordelia W. Reimers	1976-1982	1980-1981*
James N. Brown	1978-1985	1984-1985*
David Card	1983-1998	1989-1990*
Alan Krueger	1987-	2001-2006
Henry S. Farber	1991-	Fall, 1993*, 1995-1998; 2003-2004*; 2013-2017
Cecilia E. Rouse	1992-	2006-2008 (spring)
David S. Lee	2007-	2009-2013 (fall)
Alexander Mas	2009-	2014-2015*

* Acting

Dissertation Advisers

Altonji, Joseph G.

Angrist, Joshua D.

Ashenfelter, Orley

Bailey, Elizabeth E.

Baker, Laurence

Beach, Charles M.

Beaudry, Paul

Bell, Philip W.

Bloch, Howard R.

Bloom, David E.

Boozer, Michael A.

Bowen, William G.

Brown, J. Douglas

Brown, James N.

Budd, John W.

Card, David

Chay, Kenneth Y.

Coale, Ansley

Cross, John G.

Currie, Janet M.

Dahl, Gordon B.

DiNardo, John E.

Duncan, Acheson J.

Farber, Henry S.

Filer, Randall K.

Grabowski, Henry G.

Greenstone, Michael B.

Grenier, Gilles

Hallock, Kevin F.

Ham, John C.

Harbison, Frederick

Heckman, James J.

Hollander, Samuel

Holtz-Eakin, Douglas J.

Hosios, Arthur Jacob

Kiefer, Nicholas M.

Klevorick, Alvin K.

Krueger, Alan B.

Lalonde, Robert J.

Lee, David S.

Leeds, Michael A.

Lemieux, Thomas

Masters, Stanley H.

McCall, Brian Patrick

Meltz, Noah M.

Myers, Charles N.

Oaxaca, Ronald L.

Piehl, Anne Morrison

Pencavel, John H.

Pischke, Jorn-Steffen

Rees, Albert

Rosen, Harvey S.

Rouse, Cecilia Elena

Roy, Joydeep

Solon, Gary Rand

Svejnar, Jan

Worley, James S.

Faculty Associates

Orley Ashenfelter	1968-	Robinson Hollister	1970-73
Helen Baker	1937-55	Harry Kelejian	1967-73
Marianne Bertrand	1998-2000	Jeffrey Kling	1998-2006
Stanley Black	1967-71	Alan Krueger	1987-
Rebecca Blank	1983-1989	David S. Lee	2007-
Farrell Bloch	1974-78	Richard A. Lester	1945-85
William G. Bowen	1958-85	Alexandre Mas	2009-
David Bradford	1968-69	*David A. McCabe	1909-1959
J. Douglas Brown	1926-85	George de Menil	1970-75
James N. Brown	1978-85	Joseph D. Mooney	1965-67
David Card	1983-1998	Wilbert E. Moore	1962-64
George Cave	1978-85	Stephen Nickell	1978-79
John J. Corson	1962-66	Richard D. Portes	1969-72
Angus Deaton	1979-80	Cordelia W. Reimers	1978/79
Will Dobbie	2013-	Albert Rees	1966-79
Warren Eason	1955-60	Gaston V. Rimlinger	1957-60
Henry S. Farber	1991-	Harvey Rosen	1978-
T. Aldrich Finegan	1962-64	Jesse Rothstein	2003-09
Robert F. Foerster	1922-26	Cecilia Rouse	1992-
Roger H. Gordon	1975-80	Daniel Saks	1976-77
Daniel S. Hamermesh	1969-73	Sharon Smith	1974-77
Maria J. Hanratty	1993-98	Anne R. Somers	1964-89
Frederick Harbison	1955-76	Herman M. Somers	1963-89
Heinz Hartmann	1955-61	J. K. Zawodny	1957-58
Samuel E. Hill	1957-62		

* While we believe David A. McCabe was never formally listed as an Industrial Relations Faculty Associate, he was instrumental in the founding of the section and we include his name here as a tribute to him. Please refer to page 36.

Research Associates

John Abowd	1976-77	Roger Gordon	1978-79
Robert Aronson	1948-49	Frederick H. Harbison	1937-39
George W. Baldwin	1943-44	Simon Marcson	1958-62
John Ballantine	1947-48	Edward P. Moore	1940-42
W. Michael Blumenthal	1955-56	Paul Norgren	1960-64
Leahmae Brown	1937-38	William Peirce	1964-65
Arthur J. Corazzini	1964-65	Edward A. Robie	1946-48
Dorothy Dahl	1943-44	Fred Slavick	1948
Eleanor Davis	1933-34	John M. True	1946-48
Robert R. France	1948-53	Dieter K. Zschock	1964-65
Rita B. Friedman	1942-43		

Current Students, Current Post-docs, and Alumni

CURRENT POST-DOCS

2013-present
Amanda Y. Agan

2014-15
Conrad Miller

2014-15
Seth Zimmerman

CURRENT STUDENTS

Judd Cramer
Felipe M. Goncalves
Daniel Herbst
Pauline Leung
Jakob Schlockermann
David W. Zhang

ALUMNI

2015
Jacob Goldin
Inessa Liskovich
Neel Sukhatme

2014
Maria Lucia Del Carpio

2013
Marjolaine Gauthier-Loiselle
Nikolaj Harmon
Tatiana Homonoff
Yan Lau
Nicholas Lawson
Yoon Soo Park

2012
Wifag Adnan
Xiaotong Niu
Zhuan Pei

2010
Xiaoling Ang
Silvia Barcellos
Leandro Carvalho
Eleanor Choi
Ashley Miller
Francisco Perez-Arce
Nathan Wozny

2009
Robert DeForest McDuff

2008
Elaine Liu
Molly Fifer MacIntosh
Climent Quintana-Domeque
Courtney Stoddard
Elizabeth "Ty" Wilde

2007
Marie Connolly
Kirk Doran
Jane Fortson
Susan Yeh

2006
Radha Iyengar
Giovanni Mastrobuoni
Elod Takats
Fatih Unlu
Matthew Weinberg

2005
Kenneth Fortson
Pei Zhu

2004
Joydeep Roy
Claude Berrebi
Alexandre Mas
Yaron Raviv
Grace Wong

2003
Melissa Clark
Erica Field
David Linsenmeier
Mark Votruba

2002
Diane Whitmore Schanzenbach

2001
Olivier Deschenes
Harry Krashinsky

2000
Lashawn K. Richburg Hayes
Luojia Hu

1999
Lisa Barrow
David S. Lee

1998
Gordon B. Dahl
Cary A. Elliott
Michael B. Greenstone
Andrew V. Leventis
Helen G. Levy

1997
Anne-Louise Statt

1996
Jacqueline E. Berger
Kenneth Y. Chay
Mark H. Lopez
Paul E. Oyer
Geoffrey M. Rubin
Lara D. Shore-Sheppard

1995
Kevin F. Hallock
Dean R. Hyslop
Jin Heum Park
A. Abigail Payne
Michael J. Quinn
Norman K. Thurston

1994
Yukiko Abe
Laurence C. Baker
Michael A. Boozer
Alec R. Levenson
Karen Needels
John R. Penrod
Anne Piehl

1993
Kristin Butcher
Melvyn G. Coles
Kathryn J. Graddy

1992
Annamaria Lusardi
Jorn-Steffen Pischke
David Zimmerman

1991
Patricia M. Anderson
John W. Budd
Christoph M. Schmidt

1990
John E. DiNardo
Phillip B. Levine

1989
Joshua D. Angrist
Paul Beaudry
H. Dwayne Benjamin
Thomas Lemieux

1988
Brian P. McCall
Sheena M. McConnell
Janet C. Neelin

1987
James Dow
Daniel Sullivan

1986
Nicholas C. Papandreou
Jungyoll T. Yun

1985
Douglas Holtz-Eakin
Robert J. LaLonde

1984
Mehdi I. Zaidi

1983
Jesse M. Abraham
Laurie J. Bassi
David E. Card
Michael A. Leeds
Therese J. McGuire
Motty Perry
Richard G. Price
Michael R. Ransom
Gary R. Solon

1982
Gilles J. A. Grenier
Arthur J. Hosios
Mark W. Plant

1981
Joseph G. Altonji
Eleanor P. Brown
David E. Bloom
L. Denton Marks, Jr.

1980
John C. Ham
Laurence C. Morse

1979
Paul B. Bennett
Randall K. Filer
Jan Svejnar

1978
K.E. Yaeger
Christine A. Greenhalgh

1977
Edward J. Driffill
Henry S. Farber
Thorvaldur Gylfason

1976
Judith M. Gross
Nicholas M. Kiefer

1973
Ralph H. Harbison
Clifford E. Reid
Daniel H. Saks

1972
Elizabeth E. Bailey
Charles M. Beach
Donald E. Campbell
Donald E. Frey
Edward J. D. Ketchum
Thomas M. Power

1971
James E. Annable, Jr.
James J. Heckman
Stanley W. Huff
Charles N. Myers
Ronald L. Oaxaca
John D. F. Rowlatt

1970
Orley C. Ashenfelter
David C. Hershfield
Paul Offner
Robert C. Wilburn

1969
Peter Y. Comay
John W. Isbister
George N. Monsma
John H. Pencavel
Frank L. Vannerson

1967
Henry G. Grabowski
Alvin K. Klevorick

1966
Edwin F. Estle
Ronald B. Gold
Stanley H. Masters
William S. Pierce

1964
Howard R. Bloch
John G. Cross
Noah M. Meltz

1963
Peter Asch
George J. Heitmann
Samuel Hollander
Eugene M. Singer

1961
David G. Brown
Andrew J. Cooper II

1960
Benjamin B. Christopher
James H. Noren
David H. Stern

1959
Bernard Udis
W. Donald Wood

1958
William G. Bowen
James S. Worley

1957
Sherrill Cleland
I. Abdelkader Ibrahim
Jack C. Myles

1956
W. Michael Blumenthal
Benson Soffer

1954
Philip W. Bell

1953
Robert L. Aronson
Fred Slavick

1952
Marten S. Estey
Robert R. France
Thomson M. Whitin
George W. Barclay
Richard Scheuch

1951
Seymour M. Miller

1948
John E. Brigante

1947
Ansley J. Coale

1946
Matthew A. Kelly

1944
Randall W. Hinshaw

1943
Richard H. Wood

1942
Roger C. Dixon
Fred Ritchie

1941
Kenneth J. Curran
Lowell M. Pumphrey
Francis A. Spencer

1940
John D. Durand
Frederick H. Harbison

1939
Allen E. Andress
John T. Caldwell
George H. Hand
Edward F. Willett

1938
Weldon W. Welfling

1937
John R. Huber

1936
Acheson J. Duncan
Richard A. Lester
Lester V. Plum
Archibald M. Woodruff

1935
Frank T. Devyver
Everett D. Hawkins
Courtenay H. Pitt

1934
Jay W. Blum
James M. Jarrett

1933
Denzel C. Cline
Burnham N. Dell
Vernon A. Mund
Paul M. Titus

1932
George F. Luthringer
George M. Modlin

1930
Archibald M. McIsaac

1929
Howard S. Piquet

1928
Robert H. Ball
John F. Fennelly
Charles R. Whittlesey

1927
James D. Brown

1926
Frank W. Fetter

1925
Arthur F. Lucas
Shirley D. Southworth
Maurice C. Waltersdorf

1924
Arthur L. Faubel

Institutional Affiliations

Institutional Affiliations of the Industrial Relations Section's Ph.D. Recipients

Institution	Alumni Industrial Relations Section	Year of Ph.D.	Number of students
Abt Associates Inc.	Ashley R. Miller Fatih Unlu	2010 2006	2
Aix-Marseille School of Economics, France	Nicholas Lawson	2013	1
American Action Forum	Douglas Holtz-Eakin	1985	1
American Society of Training and Development	Laurie Jo Bassi	1983	1
Analysis Group, Canada	Marjolaine Gauthier-Loiselle Michael J. Quinn Laurence C. Baker	2013 1995 1994	3
Andrew P. Mellon Foundation	William G. Bowen	1958	1
APPRISE (Applied Public Policy Research Institute for Study and Evaluation)	Jacqueline E. Berger	1996	1
Asia University (Japan)	Yukiko Abe	1994	1
Author (Fiction)	Nicholas C. Papandreou James H. Noren	1986 1960	2
Bank for International Settlements	Elod Takats	2006	1
Bank of Canada	Paul Beaudry	1989	1
Bank One Corporation	James Edward Annable, Jr.	1971	1

Institution	Alumni Industrial Relations Section	Year of Ph.D.	Number of students
Bates White LLC	Cary A. Elliott	1998	1
Bendix International	Werner Michael Blumenthal	1956	1
Ben-Gurion University (Israel)	Samuel Hollander	1963	1
Boston College	Kristin F. Butcher	1993	1
Boston University	Philip W. Bell Paul Beaudry	1954 1989	2
Brandeis University	Zhuan Pei Kathryn Jo Graddy Randall K. Filer	2012 1993 1979	3
Brattle Group	James Dow Andrew V. Leventis	1987 1998	2
Brigham Young University	Michael R. Ransom Norman K. Thurston	1983 1995	2
Bristol-Meyers Squibb	John R. Penrod	1994	1
Brookings Institution	Donald E. Frey Molly Fifer McIntosh	1972 2008	2
Brown University	Kenneth Y. Chay	1996	1
Bryn Mawr College	Matthew Weinberg	2006	1
Bureau of Labor Statistics	Eleanor Jawon Choi	2010	1
Burroughs Corporation	Werner Michael Blumenthal	1956	1
Calvin College	George Norman Monsma, Jr.	1969	1
CNA	Molly Fifer McIntosh	2008	1
Capital One, Inc.	Geoffrey M. Rubin	1996	1
Carnegie Institute	Robert C. Wilburn	1970	1
Carnegie Mellon University	Robert C. Wilburn David E. Bloom	1970 1981	2
Case Western Reserve University	Mark E. Votruba William S. Pierce	2003 1966	2

Institution	Alumni Industrial Relations Section	Year of Ph.D.	Number of students
Center for European Economic Research (ZEW)	Jorn-Steffen Pischke	1992	1
Charles River Associates	Courtney Stoddard Andrew V. Leventis	2008 1998	2
Central Intelligence Agency	James H. Noren	1960	1
City of New York Independent Budget Office	Joydeep Roy	2004	1
City University of New York	David C. Hershfield	1970	1
Claremont McKenna College	Yaron Raviv	2004	1
Colby College	Clifford E. Reid	1973	1
College of William and Mary	Donald E. Campbell	1972	1
Collegio Carlo Alberto	Giovanni Mastrobuoni	2006	1
Colonial Williamsburg Foundation	Robert C. Wilburn	1970	1
Columbia University	Elizabeth Ty Wilde Janet M. Currie Douglas Holtz-Eakin David E. Bloom Joseph G. Altonji James J. Heckman David S. Lee	2008 1988 1985 1981 1981 1971 1999	7
Conference Board, Inc.	David C. Hershfield	1970	1
Congressional Budget Office	Xiaotong Niu Cary A. Elliott Douglas Holtz-Eakin	2012 1998 1985	3
Consumer Financial Protection Bureau	Xiaoling Lim Ang	2011	1
Cornell University	Tatiana Homonoff Kevin F. Hallock Jan Svejnar Nicholas M. Kiefer	2013 1995 1979 1976	4

Institution	Alumni Industrial Relations Section	Year of Ph.D.	Number of students
Cornerstone Research, Inc.	Marie Connolly	2007	1
Council of Economic Advisers	Douglas Holtz-Eakin	1985	7
	Robert J. Lalonde	1985	
	Phillip B. Levine	1990	
	Cecilia E. Rouse	1992 (Harvard)	
	Alan B. Krueger	1987 (Harvard)	
	Harvey S. Rosen	1974 (Harvard)	
	Helen G. Levy	1998	
Council on Foreign Relations	Douglas Holtz-Eakin	1985	1
CSOB Bank (Czech and Slovak Republics)	Jan Svejnar	1979	1
Dartmouth College	Annamaria Lusardi	1992	2
	Patricia M. Anderson	1991	
Data Resources, Inc.	Jesse M. Abraham	1983	1
Drake University	David G. Brown	1961	1
Drexel University	Matthew Weinberg	2006	1
Duke University	Henry G. Grabowski	1967	3
	Richard A. Lester	1936	
	Susan Yeh	2007	
Economic Policy Institute	Joydeep Roy	2004	1
European Commission, Network for the Economic Analysis of Terrorism and Anti-Terror Policies (NEAT)	Claude Berrebi	2004	1
European University Institute (Italy)	James Dow	1987	1
Ewha University (South Korea)	JungYoll Thomas Yun	1986	1
Exxon Corporation	Ronald B. Gold	1966	1
Fairview Capital Partners	Laurence C. Morse	1980	1
FDIC	Benjamin B. Christopher	1960	2
	Xiaoling Lim Ang	2011	

Institution	Alumni Industrial Relations Section	Year of Ph.D.	Number of students
Federal Advisory Council of the Board of Governors of the Federal Reserve	James Edward Annable, Jr.	1971	1
Federal Housing Finance Agency (FHFA)	Andrew V. Leventis	1998	1
Federal Reserve Bank of Chicago	Luojia Hu Lisa Barrow Daniel G. Sullivan Joseph G. Altonji Kristin F. Butcher Kevin F. Hallock	2000 1999 1987 1981 1993 1995	6
Federal Reserve Bank of New York	Paul B. Bennett	1979	1
Federal Reserve Board	Susan Yeh	2007	1
Federal Trade Commission	Matthew Weinberg	2006	1
Fisk University	Philip W. Bell	1954	1
Fordham University	Paul B. Bennett	1979	1
Freddie Mac	Jesse M. Abraham	1983	1
Fuller Theological Seminary	David Harold Stern	1960	1
FW Dodge Corporation	Jesse M. Abraham	1983	1
George Mason University	Howard R. Bloch Susan Yeh David John Zimmerman	1964 2007 1992	3
George Washington University	Annamaria Lusardi	1992	1
Georgetown University	Neel Sukhatme Joydeep Roy Paul Offner Laurie Jo Bassi	2015 2004 1970 1983	4
Georgia College and State University	David G. Brown	1961	1
Georgia Tech	Andrew Jackson Cooper III	1961	1

Institution	Alumni Industrial Relations Section	Year of Ph.D.	Number of students
Gettysburg National Battlefield Museum Foundation	Robert C. Wilburn	1970	1
Harvard University	Erica M. Field	2003	7
	Joshua D. Angrist	1989	
	David E. Bloom	1981	
	Charles Nash Myers	1971	
	Radha Iyengar	2006	
	David S. Lee	1999	
	Anne M. Piehl	1994	
Haverford College	Philip W. Bell	1954	1
Hebrew University of Jerusalem (Israel)	Joshua D. Angrist	1989	3
	Claude Berrebi	2004	
	Motty Perry	1983	
Hokkaido University (Japan)	Yukiko Abe	1994	1
Hunter College	Randall K. Filer	1979	1
Imperial Oil	William Donald Wood	1959	1
Indiana University of Pennsylvania	Robert C. Wilburn	1970	1
INSEAD	Maria Lucia Del Carpio	2014	1
International Monetary Fund	Mehdi I. Zaidi	1984	4
	Mark W. Plant	1982	
	Thorvaldur Gylfason	1977	
	Elod Takats	2006	
Israel Institute of Technology (Israel)	Peter Y. Comay	1969	1
Institute for the Study of Labor (IZA) (Germany)	Christoph Matthias Schmidt	1991	1
John D. and Catherine T. MacArthur Foundation	Kristin F. Butcher	1993	1
Joint Economics Committee	Cary A. Elliott	1998	1
JPMorgan Chase and Co.	James Edward Annable, Jr.	1971	1

Institution	Alumni Industrial Relations Section	Year of Ph.D.	Number of students
K&L Gates	Richard G. Price	1983	1
Kalamazoo College	Sherrill Cleland	1957	1
Korea Development Institute, Korea	Yoon Soo Park	2013	1
Lincoln University	Philip W. Bell	1954	1
London Business School (UK)	James Dow Kathryn Jo Graddy	1987 1993	2
London School of Economics (UK)	Radha Iyengar Jorn-Steffen Pischke Sheena Mary McConnell	2006 1992 1988	3
Marietta College	Sherrill Cleland	1957	1
Massachusetts Institute of Technology	Michael B. Greenstone Jorn-Steffen Pischke Joshua D. Angrist Janet M. Currie Henry S. Farber Thomas Lemieux	1998 1992 1989 1988 1977 1989	6
Mathematica Policy Research, Inc.	Jane Garrison Fortson Kenneth Noble Fortson Melissa A. Clark Karen Elizabeth Needels Sheena Mary McConnell Nathan Wozny	2007 2005 2003 1994 1988 2010	6
McBassi & Company	Laurie Jo Bassi	1983	1
McMaster University	Ana Abigail Payne	1995	1
MDRC	Pei Zhu Lashawn K. Richburg Hayes	2005 2000	2
Mechanics Savings Bank	Jack C. Myles	1957	1
Miami University	David G. Brown	1961	1
Michigan State University	Gary R. Solon Robert J. Lalonde	1983 1985	2
Milken Institute	Alec R. Levenson	1994	1

Institution	Alumni Industrial Relations Section	Year of Ph.D.	Number of students
Monitor Group	Elizabeth Ty Wilde	2008	1
Mount Holyoke College	Ashley R. Miller	2010	1
Mt. Lucas Management	Frank L. Vannerson	1969	1
Muhlenberg College	George J. Heitmann	1963	1
Nagoya City University (Japan)	Yukiko Abe	1994	1
National Commission on Employment and Unemployment Statistics	Gary R. Solon	1983	1
National Economic Research Associates, Inc.	Michael J. Quinn	1995	1
New York Stock Exchange	Paul B. Bennett	1979	1
Northwestern University	Diane M. Whitmore (Schanzenbach)	2002	6
	Therese J. McGuire	1983	
	Joseph G. Altonji	1981	
	Luojia Hu	2000	
	Paul E. Oyer	1996	
	Daniel G. Sullivan	1987	
Novartis AG	David M. Linsenmeier	2003	1
Office of Management and Budget	Alexandre Mas	2004	1
Office of the Governor, State of Utah	Norman K. Thurston	1995	1
Ohio State University	John C. Ham	1980	2
	Ronald B. Gold	1966	
Pardee RAND Graduate School	Silvia H. Barcellos	2010	4
	Claude Berrebi	2004	
	Leandro S. Carvalho	2010	
	Francisco Perez-Arce Novaro	2010	
Peking University (People's Republic of China)	James J. Heckman	1971	1
Pennsylvania State University	George J. Heitmann	1963	1

Institution	Alumni Industrial Relations Section	Year of Ph.D.	Number of students
Petroleum Industry Research Foundation	Ronald B. Gold	1966	1
Pew Research Center	Mark H. Lopez	1996	1
PIRA Energy Group	Ronald B. Gold	1966	1
Pomona College	Eleanor P. Brown	1981	1
Princeton University	Alexandre Mas	2004	8
	David S. Lee	1999	
	Janet M. Currie	1988	
	Henry S. Farber	1977	
	Orley C. Ashenfelter	1970	
	William G. Bowen	1958	
	David E. Card	1983	
	Richard A. Lester	1936	
Quant Economics, Inc.	Robert DeForest McDuff	2009	1
Queen's University (Canada)	Charles M. Beach	1972	2
	William Donald Wood	1959	
RAND Corporation	Francisco Perez-Arce Novaro	2010	5
	Leandro Carvalho	2010	
	Silvia H. Barcellos	2010	
	Claude Berrebi	2004	
	John E. DiNardo	1990	
Rapt	Andrew V. Leventis	1998	1
Reed College	Yan Lau	2013	1
Reis, Inc.	Geoffrey M. Rubin	1996	1
Rheinisch-Westfälisches Institut für Wirtschaftsforschung (Germany)	Christoph M. Schmidt	1991	1
Rice University	Philip W. Bell	1954	1
Rider College	David C. Hershfield	1970	1
Ropes and Gray	Susan Yeh	2007	1
Ruhr-Universität Bochum (Germany)	Christoph Matthias Schmidt	1991	1

Institution	Alumni Industrial Relations Section	Year of Ph.D.	Number of students
Russell Sage Foundation	David E. Bloom	1981	1
Rutgers University	Anne M. Piehl Peter Asch	1994 1963	2
Saba Software	Laurie Jo Bassi	1983	1
SBC Global	K.E. Yaeger	1978	1
Second Pillar Consulting	Geoffrey M. Rubin	1996	1
Stanford University	Jacob Goldin Paul E. Oyer Laurence C. Baker John H. Pencavel	2015 1996 1994 1969	4
State University of New York, Binghamton	Stanley H. Masters	1966	1
Syracuse University	Douglas Holtz-Eakin	1985	1
Temple University	Michael A. Leeds	1983	1
Tilburg University (The Netherlands)	Edward John Driffill	1977	1
Transylvania University	David G. Brown	1961	1
Treasury (of New Zealand)	Dean R. Hyslop	1995	1
University of California, Berkeley	David S. Lee Kenneth Y. Chay David E. Card Philip W. Bell Helen G. Levy Alexandre Mas	1999 1996 1983 1954 1998 2004	6
University of California, Irvine	John E. DiNardo	1990	1
University of California, San Diego	Gordon B. Dahl	1998	1
University of California, Santa Barbara	Olivier Deschenes	2001	1
University of California, Santa Cruz	John W. Isbister Ronald L. Oaxaca	1969 1971	2

Institution	Alumni Industrial Relations Section	Year of Ph.D.	Number of students
University of California, Los Angeles	David Harold Stern	1960	4
	Dean R. Hyslop	1995	
	Janet M. Currie	1988	
	Mark W. Plant	1982	
Unisys Corporation	Werner Michael Blumenthal	1956	1
Universitat D'Alacant (Spain)	Climent Quintana-Domeque	2008	1
Universität Heidelberg (Germany)	Christoph Matthias Schmidt	1991	1
Université du Québec à Montréal (Canada)	Marie Connolly	2007	1
University College Dublin (Ireland)	James J. Heckman	1971	1
University College London (UK)	James J. Heckman	1971	1
University of Albany	Ralph W. Harbison	1973	1
University of Arizona	Ronald L. Oaxaca	1971	2
	Michael R. Ransom	1983	
University of British Columbia	Paul Beaudry	1989	2
	Thomas Lemieux	1989	
University of Chicago	Robert J. Lalonde	1985	8
	Helen G. Levy	1998	
	Michael B. Greenstone	1998	
	James J. Heckman	1971	
	David E. Card	1983	
	Nicholas M. Kiefer	1976	
	Motty Perry	1983	
	Diane M. Whitmore (Schanzenbach)	2002	
University of Colorado	Bernard Udis	1959	1
University of Essex	Motty Perry	1983	2
	Melvyn G. Coles	1993	
University of Florida	Eleanor P. Brown	1981	1
University of Georgia	Matthew Weinberg	2006	1

Institution	Alumni Industrial Relations Section	Year of Ph.D.	Number of students
University of Hartford	Jack C. Myles	1957	1
University of Houston	Elaine Meichen Liu	2008	1
University of Iceland	Thorvaldur Gylfason	1977	1
University of Illinois	Kevin F. Hallock Ana Abigail Payne	1995 1995	2
University of London (UK)	Edward John Driffill	1977	1
University of Maryland	John C. Ham Mark H. Lopez	1980 1996	2
University of Massachusetts	Ronald L. Oaxaca	1971	1
University of Michigan	Gary R. Solon David C. Hershfield Helen G. Levy John G. Cross John E. DiNardo Brian P. McCall Anne-Louise Statt Jan Svejnar	1983 1970 1998 1964 1990 1988 1997 1979	8
University of Minnesota	Brian P. McCall John W. Budd	1988 1991	2
University of Montana	Thomas M. Power	1972	1
University of Montreal (Canada)	Thomas Lemieux	1989	1
University of North Carolina	David G. Brown	1961	1
University of Copenhagen, Denmark	Nikolaj Harmon	2013	
University of Notre Dame	Kirk B. Doran	2007	1
University of Ottawa (Canada)	Gilles J.A. Grenier	1982	1
University of Oxford	Kathryn Jo Graddy Christine A. Greenhalgh Paul Beaudry	1993 1978 1989	3

Institution	Alumni Industrial Relations Section	Year of Ph.D.	Number of students
University of Pennsylvania	Susan Yeh	2007	4
	Grace Wong	2004	
	Elizabeth E. Bailey	1972	
	James Dow	1987	
University of Pittsburgh	John C. Ham	1980	3
	Jan Svejnar	1979	
	Lara Shore-Sheppard	1996	
University of Rochester	Gordon B. Dahl	1998	1
University of Southampton (UK)	Edward John Driffill	1977	1
University of Southern California	Alec R. Levenson	1994	2
	John C. Ham	1980	
University of Stockholm (Institute for International Economic Studies) (Sweden)	Thorvaldur Gylfason	1977	1
University of Texas, Austin	Inessa Liskovich	2015	1
University of Toronto (Canada)	Ana Abigail Payne	1995	8
	Harry A. Krashinsky	2001	
	Harry Dwayne Benjamin	1989	
	Arthur J. Hosios	1982	
	Noah M. Meltz	1964	
	Samuel Hollander	1963	
	Donald E. Campbell	1972	
	John C. Ham	1980	
University of Utah	David C. Hershfield	1970	1
University of Victoria (Canada)	John D.F. Rowlatt	1971	1
University of Warwick	Motty Perry	1983	1
University of Washington	Richard A. Lester	1936	1
University of Western Ontario	Edward J.D. Ketchum	1972	1
University of Wisconsin	Diane M. Whitmore (Schanzenbach)	2002	2
	Louis D. Marks, Jr.	1981	
Univerzita Karlova (Czech Republic)	Randall K. Filer	1979	1

Institution	Alumni Industrial Relations Section	Year of Ph.D.	Number of students
U.S. Air Force Academy	Nathan Wozny	2010	1
U.S. Department of Commerce	Gary R. Solon Mark W. Plant	1983 1982	2
U.S. Department of Defense	Robert C. Wilburn Richard A. Lester J. Douglas Brown Frederick H. Harbison	1970 1936 1927 1940	4
U.S. Department of Labor	Gary R. Solon David C. Hershfield Alexandre Mas	1983 1970 2004	3
U.S. Department of State	Werner Michael Blumenthal	1956	1
U.S. Department of the Treasury	Werner Michael Blumenthal Cary A. Elliott Ronald B. Gold	1956 1998 1966	3
Utah Department of Health	Norman K. Thurston	1995	1
Vanderbilt University	Daniel H. Saks James S. Worley	1973 1958	2
Victoria University of Wellington	Dean R. Hyslop	1995	1
Virginia Polytechnic Institute and State University	Kristin F. Butcher	1993	1
Wake Forest University	David G. Brown Donald E. Frey	1961 1972	2
Wallace Foundation	Elizabeth Ty Wilde	2008	1
Wellesley College	Kristin F. Butcher Phillip B. Levine	1993 1990	2
Wells Fargo	Jesse M. Abraham	1983	1
Williams College	Lara Shore-Sheppard David J. Zimmerman	1996 1992	2
World Bank	Nicholas C. Papandreou	1986	1

Institution	Alumni Industrial Relations Section	Year of Ph.D.	Number of students
University of Pennsylvania	Susan Yeh Grace Wong Elizabeth E. Bailey James Dow	2007 2004 1972 1987	4
University of Pittsburgh	John C. Ham Jan Svejnar Lara Shore-Sheppard	1980 1979 1996	3
University of Rochester	Gordon B. Dahl	1998	1
University of Southampton (UK)	Edward John Driffill	1977	1
University of Southern California	Alec R. Levenson John C. Ham	1994 1980	2
University of Stockholm (Institute for International Economic Studies) (Sweden)	Thorvaldur Gylfason	1977	1
University of Texas, Austin	Inessa Liskovich	2015	1
University of Toronto (Canada)	Ana Abigail Payne Harry A. Krashinsky Harry Dwayne Benjamin Arthur J. Hosios Noah M. Meltz Samuel Hollander Donald E. Campbell John C. Ham	1995 2001 1989 1982 1964 1963 1972 1980	8
University of Utah	David C. Hershfield	1970	1
University of Victoria (Canada)	John D.F. Rowlatt	1971	1
University of Warwick	Motty Perry	1983	1
University of Washington	Richard A. Lester	1936	1
University of Western Ontario	Edward J.D. Ketchum	1972	1
University of Wisconsin	Diane M. Whitmore (Schanzenbach) Louis D. Marks, Jr.	2002 1981	2
Univerzita Karlova (Czech Republic)	Randall K. Filer	1979	1

Institution	Alumni Industrial Relations Section	Year of Ph.D.	Number of students
U.S. Air Force Academy	Nathan Wozny	2010	1
U.S. Department of Commerce	Gary R. Solon Mark W. Plant	1983 1982	2
U.S. Department of Defense	Robert C. Wilburn Richard A. Lester J. Douglas Brown Frederick H. Harbison	1970 1936 1927 1940	4
U.S. Department of Labor	Gary R. Solon David C. Hershfield Alexandre Mas	1983 1970 2004	3
U.S. Department of State	Werner Michael Blumenthal	1956	1
U.S. Department of the Treasury	Werner Michael Blumenthal Cary A. Elliott Ronald B. Gold	1956 1998 1966	3
Utah Department of Health	Norman K. Thurston	1995	1
Vanderbilt University	Daniel H. Saks James S. Worley	1973 1958	2
Victoria University of Wellington	Dean R. Hyslop	1995	1
Virginia Polytechnic Institute and State University	Kristin F. Butcher	1993	1
Wake Forest University	David G. Brown Donald E. Frey	1961 1972	2
Wallace Foundation	Elizabeth Ty Wilde	2008	1
Wellesley College	Kristin F. Butcher Phillip B. Levine	1993 1990	2
Wells Fargo	Jesse M. Abraham	1983	1
Williams College	Lara Shore-Sheppard David J. Zimmerman	1996 1992	2
World Bank	Nicholas C. Papandreou	1986	1

Institution	Alumni Industrial Relations Section	Year of Ph.D.	Number of students
Yale University	Michael A. Boozer	1994	5
	Joseph G. Altonji	1981	
	James J. Heckman	1971	
	Alvin K. Klevorick	1967	
	Henry G. Grabowski	1967	